THE COMING

of the GLORY

*HOW THE HEBREW SCRIPTURES
REVEAL THE PLAN OF GOD*

VOLUME I:
GÖBEKLI TEPE TO ELIJAH

EILEEN MADDOCKS

The Coming of the Glory Volume I: Göbekli Tepe
to Elijah © copyright 2020 by Eileen Maddocks
ISBN 13: 978-1-7324511-8-6
Library of Congress Control Number: 2020935114
Printed in the United States of America
First Printing: 2020
18 17 16 15 14 5 4 3 2 1
Edited by Mark Heinz
Illustrations by Heather Bousquet
Cover design by Dragan Bilic
SOMETHING OR OTHER PUBLISHING
Info@SOOPLLC.com
For bulk orders, e-mail Orders@SOOPLLC.com.

Contents

Acknowledgments

A WRITING PROJECT THAT takes years, like *The Coming of the Glory*, needs a lot of help and encouragement to come to fruition.

My sister, Geraldine Maddocks Whitfield, painstakingly read and reread my early drafts, catching errors and urging me forward. I could not have continued working on this book without her loving patience and endless assistance.

Several friends, including Donna Corbett, Leslie King, Angella Seesaran, and Nancy Rogers, read the manuscript and made helpful comments.

It takes a professional editor to whip a book into shape for submission to publishers. My editor, JoAnn Gometz, patiently rearranged my words and taught me the difference between passive and active sentences—and caught some egregious errors.

Wade Fransson, founder and owner of Something Or Other Publishing (SOOP), developed a unique, author-driven book publishing model that combines the best aspects of self-publishing and traditional publishing with comprehensive marketing plans. Wade's enthusiasm for my three-volume series and his wealth of publishing knowledge empowered me to keep moving along. Working with the SOOP staff has been a collaborative and consultative process. While sometimes feeling like a "driven author," I've been inspired to walk the steps of a professional writer.

The SOOP staff have been excellent partners. All stayed closely in touch with me and responded quickly to my input. Production manager

ACKNOWLEDGMENTS

Christian Lee worked tirelessly to put together all the component parts necessary for the release and marketing of Volume I. Mark Heinz, the company editor, combed through the manuscript and gave no-nonsense advice on what needed to go, what could stay, and what needed changes. The lovely cover was designed by Dragan Bilic, and the maps were illustrated by Heather Bousquet.

Thanks also go to Daphne Parsekian, the proofreader who caught the last of the elusive gremlins.

Foreword

ALL OF CREATION IS a reflection of God's image, and the Bahá'í teachings tell us God made man's inmost reality *"a mirror of His own Self."*[1] This spiritual endowment has inspired an unceasing quest since prehistoric times to know God and to respond with worship to His love.

Bahá'í scripture says God's love for His creation preceded the creation itself. *"O Son of Man! Veiled in My immemorial being and in the ancient eternity of My essence, I knew My love for thee; therefore I created thee, have engraved on thee Mine image and revealed to thee My beauty."*[2] That *"the flow of God's all-encompassing grace and plenteous mercies"*[3] might cease, *"no mind can contemplate."*[4]

From the beginning, God has revealed His love and His guidance to mankind through prophets, individuals whose reality was a perfect mirror in a human frame reflecting God's light. The light illumined the path in each age for their people to new spiritual and material heights. Who were they? We cannot know the most ancient; their names and their messages have been lost to history. *"That no records concerning them are now available, should be attributed to their extreme remoteness, as well as to the vast changes which the earth hath undergone since their time,"*[5] says the scripture. Eileen Maddocks has chronicled the ones we do know about and explains their perfect unity.

The Coming of the Glory traces the evidence of man's insatiable search for spiritual fulfillment from the remains of the most ancient temple yet

FOREWORD

discovered to the present, and demonstrates the organic unity of the quest throughout the ages.

– Thomas F. Armistead, editor and journalist

Preface

THE COMING OF THE GLORY took form because I am a curious student of biblical history. During my studies, I became intrigued by numerous references in the Hebrew Bible—the Old Testament to Christians—that seem to allude to and, though thinly veiled, even announce the coming of the Báb, Bahá'u'lláh, and the Bahá'í Era.

This book and its succeeding two volumes comprise a survey of a vast topic pursued from my Bahá'í perspective within the framework of modern biblical and archeological scholarship. It is assumed that readers have a basic familiarity with the Hebrew Bible and its accounts of the best-known people and events, such as Noah and the flood, Abraham, Joseph, Moses and the Exodus, and King David. Space permits only brief summaries of biblical history, although a basic history of ancient Israel is woven into the text and aided by timeline charts.

I started with the historical context from which emerged the revelations of Adam, Noah, Abraham, and Moses, all of whom, according to Bahá'í understanding as explained in the introduction to this book, were Prophets of God. As such, each One came to teach spiritual truths and to successively reveal aspects of God's plan for humanity.

In order to put the above Prophets in context, I found it necessary to start with the last days of the Paleolithic[1] hunter-gatherers, the Neolithic (New Stone Age)[2] era of plant and animal domestication, and the Mesopotamian city-states. Extensive archeological excavations of Middle Eastern sites from these three eras give innumerable indications of religious belief systems. The three sites I chose to focus on were

PREFACE

Göbekli Tepi, a Stone Age megalithic site in Anatolia, Turkey, active from about 10,000 to 8000 BCE; Çatalhöyük, a Neolithic village in Anatolia, inhabited from about 7400 to 6000 BCE; and Eridu, the first Sumerian village in the southern Tigris-Euphrates river valley, founded about 5000 BCE. It seems to be a constant demonstrated through archeological investigations such as these that mankind expressed spiritual or religious beliefs. These three sites introduce us to animism, ancestor veneration, animal and human sacrifice, and polytheism. Then the Prophet Adam appeared.

This first volume of *The Coming of the Glory* explores the early evolution of spiritual consciousness suggested by these excavations and continues to the early days of the kingdoms of Israel and Judah. It ends with the "still, small voice" heard by the prophet Elijah, which marks the end of divine communications accompanied by fire, thunder, and dramatic miracles.

Within this swath of history are the teachings and traditions of Adam, Noah, Abraham, and Moses—four of the Prophets of God in the Middle East recognized in the Bahá'í Writings. In addition, here we find Saul and his schools of prophets; prophetic psalms attributed to King David; and early prophets who left no written records, only memories of their service as gadflies warning the early Israelite kings of the errors of their ways.

The second and third volumes cover the lives and written works of the classical prophets—Hosea; First, Second, and Third Isaiah; Daniel, Micah, Zephaniah, Nahum, Habakkuk, Jeremiah, Ezekiel, Obadiah, Haggai, Zechariah, Joel, and Malachi—who all lived from the eighth through the late fifth centuries BCE. Summary histories of the kingdoms of Israel and Judah, and the roles of their Assyrian, Babylonian, and Persian conquerors, are entwined throughout.

PARAMETERS OF THIS WORK

To me, context within chronological history is of vital importance. However, exact dates for events were not recorded until the major Middle Eastern empires arose and started keeping written records for purposes of trade, dynastic lineage, and law. As written language developed in ancient Israel, where male literacy by the seventh century BCE was likely the highest in the region, a succession of scribes recorded oral histories of ancient events and copied and disseminated the writings of the prophets.

Approaches to the study of the Hebrew Bible are diverse. My primary approach was a search for, and then scrutiny of, the many references to the Glory of God, which is the Arabic translation for Bahá'u'lláh, the Prophet of the Bahá'í Faith. The British Bahá'í scholar Stephen Lambden found "the glory of the Lord" and "the Glory of God" thirty-six times in the Hebrew Bible.[3] From Genesis through Malachi, the Hebrew Bible abounds with references to the coming of the Glory and other terms that might refer to Him.

I tried to avoid proof texting, the dubious practice of using biblical verses out of context to prove or justify the alleged truth of unrelated verses or certain theological positions. Instead, I strove to provide the context for all cited verses within their sources, the continuity of the Hebrew experience, and the socioeconomic conditions of the times. Bahá'í texts are quoted to provide enhanced understanding of various biblical texts. My own opinions are noted as such.

Some readers will undoubtedly ask, "Who wrote the Bible?" You will find excellent approaches to this multi-faceted question in the very readable *Who Wrote the Bible?* and *The Bible with Sources Revealed* by Richard Elliott Friedman.

I encourage readers to keep a Bible or a computer at hand so that they might read beyond the quoted biblical passages. Bible Gateway (www.biblegateway.com) is easy to use and presents the Bible in more than sixty languages and numerous English translations.

Unless noted otherwise, I have used the New International Version (NIV) of the Bible throughout. There are times, though, when only the King James Version (KJV) is adequate. For example, *"Come now, let us settle this matter"* (Isa. 1:18, NIV) does not compare well with the famous phrase, *"Come now, and let us reason together"* (Isa. 1:18, KJV). Quotations from the Qur'an are from the J. M. Rodwell translation.[4]

I've used the term the "Hebrew Bible" instead of the "Old Testament" because it is more accurate and respectful. The Old Testament is only "old" when it is paired with the New Testament and when its relevance is considered secondary to the coming of Jesus. As you progress through this volume, you will discover how relevant the Hebrew Bible is to our times.

The acronyms BCE (Before the Common Era) and CE (Common Era) are used instead of BC and AD. Islamic dates are indicated by AH (Anno Hegirae). For comparison, the Islamic calendar is lunar and starts in the year 622 CE, when Muhammad and His followers fled from Mecca to Medina to escape persecution, an event called the Hegira.

Throughout this volume, there is a question as to how best to refer to God. The book of Exodus introduces the term Yahweh (YHWH) for God, and that was used for several centuries. I have simply used "God" for consistency, with the understanding that God and Yahweh are interchangeable.

The ancient people whose history is related in the Hebrew Bible are called Israelites; Israelis, in contrast, are citizens of the modern state of Israel. The term "Jews" did not come into use until postexilic times, when the former kingdom of Judah became the Persian province of Yehud.

The Manifestations of God, as understood in the Bahá'í teachings, are referred to as Prophets with a capital "P." A small "p" indicates the classical or canonical prophets. Pronouns referring to the three Central Figures of the Bahá'í Faith—the Báb, Bahá'u'lláh, and 'Abdu'l-Bahá—are capitalized, as are pronouns referring to Muḥammad and the Prophets who preceded Him. Pronouns referring to the classical prophets are not.

Quotations from sacred scriptures of all faiths are given in italics, as are quotations from the three Central Figures of the Bahá'í Faith.

Introduction

A BASIC UNDERSTANDING OF the early history and fundamental concepts of the Bahá'í Faith will help readers understand all volumes of *The Coming of the Glory*.

EXPECTANCY IN THE EAST AND THE WEST

An atmosphere of religious expectancy was reaching fever pitch simultaneously in the Christian and Shi'a Islamic worlds during the 1830s and early 1840s CE. In the West, many Christians expected the Second Coming, the return of Jesus Christ, in 1843 or 1844, based on Daniel 8:14: *"It will take 2,300 evenings and mornings; then the sanctuary will be reconsecrated."* With the biblical counting system of a day representing a year and the count starting in 457 BCE, the year Persian King Artaxerxes issued his decree to rebuild Jerusalem, the 2,300 days ended in 1844 CE. When Jesus did not return in the manner expected, His apparent nonappearance became known as the "Great Disappointment." Many of the most eager members of the movement returned to their former churches, while others joined numerous sects that quickly emerged.

Meanwhile, in Persia (today's Iran) and Iraq, Shi'a Muslims expected the imminent return of the twelfth imam, who was called the Qa'im ("He who will arise") or the Promised One. Descended from Muḥammad, he was the twelfth in the line of imams who were the Prophet's spiritual and political successors. Shi'a tradition states that the Qa'im disappeared at age five under mysterious and disputed circumstances in the year 874 CE, remained alive throughout the centuries in a state of occultation, and would return in a thousand years to usher in the Day of Judgment and establish the kingdom of God on Earth. According to the Islamic lunar calendar, the thousand years would culminate in the year 1844, or 1260 AH.

Mullá Ḥusayn (1813–1849), a Persian Shi'a Muslim and dedicated student of this prophecy, had been ardently looking for the Promised One. He felt pulled to Shiraz, Persia, where, on May 22, 1844, a young merchant named Siyyid 'Alí Muḥammad Shírází (1819–1850) divulged to Mullá Ḥusayn that He was that Messenger of God—the Báb, the Gate of the Hidden Imam, the Qa'im. A gate is a point of transition. The title of the Báb has many symbolic, layered meanings. The basic understanding is that the Báb's purpose was to serve as the gate between Islam's expectancy of the return of the Promised One, the Qa'im, and His mission to open the way for the coming of Bahá'u'lláh.

The Báb described the purpose of His Revelation as follows:

> *The purpose underlying this Revelation, as well as those that preceded it, has, in like manner, been to announce the advent of the Faith of Him Whom God will make manifest. And this Faith—the Faith of Him Whom God will make manifest—in its turn, together with all the Revelations gone before it, have as their object the Manifestation destined to succeed it. And the latter, no less than all the Revelations preceding it, prepare the way for the Revelation which is yet to follow. The process of the rise and setting of the Sun of Truth will thus indefinitely continue—a process that hath had no beginning and will have no end.*[1]

Bahá'u'lláh's great-grandson, Shoghi Effendi, who translated and edited Nabíl-i-A'ẓam's chronicle of the early years of the Bábí and Bahá'í Faiths, *The Dawn-breakers*, wrote:

> From the beginning the Báb must have divined the reception which would be accorded by His countrymen to His teachings, and the fate which awaited Him at the hands of the mullás

[Islamic clergy]. But He did not allow personal misgivings to affect the frank enunciation of His claims nor the open presentation of His Cause. The innovations which He proclaimed, though purely religious, were drastic; the announcement of His own identity startling and tremendous. He made Himself known as the Qa'im, the High Prophet or Messiah so long promised, so eagerly expected by the Muhammadan world. He added to this the declaration that he was also the Gate (that is, the Báb) through whom a greater Manifestation than Himself was to enter the human realm.[2]

THE BÁB: HIS MISSION AND MARTYRDOM

The Báb's mission was twofold—to make a complete break with Islam through a new religion that came to be called the Bábí Faith and to proclaim the coming of *"Him Whom God will make manifest."* He also made mysterious references to *"the year Nine"* and *"the year Nineteen"* (that is roughly 1852 and 1863 CE, calculated in lunar years from the year of the Báb's inauguration of His mission, 1844). The Báb also indicated to certain of His followers that they would themselves come to recognize and serve *"Him Whom God will make manifest."*[3]

Just as Jesus was severely opposed by the Jewish authorities so also was the Báb by the Islamic clergy, many of whom feared change as a threat to their station and livelihood. He was either under house arrest or imprisoned for most of His six-year ministry, while His disciples taught His Faith throughout Persia. In July 1848 the Báb was taken from His mountain prison in Chihríq to the city of Tabriz for examination before the Crown Prince of Persia and some of the foremost ecclesiastics in the country. First He seated Himself in the seat reserved for the Crown Prince. Then He started reciting verses of Divine Revelation. The clerics cut the Báb off and begged Him to abandon His mission. They asked whom He claimed to be and what was the message He brought. *"I am, I am,"* thrice exclaimed the Báb, *"I am the Promised One! I am the One whose name you have for a thousand years invoked, at whose mention you have risen, whose advent you have longed to witness, and the hour of whose Revelation you have prayed*

God to hasten."[4] Upon declaring this, He left the gathering without asking permission to do so.

The assembly was enraged, humiliated, and fearful. Its most hardened members prevailed in having the Báb sent for torture and then back to His cell in Chihríq. But the news of the Báb's proclamation spread throughout Persia and invigorated supporters of His Cause. Despite tragic upheavals and persecutions, the spirit of the new Faith continued to blaze.

Finally, the Grand Vizier for Náṣiri'd-Din Sháh succeeded in having the Báb put to death. On July 9, 1850, a firing squad executed the Báb in Tabriz in front of thousands of witnesses.[5]

The Báb appeared in one of the most morally degraded societies in the world. His announcement that humanity stood at the threshold of a new era of spiritual and moral reformation aroused excitement and hope among the population. But ruthless persecution of the Bábís, including the massacre of about 20,000 during the Báb's ministry and in the years immediately after His execution, drove this new religion underground.

The Dispensation of the Báb lasted nine years, from May 1844 to late 1852, making it the shortest in religious history. But two years before His execution, the Báb had bestowed upon one of His disciples, Mírzá Ḥusayn-'Alí Núrí (1817–1892), the name *Bahá*, which means Glory.[6] He therefore became known as Bahá'u'lláh, which translates from Arabic to "the Glory of God."

Never before in known religious history had one Manifestation of God heralded another Who was His contemporary. The renowned scholar Adib Taherzadeh (1921–2000) commented, "Because He was a Manifestation of God, the Báb had true knowledge of the station of Bahá'u'lláh, a knowledge which is beyond the reach of all humanity."[7] Interestingly, the Báb and Bahá'u'lláh never met in this world, although they lived about five hundred miles apart—the Báb in Shiraz in southwestern Persia, when He wasn't in prison, and Bahá'u'lláh in Tehran in the north. Once, Bahá'u'lláh embarked on a journey to meet the Báb, but events forcibly interrupted His effort.

As the Báb had foreseen, the "year Nine" corresponded with 1852, the year when Bahá'u'lláh received the divine confirmation of His identity and mission in a vision during His imprisonment in the infamous pit in Tehran, the Síyáh-Chál.[8]

THE MISSION AND EXILES OF BAHÁ'U'LLÁH

Bahá'u'lláh was shackled with heavy chains for four months of imprisonment in a dreaded pit of blackness, the Síyáh-Chál. Upon release, He was exiled to Baghdad in the dead of an exceptionally severe winter. Bahá'u'lláh revealed in a prayer His sufferings and those of His family and followers who went with Him.

> *My God, My Master, My Desire! … Thou hast created this atom of dust through the consummate power of Thy might, and nurtured Him with Thine hands which none can chain up…. Thou hast destined for Him trials and tribulations which no tongue can describe, nor any of Thy Tablets adequately recount. The throat Thou didst accustom to the touch of silk Thou hast, in the end, clasped with strong chains, and the body Thou didst ease with brocades and velvets Thou hast at last subjected to the abasement of a dungeon. …. How many the nights during which the weight of chains and fetters allowed Me no rest, and how numerous the days during which peace and tranquility were denied Me, by reason of that wherewith the hands and tongues of men have afflicted Me! Both bread and water which Thou hast, through Thy all-embracing mercy, allowed unto the beasts of the field, they have, for a time, forbidden unto this servant, and the things they refused to inflict upon such as have seceded from Thy Cause, the same have they suffered to be inflicted upon Me, until, finally, Thy decree was irrevocably fixed, and Thy behest summoned this servant to depart out of Persia, accompanied by a number of frail-bodied men and children of tender age, at this time when the cold is so intense that one cannot even speak, and ice and snow so abundant that it is impossible to move.*[9]

Because Bahá'u'lláh's father had been a court vizier, the authorities did not have the option of executing Him. Therefore, the Persian government persuaded the Ottoman authorities to accept Him in exile in Baghdad. January 1853 marked the beginning of Bahá'u'lláh's forty years of exile and imprisonment, ending with His death in May 1892. To the consternation of Persian authorities, however, Bahá'u'lláh attracted attention in Baghdad as a spiritual leader. After ten years, the Persian government persuaded the Ottoman authorities to exile Him farther away to Constantinople (now Istanbul), Turkey, and then to Adrianople (now Edirne) in European Turkey. Just days before His departure from Baghdad in 1863, Bahá'u'lláh publicly announced that He was the one foretold by the Báb. The year of this proclamation was 1863, "the year Nineteen" the Báb had indicated.[10]

During His exile in Adrianople, and later from Akka, Bahá'u'lláh wrote a series of tablets (letters) to the world's major religious and political leaders.[11] One was addressed to the kings of the world collectively, while others were individually addressed to 'Abdu'l-i-'Azíz, the Sultan of Turkey; Alexander II, Czar of Russia; Náṣiri'd-Din Sháh, the Shah of Persia; Napoleon III; Pope Pius IX; and Queen Victoria.

In these missives and others, Bahá'u'lláh proclaimed His station and covered many subjects, two of which were exhortations to the rulers to greatly reduce their expenditures on armaments and to care for their people with justice and mercy. For example, He wrote in a tablet addressed to the kings of the earth:

> *Fear the sighs of the poor and of the upright in heart who, at every break of day, bewail their plight, and be unto them a benignant sovereign. They, verily, are thy treasures on earth. It behoveth thee, therefore, to safeguard thy treasures from the assaults of them who wish to rob thee. Inquire into their affairs, and ascertain, every year, nay every month, their condition, and be not of them that are careless of their duty.*[12]

Bahá'u'lláh wrote repeatedly of the dawn of a new age of universal peace that would come. However, if His teachings and warnings were ignored, the establishment of that peace would be preceded by cataclysmic upheavals in the world's political, religious, and social order.

History tells us what decisions the rulers made. Today we are living with the consequences.

His exile to the prison city of Akka began in 1868. The purpose of this ultimate imprisonment with its harsh sanctions was to cause His death and, in the meantime, to cut Bahá'u'lláh off from His followers by denying Him all visitor contacts. However, in time, some of the Turkish authorities and Islamic clergy in Akka became His devoted admirers and eased the severe conditions. After nine years, two within the prison and seven within the prison city, He was allowed to live outside Akka in a country setting, where He was visited by people from all walks of life, including E. G. Browne, a distinguished English Orientalist from Oxford University. (See Appendix A.)

One might ask why a Manifestation of God would voluntarily submit to persecution, torture, and imprisonment. The answer is found in a tablet that Bahá'u'lláh wrote from Akka to an early Bahá'í, in which He stated that His sacrifices were for the advancement of mankind, thus conveying the themes of atonement and sacrifice familiar to Christians.

> *The Ancient Beauty hath consented to be bound with chains that mankind may be released from its bondage, and hath accepted to be made a prisoner within this most mighty Stronghold that the whole world may attain unto true liberty. He hath drained to its dregs the cup of sorrow, that all the peoples of the earth may attain unto abiding joy, and be filled with gladness. This is of the mercy of your Lord, the Compassionate, the Most Merciful. We have accepted to be abased, O believers in the Unity of God, that ye may be exalted, and have suffered manifold afflictions, that ye might prosper and flourish.*[13]

Taherzadeh noted that during these dire years in Akka, Bahá'u'lláh revealed some of His most momentous writings. He also explained, "And, significantly, it was during these calamitous years, and as a direct result of the afflictions and sufferings which were heaped upon the Supreme Manifestation of God in this Most Great Prison, that enormous spiritual forces were released causing humanity to be freed of all fetters which had been placed upon it in the course of past ages and centuries."[14]

Bahá'u'lláh passed away in 1892. His remains were put to rest beneath a garden room in a small house steps from the mansion of Bahji, where He spent His final years. This Shrine of Bahá'u'lláh is, for Bahá'ís, the holiest place on Earth.

'ABDU'L-BAHÁ, SHOGHI EFFENDI, AND THE BAHÁ'Í COVENANT

In His will, Bahá'u'lláh appointed His oldest son, Abbás Effendi (1844–1921), as the Head of the Faith and the authorized interpreter of the Sacred Texts. Early in life, 'Abbás Effendi took the name 'Abdu'l-Bahá, which, in Arabic, means servant ('Abdu'l) of the glory (Bahá). He chose this name to indicate his lifelong dedication to his father, which began even before He accompanied His father and family into their initial exile at age nine. When asked, He expressed the meaning of his name this way:

> *My name is 'Abdu'l-Bahá, my identity is 'Abdu'l-Bahá, my qualification is 'Abdu'l-Bahá, my reality is 'Abdu'l-Bahá, my praise is 'Abdu'l-Bahá. Thraldom to the Blessed Perfection is my glorious and refulgent diadem; and servitude to all the human race is my perpetual religion. No name, no title, no mention, no commendation hath he nor will ever have except 'Abdu'l-Bahá. This is my longing. This is my supreme apex. This is my greatest yearning. This is my eternal life. This is my everlasting glory!*[15]

'Abdu'l-Bahá's imprisonment in Ottoman custody ultimately lasted for fifty-six years, sixteen years beyond His father's death. At age sixty-four, in 1908, He was among the Ottoman Empire's religious and political prisoners freed during the Young Turks Revolution. In the years after the passing of Bahá'u'lláh, 'Abdu'l-Bahá guided the development of the Faith as it expanded from the Middle East into Asia, Africa, Europe, and North America. He became known as an ambassador of peace throughout the East and West, an exemplary human being, and the leading exponent of the Bahá'í Faith. He also devoted much of His ministry to serving the poor in Akka and its neighboring city across the bay, Haifa.

During the same period, 'Abdu'l-Bahá planned and started construction of the Shrine of the Báb for the interment of His remains that had been quietly transported from Persia to Haifa years earlier—and decades after the Báb's execution. Bahá'u'lláh Himself had shown 'Abdu'l-Bahá precisely where the Báb was to be interred on Mount Carmel.

Despite His age, 'Abdu'l-Bahá undertook a grueling three-year (1911–1913) lecture tour through Europe, Canada, and the United States. He foresaw World War I and, upon His return to Palestine, worked tirelessly to promote the cultivation and storage of grain to feed the populace during the coming conflict. He stayed in Palestine throughout the war, continuing both His local work for the poor and His guidance of the international Bahá'í community. In the process, He withstood Allied bombardments of Turkish positions and threats from the Turkish commander to crucify Him on Mount Carmel, the steep slope on which much of Haifa now stands, before the British troops entered Ottoman Palestine. In gratitude for His humanitarian efforts during the war, the British Mandate of Palestine dubbed 'Abdu'l-Bahá a knight of the British Empire (KBE) in April 1920.

'Abdu'l-Bahá died eighteen months later, in November 1921. Thousands of mourners accompanied His casket from His home in Haifa to the Shrine of the Báb on Mount Carmel, where He was laid to rest in a burial chamber next to that of the Báb. Six speakers from the Christian, Muslim, and Jewish communities offered eulogies.

The Will and Testament of 'Abdu'l-Bahá named twin successors— the Universal House of Justice, which had not yet been elected, and His eldest grandson, Shoghi Effendi Abbás (1897–1957), whom He named the "Guardian of the Faith." He also designated Shoghi Effendi the sole interpreter of the Sacred Texts of the Faith and bestowed upon him the responsibility of completing the construction of the Shrine of the Báb.

Shoghi Effendi was educated at the American School in Beirut, Lebanon, and at Oxford University, England. He had a brilliant mind and was self-disciplined beyond measure. He wrote in Arabic, Persian, and English—a language of which he displayed an exquisite, erudite, and compelling command. His writings, which include an incomparable history of the Bahá'í Faith from 1844 to 1944, *God Passes By*, and innumerable volumes of his letters and commentaries offer profound insights into the spiritual dimensions of civilization and the dynamics of social change.[16]

With infinite patience and encouragement, Shoghi Effendi guided the progress of the Faith and its global spread with painstaking attention, one small victory at a time. He labored without pause for the development of the buildings and gardens of the Bahá'í World Centre on the slopes of Mount Carmel in Haifa, which became part of the newly formed nation of Israel during his lifetime. He also translated many of the works of the Báb and Bahá'u'lláh into exquisite English. The adoration and appreciation that the Bahá'í world had for him was reflected in frequent references to the "beloved Guardian."

Shoghi Effendi's unexpected death in November 1957 left the Bahá'í world bereft. He had not been able to appoint a successor in accordance with the provisions of the Will and Testament of 'Abdu'l-Bahá, since he and his wife, Amatu'l-Bahá Rúhíyyih Khánum (the former Mary Maxwell, of Canada) had no children. Fortunately, Shoghi Effendi had continued the practice instituted by Bahá'u'lláh, and followed by 'Abdu'l-Bahá, of recognizing specific individuals for their tireless devotion to the protection and expansion of the Bahá'í Faith with the title of "Hands of the Cause of God." At the time of Shoghi Effendi's passing, there were twenty-seven surviving Hands of the Cause. All but one of them met soon after Shoghi Effendi's funeral and elected nine of their number to temporarily conduct the affairs of the Faith from the Bahá'í World Centre in Haifa. This decision was subsequently endorsed unanimously by the National Spiritual Assemblies, the highest governing bodies of the Faith at that time.

In April 1963—the centenary of the public declaration of Bahá'u'lláh—the Universal House of Justice was elected by all fifty-six National Spiritual Assemblies that were currently established in the world. The Hands of the Cause had declared themselves ineligible for election. As the highest institution of the Faith, the House of Justice is composed of nine members who are elected every five years by members of all National Assemblies. The nine-member National Assemblies themselves are elected by secret ballot by delegates who are elected by the Bahá'ís of their countries, also by secret ballot. The House of Justice is responsible for applying the principles of the Faith within the global Bahá'í community, protecting the Faith from those who wish it harm, teaching the Faith in various global endeavors, and administering the affairs of the worldwide community.

The succession after Bahá'u'lláh of 'Abdu'l-Bahá, Shoghi Effendi, and then the Universal House of Justice constitutes the Bahá'í Covenant. For the first time in the history of revealed religions, a Covenant of succession—a provision for the protection and leadership of a new faith—was enacted to prevent schism into competing sects. The Bahá'í Faith has remained undivided and free of schism—a most necessary condition for it to work effectively and credibly for global unity.

THE WRITTEN LEGACY

The Báb produced a prodigious quantity of writings. More than 2,000 of His unique works have been identified, comprising almost five million words.[17] Most of the original, handwritten writings of the Báb and Baha'u'lláh, and those that were dictated and then approved by Them, are kept in the International Bahá'í Archives at the Bahá'í World Centre, conserved in state-of-the-art conditions. To this day, descendants of individuals who received written messages from these two Prophets are still turning them over to the World Centre. This is the first time in human history that the original documents and words of Prophets of God, whether handwritten or dictated and approved, have been preserved.

Bahá'u'lláh was a prolific writer, and His works, which were mostly dictated, kept three or four secretaries busy at a time. The scope of His writings, in both Arabic and Persian, encompasses an uncountable number of subjects in about 20,000 unique works comprising more than six million words.[18] The sheer volume of His writings is referred to as the "Ocean of His Words," which He described thusly: *"Praise and glory beseem the Lord of Names and the Creator of the heavens, He, the waves of Whose ocean of Revelation surge before the eyes of the peoples of the world."*[19]

'Abdu'l-Bahá was also a prolific writer who authored several books and carried on a vast and diverse correspondence. More than 30,000 of His unique works, comprising more than five million words, have been identified and are saved in the Bahá'í Archives.[20] Well beyond 22,000 unique works of Shoghi Effendi have also been identified and added to the Archives.[21]

Who has not wished that Jesus could have traveled with a scribe whose original transcripts might have been preserved for 2,000 years? Instead, this is the first time in the history of revealed religion that written accounts of witnesses to the events surrounding a Divine Revelator have been preserved. We are extraordinarily fortunate that the Báb and Bahá'u'lláh came so relatively recently.

MANY MESSENGERS

God has sent a series of Prophets to confirm the spiritual teachings of previous Prophets and to bring new levels of those teachings, along with updated social laws appropriate for their times. Their mandates have been twofold—to liberate people from the darkness of ignorance and guide them to spiritual light and to advance the peace and tranquility of mankind by providing all the means by which that could be established.

These Prophets have appeared in all parts of the world. The best-known today include Adam, Noah, Abraham, Moses, Krishna, Buddha, Zoroaster, Jesus, Muḥammad, the Báb, and Bahá'u'lláh. However, there were many other divine teachers, and wherever they appeared, they promoted spiritual values and advancement of the local culture. Many indigenous peoples today have traditional folk tales or memories imparted from generation to generation that indicate the appearance of a Prophet to the people. Some of the teachings of the earlier Prophets have been lost, but portions of revelations from preliterate times were preserved in symbolic mythology and canonized in folklore.

There is a tendency to differentiate between the traditional Abrahamic religions (Judaism, Christianity, and Islam) and the dharmic religions (Hinduism, Buddhism, and their offshoots) that arose in the Far East. There is no one meaning for the word "dharmic," but its essence is recognition of cosmic principles and laws and living in accordance with them. And where does Zoroastrianism fit? The Gospel of Matthew tells of wise men who came from the east, searching for the one who was born king of the Jews and following His star to find and worship Him (Matt. 2:1, 9–11). They have traditionally been believed to be Zoroastrian magi. Perhaps their mystical purpose was to build a spiritual bridge between East and West. Could this story of the magi have been symbolic of the unity of East and West that must manifest for humanity to accomplish global religious unity?

AUTHENTICITY OF HOLY SCRIPTURES

Discussion of the Bible and biblical scholarship inevitably prompts the question: How authentic is the Bible? The Universal House of Justice provided additional assurance about the divine care and protection that Holy Scriptures have received:

> The Bahá'ís believe that God's Revelation is under His care and protection and that the essence, or essential elements, of what His Manifestations intended to convey has been recorded and preserved in Their Holy Books. However, as the sayings of the ancient Prophets were written down some time later, we cannot categorically state, as we do in the case of the Writings of Bahá'u'lláh, that the words and phrases attributed to Them are Their exact words.[22]

It's also important to keep in mind that, to a certain extent, the Prophets spoke to the people within the context of their culture and believed history. In these instances, their remarks cannot be taken as verifications of traditional or biblical history. The early Bahá'í scholar Mírzá Abu'l-Faḍl Gulpáypání emphasized that the prophets and Manifestations of

God were sent "to guide the nations, to improve their characters, and to bring the people nearer to their Source and ultimate Goal."[23] He then clarified that they were not sent as

> ...historians, astronomers, philosophers, or natural scientists. Therefore, the prophets have indulged the people in regard to their historical notions, folk stories, and scientific principles, and have spoken to them according to these. They conversed as was appropriate to their audience and hid certain realities behind the curtain of allusion.[24]

TWO CYCLES

Progressive revelation unfolded in human history through a succession of Prophets of God, each with His own Revelation—also called His Book. This progression formed what is called the Adamic Cycle, also called the Prophetic Cycle and the Prophetic Era, which started with Adam and culminated with the advent of the Báb.

The Bahá'í Cycle, also known as the Cycle of Fulfillment, started with the missions of the Báb and Bahá'u'lláh, whose teachings will bring humankind to spiritual maturity. The coming of the Báb in 1844 was the link between the Adamic and Bahá'í Cycles. Muḥammad was, indeed, the "Seal of the Prophets" because He was the last Prophet in the Adamic Cycle. While Prophets will continue to come at various intervals according to the will of God, they will conduct their ministries within the parameters of the Bahá'í Cycle, in the same way that Prophets from Adam to Muḥammad worked within the parameters of the Adamic Cycle.

Each Prophet foretold the coming of the next, and all of them foretold the coming of the supreme Manifestation of God, Bahá'u'lláh. 'Abdu'l-Bahá explained:

> *Each of the Manifestations of God has likewise a cycle wherein His religion and His law are in full force and effect. When His cycle is ended through the advent of a new Manifestation, a new cycle begins. Thus, cycles are*

inaugurated, concluded, and renewed, until a universal cycle is completed in the world of existence and momentous events transpire which efface every record and trace of the past; then a new universal cycle begins in the world, for the realm of existence has no beginning. ... We are in the cycle which began with Adam and whose universal Manifestation is Bahá'u'lláh.[25]

Bahá'u'lláh came for many reasons. The foremost of them was to unify humanity. The core tenet of Bahá'í belief is unity: God is one, His Prophets are one, and humankind is one. Only when these three "onenesses" are recognized will world peace be achieved. 'Abdu'l-Bahá presented the basic and distinguishing principles of the Faith of Bahá'u'lláh during His journeys to the West, speaking to Christian and Jewish audiences. Shoghi Effendi later summarized these principles. (See Appendix B.)

A basic theme of this book is that God has always been, and will always be, an actor in history. The world is vibrating with His message, if we listen.

This is the Day which the Pen of the Most High hath glorified in all the holy Scriptures. There is no verse in them that doth not declare the glory of His holy Name, and no Book that doth not testify unto the loftiness of this most exalted theme. Were We to make mention of all that hath been revealed in these heavenly Books and holy Scriptures concerning this Revelation, this Tablet would assume impossible dimensions.[26]

And lastly, let's keep in mind that the Báb wrote: *"God hath raised up Prophets and revealed Books as numerous as the creatures of the world, and will continue to do so to everlasting."*[27] While the Hebrew Bible may seem overwhelming with its vast reservoir of divine guidance and human experience, it's only a small fraction of the divine wisdom and guidance that has been poured into human history.

PROPHECIES WITHIN OUR CONCEPT OF TIME

Here on Earth, time seems to be a straightforward concept. We have minutes, hours, days, months, years, centuries, and millennia. We know the past, and we know the present. Knowledge of the future, for us, can be based on scientific trends or guesswork, the exception being tapped into a different dimension through a dream or vision. Most of us do have prophetic dreams about our own lives, regardless of whether we remember them, but generally not about other people or our society. Perhaps we can reconcile our rather pedantic understanding of time with the general attitude of physicists and other scientists that time and space are relative concepts.

In addition, the fact that countless biblical prophecies have been proven correct rather speaks for itself. This enables a pragmatic attitude that God is not bound by the earthly system of time by our differentiation of past, present, and future. Therefore, by extension, neither were His Prophets who spoke for Him.

The Hebrew prophets whom we will survey in these three volumes were speaking the Word of God received from Him, and they were operating within the Dispensation of Moses. Therefore, the prophets who received the Word of God were free of the bounds of earthly time.

Let's now explore the Revelations within the Adamic Cycle and their portents of the Day of God for our times. But first some historical background must be given.

Charts

Chart of the Kings and Named Prophets*

Rulers of united kingdom	Approx. dates of reign	Prophets
Saul	c. 1025–1005	Samuel Medium at Endor
David	c. 1095–970	Nathan
Solomon	c. 970–931	
Jeroboam I (continued as king of the northern kingdom of Israel)	c. 931–928	

The Divided Kingdoms

Kings of Israel	Approx. years BCE	Prophets of Israel	Kings of Judah	Approx. years BCE	Prophets of Judah
1. Jeroboam I	931–909	Ahijah Shemaiah			
			1. Rehoboam	931–914	
			2. Abijah	914–911	
			3. Asa	911–870	Hanani
2. Nadab	909–908				
3. Baasha	908–885	Jehu			
4. Elah	884–884				
5. Zimri	884				
6. Omri Tibni ***	884–873 884–880				
7. Ahab	873–852	Micaiah (Ahab only)			
			4. Jehoshaphat	870–846**	
8. Ahaziah	852–851				
9. Jehoram (Joram)	851–842				
			5. Jehoram (Joram)	851–843**	
			6. Ahaziah	843–842	
10. Jehu	842–814				
			7. Athaliah	842–836	
			8. Joash	836–798	
11. Jehoahaz (Joahaz)	817–800**				
12. Jehoash (Joash)	800–784				
			9. Amaziah	798–769	
13. Jeroboam II	788–747**	Jonah (to Nineveh)			

*   Dates for the kings are taken from Figure 3, p. 20, of *The Bible Unearthed* by Finkelstein and Silberman. They credit the *Anchor Bible Dictionary*, vol. 1, p. 1010, and Galel's *The Coming of the Kings of Israel and Judah*.

**   Co-regencies

***   Rival rule

The Divided Kingdoms

Kings of Israel	Approx. years BCE	Prophets of Israel	Kings of Judah	Approx. years BCE	Prophets of Judah
14. Zechariah	747	Amos (a year or two during the 750s) Hosea (Jeroboam II to Hosea, about 60 years)	10. Uzziah (Azariah)	785–733**	First Isaiah – last year of Uzziah's reign (734) through Jotham, Ahaz, and Hezekiah to 687) Micah – Jotham, Ahaz, and Hezekiah, 730s to the 690s
15. Shallum	747				
16. Menahem	747–737				
17. Pekahiah	737–735				
18. Pekah	735–732		11. Jotham	743–729**	
			12. Ahaz	743–727**	
19. Hoshea	732–722		13. Hezekiah	727–698	
			14. Manasseh	698–642	
			15. Amon	641–640	
			16. Josiah (Josias)	639–609	Hulda (Josiah only) Nahum – Josiah Zephaniah (Josiah only) Uriah – Jehoakim Habakkuk – Josiah and Jehoakim, 609–598 Jeremiah – Josiah in 626 until after Zedekiah
			17. Jehoahaz (Joahaz)	609	
			18. Jehoakim	608–598	
			19. Jehoiachin	597	
			20. Zedekiah	596–586	

*   Dates for the kings are taken from Figure 3, p. 20, of *The Bible Unearthed* by Finkelstein and Silberman. They credit the *Anchor Bible Dictionary*, vol. 1, p. 1010, and Galel's *The Coming of the Kings of Israel and Judah*.

**   Co-regencies

*** Rival rule

CHARTS

Chart of the Kings and Named Prophets*

Exilic	Prophets	Approximate Dates
Babylonian	Daniel	606–534
	Ezekiel	596–574
	Second Isaiah	No dates available, lived in the exile
	Obadiah	Early sixth century soon after the fall of Jerusalem in 586
Postexilic	**Prophets**	**Approximate Dates**
Persian	Haggai	Late sixth century
	First Zechariah	520–518, second year of reign of Darius through his fourth year
	Third Isaiah	About 520 to 500, or later
	Second Zechariah	Perhaps a century after First Zechariah
	Joel	Late fifth century, or possibly early fourth
	Malachi	Mid-fifth century, or possibly later

Maps

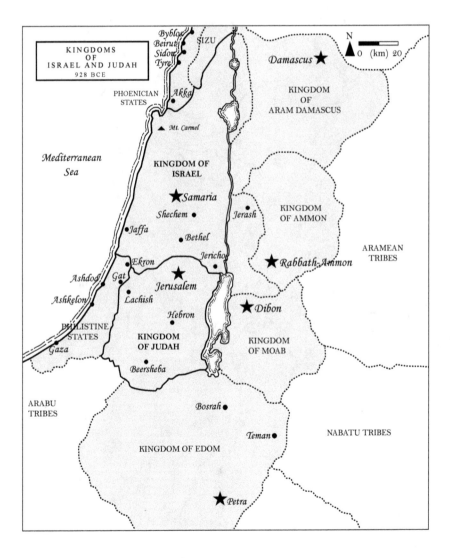

KINGDOMS
OF
ISRAEL AND JUDAH
928 BCE

Byblos
Beirut
SIZU
Sidon
Tyre

Damascus

PHOENICIAN
STATES

Akka

KINGDOM
OF
ARAM DAMASCUS

Mt. Carmel

Mediterranean
Sea

KINGDOM OF
ISRAEL

Samaria
Shechem
Jerash

KINGDOM
OF AMMON

Jaffa
Bethel

Jericho

ARAMEAN
TRIBES

Ekron

Ashdod
Gat
Jerusalem

Rabbath-Ammon

Ashkelon
Lachish

Dibon

Hebron

PHILISTINE
STATES

KINGDOM
OF JUDAH

KINGDOM
OF MOAB

Gaza

Beersheba

ARABU
TRIBES

Bosrah

Teman

NABATU TRIBES

KINGDOM OF EDOM

Petra

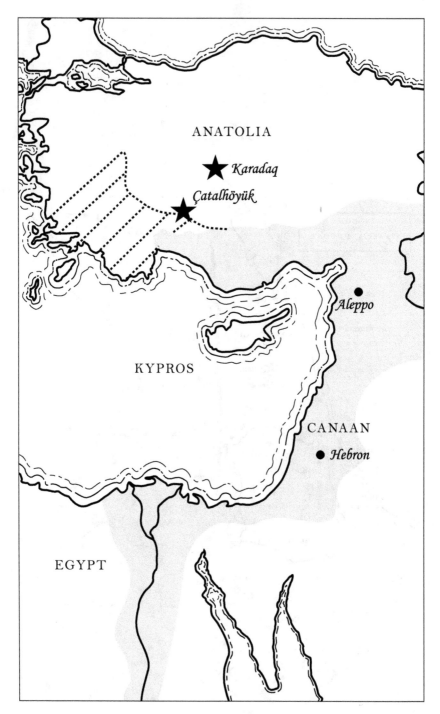

THE COMING OF THE GLORY

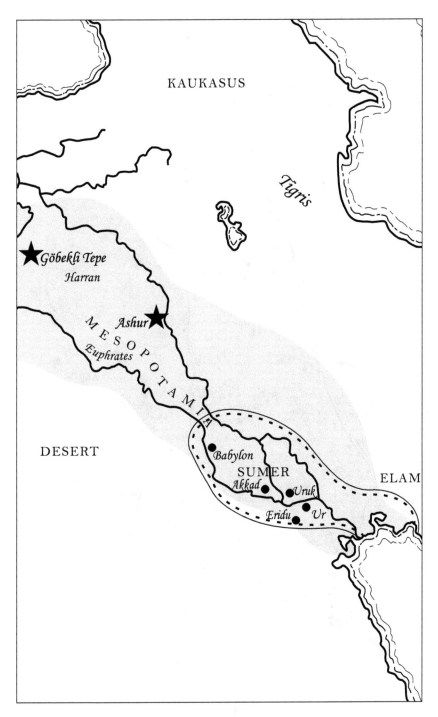

KAUKASUS

Tigris

★ *Göbekli Tepe*

Harran

M E S O P O T A M I A

Ashur ★

Euphrates

DESERT

● *Babylon*

SUMER

Akkad ●

● *Uruk*

Eridu ● ● *Ur*

ELAM

MAPS

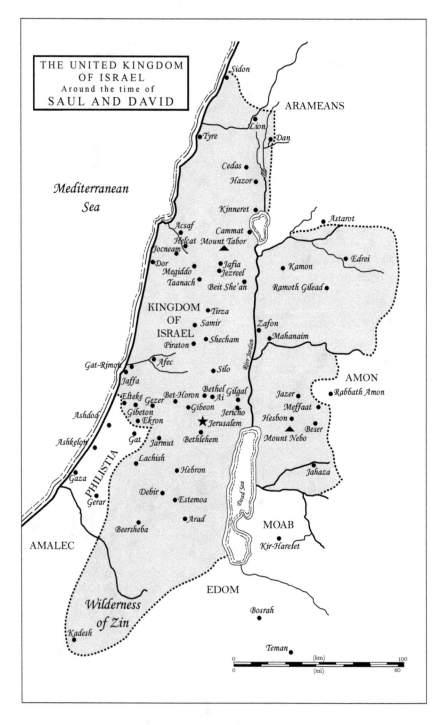

THE UNITED KINGDOM
OF ISRAEL
Around the time of
SAUL AND DAVID

ARAMEANS

Sidon

Lion

Tyre

Dan

Cedas

Hazor

Mediterranean
Sea

Kinneret

Astarot

Acsaf

Cammat
Mount Tabor

Edrei

Helcat

Jocneam

Kamon

Dor

Jafia

Megiddo

Jezreel

Taanach

Ramoth Gilead

Beit She'an

KINGDOM
OF
ISRAEL

Tirza

Samir

Zafon

Shecham

Mahanaim

Piraton

Gat-Rimon

Afec

Silo

Jriver Jordan

AMON

Jaffa

Bethel Gilgal

Jazer

Rabbath Amon

Elteke

Bet-Horon

Ai

Meffaat

Gezer

Gibeon

Jericho

Ashdod

Gibeton

Ekron

Jerusalem

Hesbon

Beser

Ashkelon

Gat

Jarmut

Bethlehem

Mount Nebo

Gaza

Lachish

PHILISTIA

Hebron

Jahaza

Gerar

Debir

Estemoa

Dead Sea

Arad

Beersheba

MOAB

AMALEC

Kir-Hareset

EDOM

Wilderness
of Zin

Bosrah

Kadesh

Teman

| 0 | (km) | 100 |
| 0 | (mi) | 60 |

Chapter 1

ANIMISM AND ATONEMENT

To appreciate the Bible properly, we cannot begin with it.

THOMAS CAHILL[1]

WHO ARE WE? WHY are we here, and what is our destiny? Did humanity evolve from the animal kingdom? Are we simply the highest of the animals? Or were we created separately from the animal kingdom?

Since time immemorial, humans have looked for signs in the heavens and in the world around them for answers about their place in creation. Initially, the animal appellation seems to fit because we mostly spend our time grooming, eating, resting, exercising, seeking sexual gratification, and generally fretting about our bodies. Animals, though, do not wonder about the meaning of life and strive to be more than they are.

'Abdu'l-Bahá shed light on this quandary by noting that there are two categories of people—those who deny the spirit and say that man is a species of animal with greater intelligence and opposable thumbs and those who recognize the spiritual nature of man. Then he said unequivocally, *"But man has always been a distinct species; he has been man, not an animal."*[2]

He continued to explain that not only are humans a distinct species but they are eternal souls created by God: *"Know that, although human souls have existed upon the earth for a myriad ages and cycles, the human soul is nonetheless originated. And since it is a sign of God, once it has come into being it is everlasting. The human spirit has a beginning but no end: It endures forever."*[3]

1

In fact, the station of the human soul is far beyond our comprehension. Bahá'u'lláh described man as *"a mine rich in gems of inestimable value."*[4]

Psalm 8 beautifully depicts the station of man:

> LORD, our Lord,
>> how majestic is your name in all the earth!
>
> You have set your glory
>> in the heavens.
>
> Through the praise of children and infants
>> you have established a stronghold against your enemies,
>> to silence the foe and the avenger.
>
> When I consider your heavens,
>> the work of your fingers,
>
> the moon and the stars,
>> which you have set in place,
>
> what is mankind that you are mindful of them,
>> human beings that you care for them?
>
> You have made them a little lower than the angels
>> and crowned them with glory and honor.
>
> You made them rulers over the works of your hands;
>> you put everything under their feet:
>
> all flocks and herds,
>> and the animals of the wild,
>
> the birds in the sky,
>> and the fish in the sea,
>> all that swim the paths of the seas.
>
> LORD, our Lord,
>> how majestic is your name in all the earth!

And God sent His Prophets to educate us, who were created a little lower than the angels, so that our potential could be released and our glory and honor claimed. The number of these divine teachers seems to be unfathomable, as Bahá'u'lláh wrote:

2

His creation hath ever existed, and the Manifestations of His Divine glory and the Day Springs of eternal holiness have been sent down from time immemorial, and been commissioned to summon mankind to the one true God. That the names of some of them are forgotten and the records of their lives lost is to be attributed to the disturbances and changes that have overtaken the world.[5]

It can therefore be assumed that many divine Messengers came to the Middle East, as well as to peoples throughout the world, and provided the sparks of consciousness that gave humans the vision to progress in all areas of life. In keeping with this assumption, a divine Messenger probably triggered the development of the first known ceremonial site that was also an architectural complex, Göbekli Tepe in southern Turkey.

The earliest vestiges of hominid activity in the Levant—the eastern Mediterranean area between Egypt and Anatolia—date to the early Paleolithic era, about a million years ago. The humans of the last migration out of Africa to the Middle East had survived the last ice age from 25,000 to 12,500 BCE and a minor ice age (the Little Dryas) from 10,800 to 9600. The earth was warming and rehydrating. The Fertile Crescent was greening, taking on the more moderate, agriculturally productive climate that it has today. Situated between the Arabian Desert and the Nile Valley to the south and the mountains of Armenia to the north, this belt of fertility extended from the Mediterranean Sea in the west to the Tigris and Euphrates Rivers and southwestern Persia in the east. Living conditions for men and animals became gentler, and life grew easier for hunter-gatherers. As it always has, ease of living freed people for learning, thinking, and pondering.

A CATHEDRAL ON A HILL

Our journey through the development of human spiritual consciousness that led to the Hebrew Bible starts with the excavations at Göbekli Tepe. Meaning *potbelly hill*, the name reflects the site's softly curving slopes a quarter mile from a large limestone outcropping in Anatolia. In approximately 10,000 BCE, a group of hunter-gatherers discovered

3

the flint they needed for knapping tools, knives, and spears embedded in the sedimentary rock composed largely of the minerals from skeletal fragments of marine organisms that lived in ancient seas and emerged as the water receded over millions of years. For more than 2,000 years, this society worked their quarry, mining flint and developing a trading post and gathering place where they could barter weapons, knives, and tools for food and goods. As the site grew into a social center, it probably became the first industrial-commercial center in the Middle East.

Twelve thousand years later, in 1963, an archeological survey by Istanbul University and the University of Chicago noted this site, but the researchers erroneously assumed that the stone slabs they found were from a Byzantine cemetery. Then, in 1994, archeologist Klaus Schmidt of the German Archaeological Institute reexamined the site, recognized the possibility that it was prehistoric, and began excavations, initially in collaboration with the Sanliurfa Archeological Museum, which was located just a few miles away. His investigation soon revealed that the site was the greatest Middle Eastern archeological discovery *ever*—one that would revolutionize the way we look at human history and the origin of religion. Schmidt has overseen excavations there since 1995 with the additional assistance of the German Archeological Institute of Istanbul.

Göbekli Tepe has unique significance not only because of its age but also because it upends the conventional belief that Neolithic domestication of grains and animals predated the building of religious sanctuaries. Science writer Patrick Symmes noted:

> The site isn't just old, it redefines old: the temple was built 11,500 years ago—a staggering 7,000 years before the Great Pyramid, and more than 6,000 years before Stonehenge first took shape. The ruins are so early that they predate villages, pottery, domesticated animals, and even agriculture—the first embers of civilization. In fact, Schmidt thinks the temple itself, built after the end of the last Ice Age by hunter-gatherers, became that ember—the spark that launched mankind toward farming, urban life, and all that followed.[6]

Unlike almost all other ancient sites, Göbekli Tepe was discovered intact and well-preserved. The site features rings of stone walls with two large, T-shaped, upright monoliths surrounded by several smaller ones within each circle. These pillars range from ten to twenty feet in height and forty to sixty tons in weight. Some of the larger ones depict clothed men with carved details such as shoulders, elbows, and jointed fingers. These figures might have represented priests or shamans or perhaps anthropomorphic depictions of nature deities.

Elaborate carvings have been found on about half of the fifty pillars that Schmidt has unearthed. A few of the carvings are abstract symbols, but most are graceful, naturalistic sculptures and bas-reliefs of the animals that were central to hunters' lives, from wild boar and aurochs, an extinct species of cattle, to totemic images of power and intelligence associated with lions, foxes, and leopards. Alongside these were images that typically instill fear, such as spiders, scorpions, snakes, fanged monsters, and carrion birds. Yet while the carvings show reverence for the animal world, depictions of domesticated animals are conspicuously absent—except for those of dogs.

There were floors of burned lime and clay within the circular walls around the pillars. Archeologists long thought that the structures at Göbekli Tepe were built without roofs. However, they later noted that large rings of monolithic T-shaped columns were paired with larger T-shaped columns at the center, a configuration that could have supported roofs.

Symmes wrote that Göbekli Tepe offers unexpected proof that "mankind emerged from the 140,000-year reign of hunter-gatherers with a ready vocabulary of spiritual imagery and a capacity for huge logistical, economic, and political efforts." [7] He endorsed Schmidt's belief that this site was a huge ceremonial site, "a 'Rome of the Ice Age' ... where hunter-gatherers met to build a complex religious community."[8] Andrew Curry, writing for *Smithsonian Magazine*, noted Schmidt's belief that this was a place of worship on an unprecedented scale—humanity's first "cathedral on a hill." [9]

Schmidt put forth the thesis that it was the urge to worship that brought mankind together in a community that was larger than typical hunter-gatherer groups. It was the drive to build and maintain this cere-monial site or temple complex that created the need for stable food sources, part of which were likely domesticated grains and animals. He wrote:

> The temple begat the city. This theory reverses a standard chronology of human origins, in which primitive man went through a "Neolithic revolution" 10,000 to 12,000 years ago. In the old model, shepherds and farmers appeared first, and then created pottery, villages, cities, specialized labor, kings, writing, art, and—somewhere on the way to the airplane—organized religion. As far back as Jean-Jacques Rousseau, thinkers have argued that the social compact of cities came first, and only then the "high" religions with their great temples, a paradigm still taught in American high schools.[10]

The massive, carved megaliths of Göbekli Tepe were crafted and arranged by prehistoric people who had not yet developed metal tools, pottery, or the wheel. How did they move such massive pillars from the nearby quarry to the site where they were carved? It has been estimated that at least 500 people were required to quarry these multi-ton stone pillars and then move them a quarter mile to the hill and erect them. How did Stone Age people achieve the level of organization necessary to do this? It seems probable that an elite class of religious leaders, such as priests or shamans, supervised the work. The archeologist Sandra Scham observed, "If so, this would be the oldest known evidence for a priestly caste—much earlier than when social distinctions became evident at other Near Eastern sites."[11]

Before the discovery of Göbekli Tepe, traditional historical and archeological belief had been that the domestication of plants and animals in the Neolithic Age preceded the building of structures for worship. This conventional certainty was based on the rational conjec-ture that only settled communities would have had the specialized labor and sufficient prosperity necessary to invest resources in constructing temples. But no signs of a village have been found at or near Göbekli Tepe. It appears that the cathedral not only predated the town but also the domestication of plants and animals.

Symmes commented, "Religion now appears so early in civilized life—earlier than civilized life, if Schmidt is correct—that some think it may be less a product of culture than a cause of it."[12] It would appear that energies were released by a Prophet of God who appeared at that time. The renewal of spiritual energy would have stimulated the building of Göbekli Tepe and the creation of its artistry as well as catalyzed cultural and civilizational development. As 'Abdu'l-Bahá told a New York audience in 1912, *"Thus there have been many holy Manifestations of God. One thousand years ago, two hundred thousand years ago, one million years ago, the bounty of God was flowing, the radiance of God was shining, the dominion of God was existing."*[13]

These pre-agricultural hunter-gatherers must have been imbued with a strong belief system that inspired them to support the luxury of several hundred workers building a temple complex. And it appears that this building endeavor, with its unprecedented and magnificent spiritual imagery and motivating consciousness, was a prompt for the development of civilization in the Middle East.

It's worth noting that the oldest known domesticated wheat was found on Karadag, a mountain eighteen miles from Göbekli Tepe. Harvesting experiments there have shown that enough wild einkorn (single-grain) wheat could easily have been harvested to support substantial hunter-gatherer settlements. Radiocarbon dating of wheat samples found at the earliest agricultural locations in the area indicates an age range from 9700 to 9500 BCE.[14] These dates mean that the beginning of the Neolithic agricultural revolution was much earlier than typically recognized.

Steven Mithen, an archeologist and scholar of prehistory, suggests that the switch to grain domestication was a direct result of the construction activities at Göbekli Tepe, which required large quantities of food to sustain the workers. During the collection of wild grain, some seeds would have fallen to the ground, sprouted, and been harvested again, thus starting the process of domestication. Mithen concluded that it might not have been a drier climactic spell that triggered Neolithic agriculture, as many researchers think. Instead, "It may have been a by-product of the ideology that drove hunter-gatherers to carve and erect massive pillars on a hilltop in southern Turkey." [15]

Worship and socialization at Göbekli Tepe came to an end about 8000 BCE. The factors that inspired the continual building of this temple site and its use for rituals and spiritual practices for more than 2,000 years had evidently waned. Perhaps the trend to domestication left too few nomads to visit the site as in centuries past, or maybe settled domesticators developed a new worldview that did not support the spirit of the site.

Inexplicably, segments of Göbekli Tepe were serially, and perhaps ritually, buried as the building continued and the hallowed ground was expanded. Before the site was abandoned, its remaining open areas were also buried. This feat of backfilling would have taken incredible effort and purpose. Perhaps the incentive was a belief that the site was too sacred to risk its profanation after abandonment.

It is likely that more definitive information will emerge from the archeological excavations. The Turkish newspaper, *The Hurriyet Daily News*, reported on July 15, 2018, that Mehmet Önal, the head of the Archeology Department at Harran University in Sanliurfa, stated that at least fifteen more mega-monumental temples with more than 200 standing stones had been discovered as part of geophysical surveys in the region. Onal also stated that the excavations in Göbekli Tepe will continue for an estimated 150 years or more.

ANIMIST SPIRITUALITY AT GÖBEKLI TEPE

What were the religious beliefs of these Stone Age hunters that inspired them to build this pilgrimage and worship site? Archeologists can work with only physical remains. As the archeologist Lewis Binford wrote, "Archeologists are poorly equipped to be paleo-psychologists." [16] No hints are left of the nature of the rituals that were probably performed at Göbekli Tepe. No traces of altars or blood from animal sacrifice have been found, which suggests that blood sacrifice was introduced later by Neolithic pastoralists. The stone walls and the pillars with their carvings are silent witnesses to whatever occurred there.

However, the reverence for animal life indicated in the carvings strongly suggests animism, a belief system that attributes a spiritual essence to nonhuman life. In animist thought, nonhuman entities are spiritual beings that could be either good or evil. Sometimes these spirits are thought to be the souls of the deceased. In this belief system, humans are an intrinsic part of nature rather than superior to it or separate from it, thereby putting them on equal footing with natural forces. Therefore, these forces, especially those of animals and the weather, must be treated with respect. Goodwill in rituals would have been essential to gaining the cooperation of spirits that could help worshippers find food and shelter and maintain fertility.

If animism was the ideology of Göbekli Tepe, there would almost certainly have been a parallel development of shamanism. Sometimes called medicine men, shamans serve as intermediaries between the seen and the unseen worlds in curing illness, foretelling the future, and controlling natural forces. Shamans would have been responsible for finding increasingly scarce meals-on-the-hoof. The glaciers of the ice ages once provided walls of ice that kept animals in the valley, but as they melted, game wandered farther away into the Zagros and Taurus mountains. At the same time, human population growth would have contributed to thinning the herds. Shamans would also have guided the continual construction of Göbekli Tepe and developed the rituals for worship there.

Karl W. Luckert, Professor Emeritus of the History of Religions at Missouri State University, visited and studied Göbekli Tepe. He advanced a guilt theory that the killing of animals was a serious matter to these hunters because the spirits of animals were possibly identified as spirit siblings to man. There might also have been a reverence for the earth that caused guilt about extracting flint nodules from it. Luckert concluded that rituals of atonement were practiced at Göbekli Tepe because he believed that early religions usually evolved as answers to problems stemming from hunting, domestication, and what he called "hyper-domestication," which will be discussed later. Luckert was forcefully direct in his comments as he considered these difficult concepts:

> The great conflicts that have been engulfing cultures, tribes, and civilizations were generated predominantly by men. While writing "by men" I specifically refer to "huntsmen, domesticators, butcher-priests, executioners, kings, warriors, craftsmen, manufacturers, merchants, scientists and technicians." Indeed, what a latter-day holy book confirms may be read gender-specific in English, to the effect that "by man came death" (1 Cor. 15:21). By males was amplified the art of killing, and consequently life and salvation needed to be brought back, or at least permitted to return, by men who had become obstacles to life.[17]

Luckert was emphatic that hunter-gatherers were rigidly separated into killers (men) and foragers (women), almost to the point of males and females being culturally distinct subspecies to each other. Within this culture, however, there could have been a considerable degree of freedom for women, whose men were often absent on hunting trips. They would have been self-sufficient and made their own decisions while the men were absent. It is doubtful that guilt and atonement were part of the psyche of women foragers. Their pursuits and concerns would more likely have birthed ideologies and rituals that held meaning in their lives as gatherers and mothers.

ATONEMENT AND ONEMENT

Some archeologists theorize that when hunters arrived at Göbekli Tepe to replenish their tools and weapons and to share their stories of the hunt, they may also have shared shades of guilt about the slaughter of animals. The conundrum was that even if animals were spirit siblings to people, killing them was necessary for survival. Therefore, rituals of atonement might have evolved to assuage this guilt. These hunters were caught in a seemingly irreconcilable situation, a dichotomy between reconciliation with the forces of nature and the necessity to petition these forces for assistance in the hunt.

Despite the dilemma of killing to live, the architecture, sculptures, and art at Göbekli Tepe were life affirming. They also reflected a society where men had the leisure time to become accomplished artists. Luckert sympathetically portrayed the men at Göbekli Tepe as having tried to come to grips with death, perhaps their own as well as that of the animals they killed. Luckert saw their attunement with nature as containing the seeds of nurturance, which was a key quality for the Neolithic revolution:

> They lived, they killed, they ate and they died. But at the Göbekli Tepe sanctuaries, for a time, they succeeded in ritually discounting and defeating death. With the skills they had they could not win immortality for themselves. But then, not all was lost. The education and enthusiasm for life, which they perpetuated in their rituals, eventually enabled some of them to convert to a strategy of nurturing living things. Learning thus, they invented domestication and helped themselves and their offspring prosper. We have here, in a brief moment in evolutionary time, the glimpse of a religious intuition that enabled human minds, and hands, to begin resolving the self-inflicted crisis of the Neolithic.[18]

Theories of religious practice and belief at Göbekli Tepe cannot be proven with available data. Still, it appears that the driving force was a spiritual one that took the people through an arc of religious and cultural development. After this force dwindled, a new one would propel the people in early settlements to further progress. The town of Çatalhöyük, with its own mysteries, awaits us.

Chapter 2
AUROCHS AND ANCESTORS

Why farm? Why give up the 20-hour work week and the fun of hunting in order to toil in the sun? Why work harder for food less nutritious and a supply more capricious? Why invite famine, plague, pestilence and crowded living conditions?

JACK R. HARLAN[1]

THE MIDDLE EAST IS unique, both geographically and spiritually. When the globe is presented as a cylindrical Mercator projection, flat and rectangular, the Middle East is in the center of the earth's land mass. This small region is the intersection of three continents—Africa, Asia, and Europe. It was here that our known history of the magnificent drama of six of the world's major religions unfolded. A recognized succession of God's Prophets—Adam, Noah, Abraham, Moses, Zoroaster, Jesus, Muḥammad, the Báb, and Baháʼuʼlláh—walked among the people in the Middle East. What a tremendous amount of spiritual capital was invested in this small area of the world!

Before this infusion of divine spiritual education could unfold, however, humanity had to progress from hunter-gatherer nomadic groups to more complex societies. The Neolithic Revolution, the transition from foraging and hunting to domestication of plants and animals, developed first in the Middle East. The nomadic hunter-gatherer lifestyle had, to that point, characterized more than ninety-nine

13

percent of humanity's tenure on Earth. The shift from nomadism to agricultural settlements took only a few thousand years in Europe and the Middle East. This change also fostered new spiritual beliefs and challenges.

ENTRAPMENTS OF DOMESTICATION

The ramifications of the transition from nomadic life to farming and village dwelling have been preserved in scripture and folklore. The renowned anthropologist Alan H. Simmons described the Eden story in Genesis as an allegory of the move from the freedom of hunting and gathering to the discipline and back-breaking work of farming:

> The socioeconomic transition from foraging to farming left its imprint on the collective human memory, expressed in various parts of the world in mythological stories. Judging by the myths, the transition from the seemingly leisurely lifeways of hunting and gathering to toiling on the land, sowing, planting, harvesting, and storing surplus grain, was a major shift in the role of both work and gender in society. In the biblical story it is retold as the expulsion of Adam and Eve from the Garden of Eden. Thus, the transition in lifeways caused by the Neolithic Revolution resulted in deep-seated cultural shock retained in the oral history of the populations of the Near East.[2]

It's ironic that Göbekli Tepe, which venerated the comparatively leisurely hunter-gatherer lifestyle, would stimulate the start of domestication and the hard existence of subsistence farming. When the weather was within normal parameters and nature was bountiful, hunter-gatherers could have a two-day workweek and a five-day weekend with leisure time for cultural activities and socializing, while farmers labored seven days a week from sunrise to sundown. Eminent anthropologist Marshall Sahlins concluded that agriculturists work much harder than hunter-gatherers and compared their values with our modern ones:

14

Hunter-gatherers consume [use] less energy per capita per year than any other group of human beings. Yet when you come to examine it the original affluent society was none other than the hunter's—in which all the people's material wants were easily satisfied. To accept that hunters are affluent is therefore to recognize that the present human condition of man slaving to bridge the gap between his unlimited wants and his insufficient means is a tragedy of modern times.[3]

Other academics in the fields of history, anthropology, and archeology have also recognized the problems brought by domestication. For example, archaeologists David Lewis-Williams and David Pearce questioned the generally held belief that domestication improved the quality of life.

On the one hand, agriculture seems to Westerners to be a good idea, an advance toward civilization. On the other hand, it could be pointed out that domesticated plants and animals were more prone to catastrophic disease, and, in any event, farmers work harder and longer hours than hunter-gatherers. Perhaps this change was humankind's first Big Mistake.[4]

The hunter traveled light and kept his tool kit simple. Most of his efforts went into tracking, ambushing, and red-hot pursuit. Successful hunts were celebrated with feasts and reenactments of the hunt. Meat from the kill was divided among the family and clan members. Although a skilled hunter could win extra status by showing extraordinary valor on the hunting range, hunter-gatherer societies were basically egalitarian in nature. This belief is based on extensive research of today's Stone Age cultures. As reported in the international newsletter *New Scientist*:

For 5,000 years, humans have grown accustomed to living in societies dominated by the privileged few. But it wasn't always this way. For tens of thousands of years, egalitarian hunter-gatherer societies were widespread. And as a large body of anthropological research shows, long before we organized ourselves into hierarchies of wealth, social status and power, these groups rigorously enforced norms that prevented any individual or group from acquiring more status, authority or resources than others.

Decision-making was decentralized and leadership ad hoc; there weren't any chiefs. There were sporadic hot-blooded fights between individuals, of course, but there was no organized conflict between groups. Nor were there strong notions of private property and therefore any need for territorial defense. These social norms affected gender roles as well; women were important producers and relatively empowered, and marriages were typically monogamous.

Keeping the playing field level was a matter of survival... sharing and cooperation were required to ensure everyone got enough to eat. Anyone who made a bid for higher status or attempted to take more than their share would be ridiculed or ostracized for their audacity.[5]

The decision to farm could have been a response to drought brought on by climate change that caused the forests and herds to retreat as well as the need to feed an increasing population. But settled village life trapped the domesticators in the boredom of methodical and ritualized work habits dictated by future requirements for sustaining the family and community. Farmers could accumulate larger quantities of food and establish elaborate procedures for the building and maintenance of equipment, but that work had none of the excitement of red-hot pursuits. As man no longer took from nature everything he needed, a new sense of ownership and social stratification developed. Yet a certain need to keep matters right with the spirit world may have remained. This would explain the origination of animal sacrifice as a ritual. Luckert explains that ritual procedures were still needed for justification of killing and alleviation of the guilt of killing, even though hunting was assisted by the spirits of nature. Domestic butchering shifted the weight of ceremonial justification to claims of divinely guaranteed ownership of animals, thereby raising new problems:

> The guilt of killing and eating, among domesticators, became a problem of cult and culture-defined economics which, in turn, was based on divinely granted status and property rights.
>
> Ownership of possessions could be demonstrated among domesticators by offering advance-share sacrifices to the gods and contracting divine-human covenants for acquisition. For the legitimate acquisition of entire herds, in some early herder cultures, whole individual share-animals needed to be paid to an original divine owner. The price that had to be paid to the gods was often higher than what poorer people could afford. Thus, religiously justified status, demonstrated in the presence of some deity, might then justify and stabilize a lopsided social order. Full share payments legitimatized owning the original breeding stock, not so much because a deity really needed food shares, but to stabilize ownership rights among humankind in a somewhat orderly manner. Theologically, the situation can be understood as the gods having played along in the rituals of humankind, by their grace, to enable human economies, trade, and exchange to begin.[6]

The development of animal sacrifice was a social innovation that had the pragmatic function of balancing a society of early domesticators where every man was still a hunter in his consciousness. There was little work to be done on the farm that was not demeaning to male-hunter egos. The thrill of the hunt remained within his memory as he bent his back to breaking the soil, planting and harvesting, and caring for domesticated animals.

Another far-reaching effect of domestication was its deleterious effect on general physical welfare. Agriculture is more productive than foraging because it produces more food per unit of land. However,

17

agriculture is far less productive than foraging when the food produced is measured by the hours of effort and lack of variety.

Tom Standage, a journalist who covers culture, science, and technology, wrote an eye-opening summary of the dietary effects of domestication in his book, *An Edible History of Humanity*. He reports that the teeth of Neolithic farmers often show dental-enamel hypoplasia, a horizontal striping caused by nutritional distress, but the teeth of hunter-gatherers do not. Dental remains also indicate that farmers suffered from tooth decay caused by carbohydrates in cereal-based diets, but the teeth of hunter-gatherers indicate that they did not. The bones of these farmers often show evidence of rickets, scurvy, and anemia, all caused by malnutrition—but again, the skeletons of ancient hunter-gatherers do not, nor do they show evidence of endemic diseases. The diet of cereal grains did not provide the full range of essential nutrients.[7]

Height was also affected. Dental age in relation to the length of long bones illustrates that farmers were considerably shorter than contemporary hunter-gatherers. Spencer Wells, an expert in biological anthropology and genetics, cited data developed by anthropologist J. Lawrence Angel indicating that the height of hunter-gatherers in about 12,000 BCE averaged 5 feet, 9.7 inches for men and 5 feet, 5.6 inches for women. By 3000 BCE, when farming was the norm, these heights had fallen to 5 feet, 3.5 inches for men and 5 feet, 0.7 inches for women. This loss of height has only recently been regained in richer countries.[8]

Longevity for farmers also declined significantly. During the Late Paleolithic era (30,000 to 9000 BCE), the median life span was 35.4 years for men and 30 years for women. By the late Neolithic Age (5000 to 3000), those averages were 33.1 and 29.2 years, respectively. By the mid-nineteenth century, they had risen to 40 and 38.4 years and by the late twentieth century to 71 and 78.5 years.[9]

Hard manual labor took its toll on both Neolithic men and women, but women seem to have suffered more. Their skeletons often show evidence of arthritis and deformities of the low back, knees, and toes caused by using a saddle quern, a primitive hand mill for grinding grain. Even more critical for women was the decreased size of the pelvic inlet depth, a measurement of the size of the pelvic canal through which a baby passes during birth. Again citing data from Angel, Wells reported that the average size of the pelvic inlet for late Paleolithic women was 97.7 millimeters (3.85 inches). The size decreased in the late Neolithic period to 75.6 millimeters (2.98 inches) and increased to 81 millimeters (3.2 inches) during the Bronze and Iron ages. Size continued to fluctuate, reaching 82.9 millimeters (3.26 inches) at the end of the nineteenth century, a drop from 85.9 millimeters (3.38 inches) during medieval times. By the end of the twentieth century in the United States, it averaged 92.1 millimeters (3.63 inches). A narrower pelvic inlet makes childbirth more difficult, excruciatingly painful, and sometimes lethal.[10] Even today many women and babies would not survive childbirth without Caesarean sections and other modern interventions.

Domesticators were also vulnerable to many diseases that hunter-gatherers escaped by living in small, widely dispersed nomadic groups. Working with domestic animals triggered the process of zoonosis, the spread of disease from animal to man. Viruses and bacteria that were harmless to animals became sources of mumps, measles, smallpox, cowpox, tuberculosis, and undulant fever for humans. Keeping animals in close quarters also heightened contact with parasitic worms as well as insects that carried yellow fever and sleeping sickness. When populations increased in crowded settings, primitive sanitation became a major threat, along with infectious diseases. Perhaps the final insult was the waste from domestic animals that often fouled water supplies.

Continuing with Simmons' allegory mentioned previously about domestication and the expulsion from the Garden of Eden, he noted how prescient it was that God told Eve:

> *I will make your pains in childbearing very severe;*
> *with painful labor you will give birth to children.*
> *Your desire will be for your husband,*
> *and he will rule over you.* (Gen. 3:16)

And that He told Adam:

> *Cursed is the ground because of you;*
> *   through painful toil you will eat food from it*
> *   all the days of your life.*
> *It will produce thorns and thistles for you,*
> *   and you will eat the plants of the field.*
> *By the sweat of your brow*
> *   you will eat your food*
> *until you return to the ground,*
> *   since from it you were taken;*
> *for dust you are*
> *   and to dust you will return.*
> (Gen. 3:17–19)

On a more positive note, Neolithic society in the Middle East was peaceful, as evidenced by excavated villages and towns that showed no evidence of walls. Despite the health hazards of domesticator life, more dependable food sources combined with a relatively peaceful lifestyle resulted in population growth, economic transformation, and social reorganization.

Given the difficulties and setbacks of transitioning from a nomadic life to a settled one, one wonders: Why did humanity go down such a problematic path? One response comes from a perspective of the need for social and spiritual growth. Nomadism had severe limitations for human experience and progress. It was time to move on. 'Abdu'l-Bahá explained, *"The wisdom of the appearance of the spirit in the body is this: The human spirit is a divine trust which must traverse every degree, for traversing and passing through the degrees of existence is the means of its acquiring perfections."*[11]

Stone Age people would not progress by traversing all conditions because they had neither the reason nor the opportunity to do so within their limited worldview—until something nudged or forced them. Did divine educators appear among the hunter-gatherers at the quarry at Göbekli Tepe to foster change and inspire hearts to spiritual progress? In all probability, Prophets unknown to us, forgotten in the mists of time, came to catalyze the social and spiritual evolution of Middle Eastern societies according to their needs.

THE WORLD OF ÇATALHÖYÜK

At the excavated site of Çatalhöyük, about 200 miles west of Göbekli Tepe, a well-established village of domesticators offers insights into the Neolithic concept of the universe. Archeologists believe that this village was representative of Neolithic settlements throughout the Middle East. The mound covering it was first excavated from 1961 to 1965 by James Mellaart, an archeologist associated with the British Institute of Archeology in Ankara, Turkey, who discovered the site. Since 1993 Ian Hodder has led an international team of archeologists and other specialists in further excavations of the settlement as the Director of the Çatalhöyük Archaeological Project.

Çatalhöyük was strategically located on 34 acres on the Konya Plain in Anatolia and was occupied from about 7500 to 5700 BCE. Situated on a hill by the banks of a river, the village was close to marshes where lime-rich soil could be gathered for frequent plastering of floors and walls and where reeds were easily harvested for mats and baskets. The dry lands of the agricultural fields were seven miles away, which indicates that some members of the village lived in field huts during the growing and harvesting seasons.

Roughly 3,000 to 8,000 people lived in Çatalhöyük at any given time. Excavations uncovered eighteen levels of tightly packed, multi-room homes built from mud bricks and timber. "Crowded" does not begin to describe the layout. These "condos" did not share all of their outside walls, but the distances between them could sometimes be measured in centimeters. There were no alleys or footpaths between buildings. Homes were accessed through a hole in the roof and an internal ladder or, if they had an outside wall, by doorways with exterior ladders. With no streets or ground-level walkways, roofs served as thoroughfares—up and down through the roof holes, over and across the roofs. The only source of daylight seems to have been those roof entries, while protection from the elements took the form of wooden barriers mounted on slanted frames. Domed ovens provided both heat and light.

Close to living units, livestock pens housed goats and sheep. Empty houses served as middens, or garbage heaps. The stench from such a closely-packed population, the middens, and the livestock would have been overwhelming to our senses. Epidemics must have been rampant in the crowded, unsanitary conditions. And one can only imagine the cacophony. One wonders if children and less-than-nimble adults injured themselves climbing up and down ladders or falling through rooftop entryways.

Skulls, tusks, and horns of aurochs and boars' teeth, and other parts of wild animals were fastened to interior walls, which also bore the sculpted figures of wild animals. Why were homes constructed in such an inconvenient manner, and why were they decorated in such a wild, even dangerous, fashion? Perhaps the hunt was sanctified in some way, or maybe the fear of the afterlife was portrayed in the tiered levels.

The wildness of nature was not limited to the mounting of horns and tusks on, or in, the walls. An amazing concentration of wall art adorned the north walls of the houses, depicting the collective hunting of dangerous animals, such as big cats, vultures, boars, and auroch bulls. Wild animal artifacts were set into walls and then repeatedly plastered over, and niches, sometimes painted red, went deep into the walls. Images of people dancing around agitated aurochs might represent a ritual of the hunt. Geometric symbols, whose meanings remain unknown, were included in the paintings. As in Göbekli Tepe, representations of agriculture and domesticated animals were conspicuously absent, which could reflect an inner conflict about domesticated life and an idealization of the hunter lifestyle.

David Lewis-Williams studied the excavations at Çatalhöyük and saw in its architecture symbolism of belief in a tiered cosmos. Typical of this belief would be a subterranean level inhabited by spirits and spirit-animals, an upper level in or above the sky with its own spirits or creatures, and an intermediate level where humans live. He noted that the outside ladders were not only functional but, in accordance with much shamanistic lore, could have represented ascent to an upper realm. Platforms within these small homes might have been associated with transitions within cosmic levels. It's probable that strict traditions and taboos were observed in movements within the homes and that usages of various spaces were firmly defined in keeping with belief in a multi-tiered cosmos and one's need to either access or avoid aspects of it. Certain persons were buried underneath platforms, possibly to protect the home from negative spirits of the underworld. Walls seemed to be considered permeable to other levels of reality. Rooms were not accessed by doors but by small portholes that could be passed through only by bending or crawling. The walls, floors, and animal artifacts were plastered repeatedly. Whatever points of theology were reflected in the architecture, treatment of the homes when abandoned was telling:

> Not only were the plaster figures defaced by having their hands, feet and faces broken, but the small porthole-like "doorways" between rooms were bricked up. Any further emergency of figures from the walls, as well as the possibility of human beings or, more probably, spirit beings crawling through walls, was thus both literally and symbolically terminated before a new room was built. Clearly, there was more to these structures than mundane living quarters.[12]

Surprisingly, Çatalhöyük lacked public buildings and any evidence of a priesthood. No remains of administrative centers, temples, or elite quarters have been found. Excavations indicate a relative equality of status as all the houses were of a similar size. Life revolved around and inside the houses, so social restrictions must have been severe to preserve harmonious living in such a densely populated environment.

With no public places to produce household or trade goods, these tasks must also have taken place in the houses amid specific and practical restrictions and taboos for uses of different spaces in the home. Hodder equated the hold that the homes had on their occupants with entanglement in the materiality they represented:

People and society had become thoroughly entangled in the materiality of the house—in its construction, use, abandonment, rebuilding and so on. Children grew up in a world in which small things mattered—where one cooked, how one swept up, where one hid little figurines, and so on. There were new relationships with a more historical past, and new senses of individual and material agency. Social life centered upon the house and a set of values associated with hunting, sexual and other prowess, feasting and ancestry. All these went alongside settled "town" life and the domestication of plants and animals.

The smallest of actions, such as the decision to plaster the house floors with fine muds, or the decision to keep obsidian pre-forms below the floors, had as much impact as the first planting of a seed or the first tethering of a cow. This is because the small decisions involved changes in material-human relations that also changed the ways people interacted with each other and with the spirit world.[13]

Çatalhöyük, with its tiny homes and restricted modes of conduct, suggests fear of the unknown. Uniformity of thought seems to have replaced the creativity of Göbekli Tepe and probably the free-wheeling sharing that resulted from meetings with diverse people who came from long distances on foot.

Some of the deceased were buried beneath the floors and platforms on the north side of the houses, where most of the wall art and animal artifacts were located. Perhaps space below the floors represented the lower third of the cosmos and the afterlife so that spirits of buried relatives could protect the house or intercede for the family in some way. Whatever the beliefs were, this burial practice suggests ancestor veneration, if not worship, and gives evidence to a belief in some form of survival after death.

Another indication of ancestor veneration is the symbolic decoration of skulls, a practice that was prevalent throughout the Middle East during Neolithic times. Human skulls were plastered to replicate life and then painted in several layers of red. Some skulls were probably displayed in wall niches and others reburied, perhaps at the time a house was rebuilt since a few skulls were found at the bottom of house posts, for what were probably ritual reasons. At least one skull was found cradled in the arms of a full skeleton.

Archeology focuses on the tangible remains of a culture. Theories about the intangible, such as religious beliefs and rituals, always carry a degree of uncertainty. Some artifacts provide obvious information, such as pig bones in the midden. But Neolithic beliefs remain vague because there is a total lack of written records and a complete loss of the language. Even so, Hodder recognizes religion as a vital aspect of life at Çatalhöyük:

> Humans at Çatalhöyük lived religion in all aspects of their lives as part of a seamless world. In everything they did there was an understanding that the world had vitality and power. The world was replete with substances that flowed and transformed and with surfaces that could be passed through. According to this view, religion was an ever-present component of the life process. For example, both ancestors and wild animals were necessary for daily life, and they protected each other in the context of the home.[14]

In Çatalhöyük, as in other Neolithic settlements, materialism started gaining a pernicious hold that would strengthen for thousands of years. Perhaps this was a consequence of humans trying to manage and control forces they did not understand.

The Neolithic bridge from hunter-gatherers to the beginning of Sumerian city-states ran its course for 5,000 or 6,000 years with continued advances in art and technology. Cereal crops and animal husbandry continued to make population growth possible.

As the late Neolithic age gradually gave way to early Sumerian civilization, priests replaced shamans to serve the gods and function as exalted killers of sacrificial animals. Social stratification became more complex, and there was a greater preoccupation with wealth and status. For the first time in recorded human history, war and slavery became common-place. These developments are what Luckert meant by "hyper-domesti-cation," a process that continued to develop into our time.

City-states replaced Neolithic villages. Trade developed, and skills diversified to meet the new needs of an advancing civilization, which brought new temptations for entrapment in materiality. The stage was being set for the coming of Adam and religious beliefs more familiar to us.

Chapter 3

GODS AND GODDESSES

The real challenge for biblical archeologists today is not to search for long-lost cities but to understand why the ancient Israelites formulated these powerful myths.

Eric H. Cline[1]

HISTORIANS GENERALLY REGARD THE Neolithic Revolution in the Middle East as the most significant turning point in ancient human history. In contrast to the Paleolithic period, which lasted from about 2.6 million years to 12,000 BCE, the Neolithic period lasted only 5,000 or 6,000 years. The transition to a settled farming lifestyle, with its accompanying population increase, gradually led to the development of more complex societies and belief systems, probably catalyzed by various divine Messengers at critical points. Specialized labor evolved and, with it, more complicated social relationships, hierarchies, and interdependence. These settlements were initially autonomous and were not threats to each other.

Paleolithic hunter-gatherer groups undoubtedly skirmished with each other, but the population density was low, and the land was bountiful. An animistic kinship with nature would have dictated taking only what they needed from the land and leaving the rest, knowing that nature's surplus would be waiting for them when they returned. As a result, there would have been little need to fight for resources. However, domesticators tried to impose a hitherto unknown degree of control over nature to guarantee plenty. They planted crops on a seasonal or yearly basis and raised animals to be slaughtered at foreseen, regular intervals. In the process, farmers began to reduce the status of these resources from spiritual kin to objects. The egalitarianism of the hunter-gatherer heritage declined as a mode of survival.

The culture of the city-states led to increasing inequality and ultimately to recognition of kings, chieftains, and priests at the top tier of society, who assumed that they were entitled to own and control the land, its mines and farms, and even their fellow humans. Artisans and merchants bowed to these authorities, while the lower classes were progressively dehumanized as slaves, indentured servants, serfs, peasants, or simply "the poor." Each neighboring village or town represented a new source of land, livestock, and subservient people. Hunting, once limited to the killing of wild prey for survival, became a tool to subjugate or remove other humans.

CITY-STATES AND EMPIRES

A settlement called Eridu, which was founded about 5300 BCE, marked the beginning of the city-state era. Long considered the earliest city in southern Mesopotamia, in a region called Sumer, Eridu is considered by some archeologists to be the oldest city in the world. It was located on the river delta of the Persian Gulf, on the west side of the mouth of the Euphrates River, a few miles south of Ur, the traditional birthplace of Abraham. The Tigris and Euphrates delta became the center of life for Mesopotamian civilization just as the Nile River did in Egypt. Mesopotamia has often been called the "cradle of civilization" because it was the first place where evidence of complex cities was found.

Gwendolyn Leick, an anthropologist who specializes in Assyriology, reports that the first structure found at the lowest level of Eridu included a primitive chapel no more than three meters (about ten feet) square, with a pedestal facing the entrance and a recessed wall niche. Wooden images of gods were often displayed in wall niches of Sumerian temples. This shrine was rebuilt with sun-dried bricks many times

over 1,000 years until it became a *ziggurat*, a monumentally sized plat-
form temple featuring a large central room with a pedestal and several
side rooms.[2]

Like the Neolithic people who sealed their houses when building new
ones on top, the Sumerians sealed the earlier temples before building on
top of them. Unlike their forebearers, who had no public buildings or
shrines, the people of Eridu and the other city-states built public temples
as the seats of their many gods. Worship of the deities was both public in
the temples and private at home shrines.

The early city-states showed no archeological evidence of city
walls, indicating peaceful trade relations with other settlements. In time,
though, hostilities developed, and city-states took turns conquering
each other. City walls began to appear in the early third millennium,
indicating a rise in intercity strife and incursions from the outside—the
beginning of warfare as we know it. A succession of Mesopotamian
city-states rose and fell, including Eridu, Uruk, Shuruppak, Akkad, Ur,
Nippur, Sippar, Ashur, Nineveh, and Babylon. Empires evolved. The
hyper-domestication described by Luckert developed from the city-states
into the fearsome empires and conquering armies of Akkadia, Assyria,
and Babylonia. At its height, the Assyrian Empire stretched from the
Mediterranean Sea to the Caspian Sea and from the foothills of the
Caucasus Mountains to Egypt.

Robert N. Bellah, a preeminent sociologist of religion, noted that
the alluvial plains of southern Mesopotamia were only sparsely settled
until about 3200 BCE, when true cities started emerging. These early
urban sites focused on monumental temple compounds, but they also
had palaces, markets, and extensive housing. New levels of population
density were supported by irrigation agriculture, and the growth of these
cities was also supported by another revolution:

> The economic basis of these cities was not just local irriga-
> tion agriculture, but area-wide economic innovations that
> Andrew Sherratt has called the secondary products revolu-
> tion, a transformation that he believes was as significant as the

29

beginnings of plant and animal domestication themselves, at least 4,000 years earlier.[3]

The secondary products revolution made domestication far more efficient and productive. For example, the invention of yokes and harnesses made it possible for animal power to replace human power in agriculture. The plow could go four times deeper than the hoe and was therefore far more efficient. Animal-drawn carts facilitated trade. A new kind of pastoralism emerged as well. The use of milk and milk products, such as yogurt and cheese, originated about this time. Herds used for milk were several times more efficient at producing protein using the same feed than animals raised only for meat. The same was true for sheep that supplied wool for textiles as well as serving as food. Earlier textiles had been woven from vegetable fiber.

Bellah pulled the various factors together: "In spite of great ingenuity in the use of resources indigenous to the area, it is clear that trade, including long-distance trade, was essential from the very beginning. Thus, a region-wide economy, involving plow agriculture and intensive pastoralism, together with a considerable amount of trade, had appeared by the end of the fourth millennium BCE."[4]

There was also an explosion of learning and technology in the land between the Tigris and Euphrates Rivers. Innumerable inventions included the sailboat, the potter's wheel, and wheeled vehicles. The wheel was either invented in Sumer or developed there for use in irrigation machinery and other mechanisms. The most extensive irrigation system ever known in the Middle East was built in Sumer. The donkey-drawn cart and horse-drawn chariot revolutionized trade and warfare.

Cuneiform, or wedge writing, was the world's first system of writing, invented as early as 3800 BCE for commercial use. Accounting systems were created to handle the needs of commerce and centralized administrations.

The breakthrough in mathematics was staggering. The Sumerians developed a mathematical system based on the number 60, which is the base still used globally today for the minutes in an hour and the seconds in a minute. The original sexagesimal system enabled the Sumerians to calculate roots, multiply into millions, and use fractions. Our math still uses 360 degrees in a circle and 12 inches in a foot. The Sumerians also invented the astrolabe, an astronomical device used in ocean navigation. It was used for solving problems relating to time and the positions of the sun and stars. They looked to the skies and developed astronomy, the lunar calendar, and the sun dial.

At the same time, architecture advanced rapidly with the invention of the pulley, lever, saw, chisel, and other tools. The Sumerians built monumental stone sculptures and stepped temples. They invented engraving and inlay work as well as the brick mold, arch, vault, and dome.

Why did such an outburst of creativity and learning seemingly come out of nowhere? To find the answer, we will first digress to, of all people, Bishop James Ussher.

THE COMING OF ADAM

James Ussher (1581–1656 CE) was Archbishop of Armagh, Primate of All Ireland, and Vice-Chancellor of Trinity College in Dublin, Ireland, before spending most of his life in England. Bishop Ussher was highly regarded in his day as a churchman and scholar who read biblical texts in their original languages. He assembled a timeline of biblical events through a literal reading of the Hebrew Bible. By tracing the "begats" and biblical time references during the monarchies and postexilic times, Ussher dated the creation of the universe and Adam's sojourn in the Garden of Eden to 4004 BCE. Ussher's conclusion reflected the widely held belief of his time that the earth had been created in six days, as told in the book of Genesis. This belief was reinforced by 2 Peter 3:8: *"With the Lord a day is like a thousand years, and a thousand years are like a day."* Ussher's date for the creation 6,000 years ago was broadly accepted for two centuries, until early geologists and other scientists demonstrated that the earth was billions of years old and life on it was millions of years old, as well as constantly evolving in response to changing conditions.

While Ussher's calculations for the creation of the earth and the duration of humanity's time on it were incorrect, they might have closely approximated the time when the Prophet Adam appeared. Six thousand years before the end of the Prophetic Cycle is approximately 4156 BCE. The Bahá'í Writings indicate that the Adamic Cycle lasted 6,000 years, closing in 1844 CE at the beginning of the Bahá'í Cycle. Shoghi Effendi mentioned this when he referred to the Báb as "Prophet and Herald of the Faith of Bahá'u'lláh, Founder of the Dispensation marking the culmination of the six-thousand-year-old Adamic Cycle, Inaugurator of the five thousand century Bahá'í Cycle." [5]

Is it only a coincidence that the growth and flowering of Sumerian civilization occurred in the fourth and third millennia BCE? I think not. Adam, like every Prophet of God, released spiritual energy that triggered a divine springtime that expressed itself not only spiritually but in an accelerated advancement of civilization. In April 1912, in New York City, 'Abdu'l-Bahá explained this outpouring to a Christian audience:

The spiritual world is like unto the phenomenal world. They are the exact counterpart of each other. Whatever objects appear in this world of existence are the outer pictures of the world of heaven. When we look upon the phenomenal world, we perceive that it is divided into four seasons; one is the season of spring, another the season of summer, another autumn and then these three seasons are followed by winter. When the season of spring appears in the arena of existence, the whole world is rejuvenated and finds new life. The soul-refreshing breeze is wafted from every direction; the soul-quickening bounty is everywhere; the cloud of mercy showers down its rain, and the sun shines upon everything. Day by day we perceive that the signs of vegetation are all about us. Wonderful flowers, hyacinths and roses perfume the nostrils. The trees are full of leaves and blossoms, and the blossoms are followed by fruit. The spring and summer are followed by autumn and winter. The flowers wither and are no more; the leaves turn gray and life has gone. Then comes another springtime; the former springtime is renewed; again a new life stirs within everything.

The appearances of the Manifestations of God are the divine springtime. When Christ appeared in this world, it was like the vernal bounty;

the outpouring descended; the effulgences of the Merciful encircled all things; the human world found new life. Even the physical world partook of it. The divine perfections were upraised; souls were trained in the school of heaven so that all grades of human existence received life and light. Then by degrees these fragrances of heaven were discontinued; the season of winter came upon the world; the beauties of spring vanished; the excellences and perfections passed away; the lights and quickening were no longer evident; the phenomenal world and its materialities conquered everything; the spiritualities of life were lost; the world of existence became life unto a lifeless body; there was no trace of the spring left.[6]

In all probability, there was a connection between the coming of Adam about 4000 BCE and the flowering of Mesopotamian civilization over the next millennium. Following the pattern outlined by ʻAbduʼl-Bahá, Mesopotamia experienced an incredible divine springtime. Comparatively speaking, it was the greatest explosion of knowledge until that of the nineteenth and twentieth centuries—which makes sense when one remembers that Adam initiated the Prophetic Cycle and Baháʼuʼlláh initiated the Cycle of Fulfillment.

Gradually, the pace of creative change slowed, and Mesopotamia experienced the plateau of divine summer. After this stable period, Adam's message and teachings would inevitably have become distorted and perverted, leading to the fall and winter of His revelation and accompanied by a decrease in moral vitality, social cohesion, and the memory of His spiritual fragrance. Then the next Prophet of God would have initiated another leap forward, with a new increase in spiritual understanding, a resulting burst of creativity, and another advance in civilization.

MESOPOTAMIAN POLYTHEISM

There is no record of what Adam taught, but like all Prophets of God, He would have wisely worked within the belief system of the people he taught, starting with the culturally familiar and then moving forward. Perhaps He did not teach against polytheism but left the practice alone

33

for that time and place, leaving this issue for the Prophet Abraham to handle. However, by the second millennium BCE, an elaborate pantheon of deities had evolved that was probably symptomatic of the autumn of Adam's Dispensation. Assyriologist John Bottéro, an expert on the ancient Middle East, wrote that no one has yet reached an exact count of the Mesopotamian deities:

> ... but even in round numbers we reach figures that appear totally unbelievable. The most complete count that was ever done in the second millennium by Babylonian scholars came up with almost two thousand names. In his Pantheon babylon-icum of 1914, A. Deimel counts three thousand three hundred names; and the inventory of K. Vallqvist, Akkadische Gőtterep-itheca, compiled in 1938 on stricter criteria, includes around two thousand four hundred! I know of no more recent listing, but the list was not, and still is not, complete: new documents, as they are discovered, continue to present us with the names of deities that were hitherto unknown.[7]

One can get lost in the various legends, identities, and domains of the gods and goddesses. The mythologies and religious beliefs of the people between the rivers were, in a word, complicated. A simplified version of the mythology of the gods indicates that each of the numerous gods was related to a particular aspect of nature and was responsible for keeping the natural systems functioning, and at the same time, each bore part of a collective responsibility for their created servants, the humans. This was a symbiotic relationship between the deities and humans.

There were four major gods. Anu was the father of the gods; his son Enlil was the ruler of the gods; Ninhursaga was the goddess of birth; and Enki was the god of fresh water, of intellect and cunning, and of all productive arts. According to legend, Enlil put the legions of lesser gods to work digging the irrigation canals from the Tigris and Euphrates Rivers. Understandably, they rebelled at the hard task, burned their work tools, and threatened Enlil. Being a god had to count for something! So

Enlil turned to Anu and Enki for help. Enki suggested creating men to do the toilsome work. He killed one of the lesser gods and mixed his blood with clay to fashion the first human beings.

The story continues that humans multiplied and did the work, but overpopulation caused them to become very noisy. Enlil could get no sleep, so he sent a plague to wipe them out. But the wise man Atrahasis consulted Enki, who told him to keep the people quiet and counseled them to give more offerings to the gods. The plague stopped. When the people got noisy again, Enlil sent a drought. Again, Atrahasis persuaded Enki to intervene. The cycle repeated a third time with a flood. As Bellah narrated:

> The third time was really too much and Enlil sent a great flood to kill every human being. Enki, however, was one step ahead of him and had Atrahasis construct an unsinkable boat, load it with every kind of animal, and last out the flood. When Enlil discovered what Enki had done he was furious, but meantime the decimation of the people had left the gods with no offerings, and they were beginning to starve. Enlil finally realized that humans were indispensable to the gods, and, having arranged several methods of birth control, allowed Atrahasis and his people to resettle the earth.[8]

The survivors of the ark disembarked and made a food sacrifice to the gods, which they ravenously devoured. The deities made a covenant with humankind—the gods would never again wipe out humans, and humans would serve the gods while the gods ran the world and looked after them. However, the gods' manner of caretaking would prove to be temperamental and inscrutable. After all, Enlil was a "storm god," a deity who had absolute power and sometimes got out of control. Sensitivity and altruism were not his strongest attributes.

The essence of Mesopotamian religion was service to the gods, whose representations were carved from wood, painted or gilded, and then put on pedestals in temples. A theocratic cult developed in connection with their care and maintenance, which figured prominently in the social hierarchy and economy. Each god and goddess had an individual temple where they lived in peace, dignity, and sumptuous splendor.

Temples became complexes of multiple buildings for administration, storerooms, and housing for the priests and priestesses. The largest temple compounds were virtual cities that became economic centers wielding tremendous power gained from exploitation of the land, herds and agriculture, and commerce. All levels of society contributed to the temples. The wooden deities, which were treated like kings, were given the best of everything.

Almost constant devotion and service to the gods were recommended for secular well-being, not for spiritual betterment as we understand that concept. Such service was viewed as *"beneficial,* reflecting a hedonistic life that was above all geared for success."[9] Was spiritual behavior as we understand it a value in this religion? Bottéro found no such evidence:

> They had, of course, like everyone else, their "moral code," which if not explicitly detailed or conscious, was at least sufficiently known and integrated into their culture. But the reason for following it, beyond the guarantee of a good social order, was ... only to avoid the disadvantages that came from forgetting or ignoring it: the observance of moral laws did not stem from piety but from prudence, precaution (for "success"!). It had absolutely no role in the cult to the glory and benefit of the gods; rather, its sole purpose was to ensure a healthy balance sheet for one's own existence. The only way one could serve the gods and render homage to them was by providing them with opulent goods and services through one's daily work and by serving them or having them served by the appropriate person; all of this was, as the Mesopotamians believed, agreeable and indispensable to the gods, and it was for the preparation, manufacture, and delivery of those goods and services that human beings had been created and put on Earth. Once that fundamental duty had been fulfilled, each person was free, and the gods expected

nothing more from them, although a person might naturally be inclined to expect the gods to return some deserved favor—*do ut des* [something is given so that something may be received].[10]

In light of ancient writings currently available, the gods appear to have been revered but not held close to the heart, glorified but feared, worshipped but not trusted. They were beseeched, cajoled, and supplicated. There seems to have been nothing mystical in this devotion. The world was unstable and unreliable because it was ruled by gods who squabbled among themselves. The theology of Mesopotamian polytheism was an intricate, expensive, and pragmatic balancing act between the gods who ran the world and the humans who served them.

From what is known of Mesopotamian beliefs, death seems to have offered little solace. Bottéro notes that Mesopotamian belief did not include a soul that animated the body but that the deceased turned into phantoms.

> However, death was not nothingness, a notion that was too unimaginable ... for the ancient Mesopotamians ever to have considered.... But foremost, the deceased had not completely disappeared from the existence of the survivors: in their memories, in their dreams, or in their obsessions that the dead person came to them, not only so they would think of him, but so they could see him again, vaguely, and even believe that they heard him speak, cry, wail ... they were convinced that that vague profile, aerial, foggy, evanescent, and untouchable, truly was all that remained of the deceased himself, in his new condition as "shadow," as "specter," as "phantom."[11]

Bottéro likened burial of the body in the earth as sending the "phantom" into the netherworld below, a place of endless, weighty sleep. "Each person upon dying automatically went there, without undergoing any form of 'judgment' in order to be granted a more or less bearable 'fortunate' condition: the last sleep was for everyone."[12] Since the afterlife held no promise of reward or punishment, it was reasonable to believe that only earthly life mattered, with its material goods, pleasures, status, and success.

Scholars of Mesopotamian religion generally consider it to be cyclical and repetitious, with time as a closed circle and life like the revolution of the wheel. Thomas Cahill, author of the *Hinges of History* series, expressed this viewpoint when he wrote, "Cyclical religion goes nowhere because, within its comprehension, there is no future as we have come to understand it, only the next revolution of the Wheel."[13] However, change does occur in a closed system, albeit slowly, and a major change arose out of Mesopotamia when a young man named Abram rejected the idol worship, challenged the emperor on the subject, and was exiled. In time, five religions came to be called Abrahamic—Judaism, Christianity, Islam, the Bábí Faith, and the Bahá'í Faith.

PARALLELS OF MESOPOTAMIAN AND HEBREW MYTHOLOGY

Aspects of Mesopotamian mythology and culture permeate the early Hebrew Scriptures. Enlil mixed blood with clay to fashion the first humans, while Adam was created from the dust of the ground with God's breath breathed into his nostrils. Enlil sent the flood to kill humanity and a few people survived with their animals in a boat, while Noah built an ark to save his family and every species of animal. The reverence of the *cella*, the sacred residence of the deity in the temple, is reminiscent of the inner sanctuary of the Tabernacle and later of the Temple in Jerusalem.

The legend of Sargon the Great of Akkad, who ruled from about 2340 to 2284 BCE, parallels that of Moses. Tradition has it that Sargon was born an illegitimate son of a temple priestess, who set him adrift in a basket on the Euphrates River, where he was found by the gardener Akki. He was appointed as the cupbearer to the king of Kish, who then sent him to work for Lugalzagesi of Uruk. He promptly overthrew Lugalzagesi, conquered Kish and became its king, and founded the city of Akkad (Agade). Then he conquered the Sumerian city-states and forged the first great Semitic kingdom, the Akkadian Empire. Sargon was considered the greatest man who ever lived, and he was celebrated in glorious tales until the days of the ancient Persian Empire.[14]

The Mesopotamian empires gradually collapsed into the proverbial dustbin of history, and their cultures faded from the land between the rivers.

And what had been Adam's mission? Let's backtrack to approximately 4000 BCE and consider the possibilities.

Chapter 4

ADAM, EVE, AND EDEN

For had the embryo not existed, how could he have reached
his present state? Likewise had the religion taught by
Adam not existed, this Faith would not have attained
its present stage. Thus consider thou the development
of God's Faith until the end that hath no end.

The Báb[1]

NOW WE COME TO the Hebrew Bible, which records a people's extraordinary spiritual journey. The inevitable question arises: "How true is the Bible?" 'Abdu'l-Bahá inscribed a Bible in London as follows: *"This Book is the Holy Book of God, of celestial inspiration. It is the Bible of Salvation, the Noble Gospel. It is the Mystery of the Kingdom and its light. It is the Divine Bounty, the sign of guidance of God."*[2]

The Bahá'í approach is, as a letter written from the Universal House of Justice to an individual states, as follows: "The Bahá'ís believe what is in the Bible to be true in substance."[3]

Determining the substance of biblical verses can be daunting because, as 'Abdu'l-Bahá wrote, *"Divine things are too deep to be expressed by common words. The heavenly teachings are expressed in parable in order to be understood and preserved for ages to come."*[4] He also stretched our limits of comprehension by writing that *"the Words of God have innumerable significances and mysteries of meanings—each one a thousand and more."*[5]

Thus cautioned, Bahá'ís first look to the Bahá'í Writings for guidance about the meanings of various biblical verses. Then Bahá'í independent scholarship is encouraged as a valuable part of the development of the intellectual life of the Bahá'í community. Although these efforts have no authority of their own, they add to spiritual knowledge and understanding, like meaty chunks simmering in the interpretive stew.

THE EPIC OF GILGAMESH

There are no historical records of Adam or what He taught because His coming was 6,000 years ago, before the invention of writing. However, it's possible that threads of His teachings were remembered in mythology. The epic mythological poem, *The Epic of Gilgamesh*, is a case in point because it depicts the transition from animal consciousness to human self-awareness. Believed to have been written by 2700 BCE and based on the historical King Gilgamesh, who ruled the city-state of Uruk at that time, this epic poem is the oldest known written story. The oldest existing version of it, written in Sumerian cuneiform, dates to about 2000 BCE.

According to this epic poem, Gilgamesh's exploits became the province of legend and his status that of a god. This classic tale tells how Gilgamesh was a tyrannical ruler who irritated the divine assembly of the gods with his oppression of the people. The gods asked Aruru, the goddess of creation, to create a companion for Gilgamesh to take him on adventures away from Uruk, which led to Enkidu's formation from clay and water. However, Enkidu preferred to run with wild animals, so the divine assembly assigned Shamhat, the Wise Woman, to teach Enkidu how to be human.

Enkidu and the Wise Woman spent several passionate days together. Then, when he tried to rejoin the animals, they rejected him. Enkidu no longer had the strength of an animal, and his mind was filled with a new wisdom. The Wise Woman now made her move. She reproved him for his animal ways and invited him to come to the sanctuary of the gods Anu and Ishtar. She dressed him and taught him how to drink and eat bread and to relate to others.

He became cheerful and playful.
>His heart rejoiced and his face glowed.
He bathed and oiled his body,
>He combed his hair.
Enkidu became human.[6]

The symbology is straightforward. Enkidu was formed from clay, representing the earth and lower consciousness, and water, representing the
spiritual. He had been living only on the lower, animal level, unaware
of his soul. After union with a woman, who represented his soul, and
education by her, he awakened and found the balance between his physical and human selves. He was nurtured with the bread of life, which
was spiritual sustenance, and with beer, which was the fruit of the earth.
Perhaps the Prophet Adam had taught the people about their dual identity and this teaching was remembered throughout the ages in mythology.
And perhaps its symbology was borrowed in part for the Genesis story of
the creation of Adam and Eve.

THE GENESIS STORY OF CREATION

The story of Adam and Eve in the Hebrew Bible is fundamental to most
streams of Christian theology because the belief in the "original sin"
of humanity that required the sacrifice and redemption of Christ came
from it.

The reality of Adam as a Prophet of God bringing divine wisdom
and guidance is an entirely new perspective. About 4,000 years before
Christ and 2,500 years before Abraham, Adam launched a process of
spiritual education of mankind within the cycle named after Him.

Adam was not the innocent man-child of nature depicted in Genesis.
On the contrary, He was at the other end of the spectrum. The Báb
wrote that Adam was the first Prophet of God in this Cycle and provided
insight into His station and His relationship to later Prophets:

*In the time of the First Manifestation the Primal Will appeared in Adam;
in the day of Noah It became known in Noah; in the day of Abraham in*

43

Him; and so in the day of Moses; the day of Jesus; the day of Muḥammad,
the Apostle of God; the day of the "Point of the Bayán" [the Báb]; the day
of Him Whom God shall make manifest [Bahá'u'lláh]; and the day of the
One Who will appear after Him Whom God shall make manifest. Hence
the inner meaning of the words uttered by the Apostle of God [Muḥammad],
"I am all the Prophets," inasmuch as what shineth resplendent in each one
of Them hath been and will ever remain the one and the same sun.[7]

Bahá'u'lláh commented on creation and the Prophet Adam, emphasizing the role of the Word of God as the dawning place of human
intellect and the catalyst for creation:

The entire creation hath been called into being through the Will of God, magni-
fied be His glory, and peerless Adam hath been fashioned through the agency
of His all-compelling Word, a Word which is the source, the wellspring, the
repository, and the dawning-place of the intellect. From it all creation hath
proceeded, and it is the channel of God's primal grace. None can grasp the
reality of the origin of creation save God, exalted be His glory, Whose knowl-
edge embraceth all things both before and after they come into being. Creation
hath neither beginning nor end, and none hath ever unravelled its mystery.[8]

The advent of Adam was a critical marker in human spiritual history
because it initiated the beginning of a cycle that would unfold through
a succession of Prophets over succeeding centuries and millennia. Each
Prophet would inaugurate His own Dispensation by bringing His own
Book, whether written or oral, to educate humanity. Each would confirm
the eternal verities but would have His own mandate specific to the needs
and conditions of society at the time; each would also make references to
future Messengers from God. This chain of progressive revelation would
eventually link Adam with the Báb and Bahá'u'lláh, Who wrote:

Contemplate with thine inward eye the chain of successive Revelations that
hath linked the Manifestation of Adam with that of the Báb. I testify before
God that each one of these Manifestations hath been sent down through the

operation of the Divine Will and Purpose, that each hath been the bearer of a specific Message, that each hath been entrusted with a divinely-revealed Book and been commissioned to unravel the mysteries of a mighty Tablet. The measure of the Revelation with which every one of them hath been identified had been definitely fore-ordained.[9]

An endnote specifically pertaining to the above quotation states, "In the Bahá'í Writings the term 'Adam' is used symbolically in two different senses. The one refers to the emergence of humans, while the other designates the first of the Manifestations of God."[10] Adam in the first instance does not mean the literal creation of a first, singular human being but rather is a symbol for humans reaching a milestone of self-awareness. Adam in the second instance is a Prophet of God.

THE GENESIS NARRATIVES OF
CREATION AND OF ADAM AND EVE

Genesis offers two creation stories, each with a separate sequence of events and area of emphasis. The first version (Gen. 1:1–31, 2:1–3) is often called the *general creation*. It states that in the beginning, the earth was formless, empty, and dark, with the Spirit of God hovering over the waters. Then, six times we read "God said" as He brought about the events of each day of creation. First, God produced light and divided time into darkness and light; then He created a vault, the sky, between the waters to separate them. On the third day, God gathered the water under the sky into the seas so that dry land could appear and be covered with vegetation; then He created the firmament of stars in the sky, along with the sun to preside over day and the moon to rule over night. On Day Five, He made the fish and birds, followed by the animals and, lastly, man in His own image to be the master of all life upon the earth, in the skies, and in the seas. On Day Seven, God rested.

The second version of the creation story (Gen. 2:4–25, 3:1–24), which is often referred to as the *special creation*, starts when there is light and the earth but no vegetation because God has not yet sent rain. Although streams came up from the earth to water the garden, there was no one to work the ground. Then God formed man from the dust of the earth and breathed into his nostrils the breath of life. He put Adam in a garden called Eden, where two particular trees grew among the others—the Tree of Life and the Tree of Knowledge of good and evil. He was to work in the garden and nurture it. Adam was free to eat from any tree there except the Tree of the Knowledge of good and evil because eating from this tree would bring death. God formed the animals and birds out of the ground, and He brought them to Adam to name them. Then God caused Adam to fall into a deep sleep, and He created Eve from one of Adam's ribs. Adam and Eve then lived happily, unashamed of their nakedness, which was a metaphor for spiritual innocence.

Life was good in the garden, but then came the crafty serpent who beguiled Eve. She initially protested eating from the Tree of Knowledge of good and evil, but the serpent assured her that the tree's fruit would not kill her but would instead open her eyes so that she would be like God, knowing good and evil. That sounded wonderful; she ate the fruit of the tree and then offered it to Adam, who also ate. They would never be able to return to their childlike innocence.

When God came looking for them, He deduced what had happened. Adam blamed Eve, while Eve blamed the snake. Who would God chastise first? The snake, who would crawl on his belly, eat dust all his days, and experience enmity between him and Eve and her offspring for generations. Then God declared that He would make Eve's pains in childbirth severe, and her desire would be for her husband, who would rule over her. Turning to Adam, who was probably hoping for the best but fearing the worst, God decreed that the ground would be cursed because of him and that he would toil on it painfully all his life. By the sweat of his brow, Adam would eat his food until he was returned to the ground from whence he had come, *"for dust you are and to dust you will return"* (Gen. 3:19).

But there was also mercy. God prepared Adam and Eve for their departure from Eden by making them garments from the skins of animals. Adam and Eve went forth prepared for a primitive existence.

Then God said, *"The man has now become like one of us, knowing good and evil. He must not be allowed to reach out his hand and take also from the Tree of Life and eat and live forever"* (Gen. 3:22). He placed cherubim and a flaming sword flashing back and forth on the east side of the Garden to guard the way to the Tree of Life.

The theology that developed from a literal interpretation of the Genesis story was never logical. For millennia, the conventional understanding of Adam and Eve engendered many unfortunate consequences for women as it was used to subjugate them to men and to justify belief in their inherent inferiority, emotional instability, and lack of judgment. In *The Legends of the Jews*, Rabbi Louis Ginzburg wrote, "Adam was the heave offering of the world, and Eve defiled it. As expiation, all women are commanded to separate a heave offering from the dough. And because woman extinguished the light of man's soul, she is bidden to kindle the Sabbath light." [11]

Traditional Christian theology, largely formulated by Augustine (354–430 CE), burdened Christianity with the doctrine of original sin, a state of innate sinfulness into which everyone was born and from which everyone had to be saved. Original sin was laid at Eve's door because she had tempted Adam, who in turn was blamed for bringing original sin to mankind. "In Adam's fall, we sinned all." [12] Traditional Christian doctrine has maintained that every soul must be redeemed from original sin or face eternal hell and damnation. This caused guilt and immense fear of the hereafter. Even today, many Christians agonize over whether they are "saved."

THE SYMBOLOGY OF THE
CREATION NARRATIVES

A further search for truth is needed to decipher the two creation stories because the literal approach so fetters the mind and spirit. 'Abdu'l-Bahá explained that only a symbolic approach to this mythic account of creation would reveal its truths:

> *As to the record in the Bible concerning Adam's entering paradise, His eating from the tree and His expulsion through the temptation of Satan: These are all symbols beneath which there are wonderful and divine meanings not to be calculated in years, dates and measurement of time. Likewise, the statement*

47

that God created the heaven and the earth in six days is symbolic. The texts of the Holy Books are all symbolical, needing authoritative interpretation.[13]

'Abdu'l-Bahá gave an extensive account of the symbology of Adam and Eden in answer to questions posed from pilgrims who visited Him in Akka, Palestine. In this account, 'Abdu'l-Bahá also elaborated on the teachings of Jesus. His comments here are not edited or shortened, because there is no substitute for His breadth and clarity of thought:

If we were to take this account according to the literal meaning of the words, as indicated by their common usage, it would indeed be exceedingly strange, and human minds would be excused from accepting, affirming, or imagining it. For such elaborate arrangements and details, such statements and reproaches, would be implausible even coming from an intelligent person, let alone from the Divinity Himself, Who has arranged this infinite universe in the most perfect form and arrayed its countless beings in the utmost order, soundness, and perfection.

One must pause awhile to reflect: If the outward meaning of this account were to be attributed to a wise man, all men of wisdom would assuredly deny it, arguing that such a scheme and arrangement could not possibly have proceeded from such a person. The account of Adam and Eve, their eating from the tree, and their expulsion from Paradise, are therefore symbols and divine mysteries. They have all-embracing meanings and marvelous interpretations; but only the intimates of the divine mysteries and the well-favored of the all-sufficing Lord are aware of the true significance of these symbols.

These verses of the Torah have therefore numerous meanings. We will explain one of them and will say that by Adam is meant the spirit of Adam and by Eve is meant His self. For in certain passages of the sacred scriptures where women are mentioned, the intended meaning is the human self. By the tree of good and evil is meant the material world, for the heavenly realm of the spirit is pure goodness and absolute radiance, but in the material world light and darkness, good and evil, and all manner of opposing realities are to be found.

The meaning of the serpent is attachment to the material world. This attachment of the spirit to the material world led to the banishment of the self and spirit of Adam from the realm of freedom to the world of bondage and caused Him to turn from the kingdom of Divine Unity to the world of human existence. When once the self and spirit of Adam entered the material world, He departed from the paradise of freedom and descended into the realm of bondage. He had abided in the heights of sanctity and absolute goodness, and set foot thereafter in the world of good and evil.

By the tree of life is meant the highest degree of the world of existence, that is, the station of the Word of God and His universal Manifestation. That station was indeed well-guarded, until it appeared and shone forth in the supreme revelation of His universal Manifestation. For the station of Adam, with regard to the appearance and manifestation of the divine perfections, was that of the embryo; the station of Christ was that of coming of age and maturation; and the dawning of the Most Great Luminary* was the station of the perfection of the essence and the attributes. That is why in the all-highest Paradise the tree of life alludes to the focal centre of absolute sanctity and purity, that is, the universal Manifestation of God. For from the days of Adam until the time of Christ there was little mention of life eternal and of the all-embracing perfections of the kingdom on high. This tree of life alludes to the station of the reality of Christ: it was planted in His Dispensation and adorned with everlasting fruits.

Now consider how closely this interpretation conforms to reality: For when the spirit and the self of Adam became attached to the material world, they passed from the realm of freedom into the realm of bondage, this condition was perpetuated with each succeeding generation, and this attachment of spirit and self to the material world, which is sin, was inherited by His descendants. This attachment is the serpent which will forever be in the midst of, and at enmity with, the spirits of the descendants of Adam, for attachment to the world has become the cause of the bondage of the spirits. This bondage is that sin which has been transmitted from Adam to His descendants, for it has deprived men of recognizing their essential spirituality and attaining to exalted stations.

49

When the holy breaths of Christ and the sanctified lights of the Most Great Luminary were spread abroad, human realities—that is, those souls who turned toward the Word of God and partook of His manifold grace—were saved from this attachment and sin, were granted eternal life, were delivered from the chains of bondage and entered the realm of freedom. They were purged of earthly vices and endowed with heavenly virtues. This is the meaning of Christ's words that I gave My blood for the life of the world. That is, I chose to bear all these trials, afflictions and calamities, even the most great martyrdom, to attain this ultimate objective and to ensure the remission of sins—that is, the detachment of spirits from the material world and their attraction to the divine realm—that souls may arise who will be the very essence of guidance and the manifestations of the perfections of the Kingdom on high.

Note that if these words were taken literally, as imagined by the people of the Book,** it would be sheer injustice and absolute predestination. If Adam sinned in approaching the forbidden tree, what then was the sin of glorious Abraham, the Friend of God, and the error of Moses, Who conversed with God? What was the offence of Noah the Prophet and the transgression of truth-speaking Joseph? What was the fault of the Prophets of God and the failure of John the Chaste? Would divine justice have suffered these luminous Manifestations to endure, by reason of Adam's sin, the torment of hell until such time as Christ should come and by His sacrifice rescue them from the nethermost fire? Such a notion is beyond the pale of every rule and principle and no rational person can ever accept it.

Rather, the meaning is that which was already mentioned: Adam is the spirit of Adam and Eve His self; the tree is the material world and the serpent is attachment to it. This attachment, which is sin, has been transmitted to the descendants of Adam. Through the breaths of holiness Christ rescued souls from this attachment and delivered them from this sin.

This sin in Adam, moreover, is relative to His station: Although this worldly attachment produced substantial results, yet in relation to attachment to the spiritual realm it is nonetheless regarded as a sin, and the truth of the saying "The good deeds of the righteous are the sins of the near ones" is established. Again, it is like the power of the body, which is imperfect in relation to the power of the spirit—indeed, it is sheer weakness in comparison.

50

Likewise, material life, compared to eternal existence and the life of the Kingdom, is regarded as death. Thus Christ referred to this material life as death and said, "Let the dead bury their dead." Although those souls enjoyed material life, yet in His eyes that life was even as death.

This is but one of the meanings of the biblical account of Adam. Reflect, that you may discover the others.[14]

* *"By the righteousness of God! The world's horizon is resplendent with the light of the Most Great Luminary, yet the generality of mankind perceive it not."* (Bahá'u'lláh, *Tablets of Bahá'u'lláh Revealed After the Kitáb-i-Aqdas, 236*)

** Jews and Christians

Adam did not *fall*. He *entered!* The Prophet Adam voluntarily left the spiritual realm of His preexistence behind the mystic veil to enter human society in order to start a major cycle, the Prophetic Cycle, of the spiritual education of mankind.

The Paleolithic and the Neolithic societies would have had social laws and taboos that eased the tensions of group life and promoted the common welfare. Some were undoubtedly based on pragmatic considerations for survival through social cooperation. But they also had received divine guidance, as Shoghi Effendi wrote: "We are taught there always have been [other] Manifestations of God, but we do not have any record of their names."[15] As more becomes known about prehistoric times, the clues might become clearer as to when and where these Messengers appeared and what their seeds were—perhaps the migrations from Africa to Europe and Asia, the development of cave art and other artistry, and evolving forms of communal life. One can only speculate. But apparently a major shift, or focus, in God's plan for humanity was inaugurated by the Prophet Adam.

THE TREE OF LIFE

The second tree in Eden, the Tree of Life, was figuratively guarded from humanity by cherubim and a flaming sword because mankind was not ready for it. As quoted above from 'Abdu'l-Bahá with regard to the Tree of Life, *the station of Christ was that of coming of age and maturation.* Human maturation is relative and unfolds by degrees. Eternal life and the heavenly perfections were little mentioned from the days of Adam until those of Christ. All the Prophets have represented the Tree of Life in accordance with the circumstances of their times. But it was Jesus who emphasized the concept of eternal life. Before then, people were not ready for this level of spiritual understanding, even though they were eternal souls who would enter the Kingdoms of God upon death.

Moses introduced a code of moral laws to improve the ethical and social order, but the reward for following them was a good life on Earth. It was Jesus who brought the Tree of Life to fruition within the context of eternal life. In this sense, He "planted" the Tree of Life in His ministry by correlating it with the eternal life of the soul, the life everlasting. The Báb, whose ministry closed the Adamic Cycle and opened the Cycle of Fulfillment, beseeched God that His station as the tree would be fulfilled: *"Consecrate Thou, O my God, the whole of this Tree unto Him, that from it may be revealed all the fruits created by God within it for Him through Whom God hath willed to reveal all that He pleaseth."*[16]

The Tree of Life is also understood as the station of the Universal Manifestation of the Cycle of Fulfillment, Bahá'u'lláh, Who referred to Himself as the Tree of Life in the Tablet of Aḥmad:

> *Verily this is that Most Great Beauty, foretold in the Books of the Messengers, through Whom truth shall be distinguished from error and the wisdom of every command shall be tested. Verily He is the Tree of Life that bringeth forth the fruits of God, the Exalted, the Powerful, the Great.*[17]

Divine education unfolded progressively to the point where the Tree of Life could blossom globally for all mankind, though perhaps incrementally, one leaf at a time.

REFLECTIONS OF ELENA MARIA MARSELLA

Individual Bahá'ís have pondered 'Abdu'l-Bahá's comments on the biblical account of Adam and responded to his challenge: *"Reflect, that you may discover the others."* Elena Maria Marsella reflected on the symbology of the Eden story and approached the tree of knowledge as a moral code:

> At the time of Adam's appearance, Good and Evil, as a purely moral code, had (1) never been introduced to the particular society in which he lived, or (2) had been lost through the deterioration and destruction of a former "world." In either case he would have been nurtured in a culture similar to thousands which still exist today in isolated pockets of the earth—a culture dominated by priests, shamans, and witch doctors and held solidly together by sheer terror of their magical powers.[18]

Next, Marsella approached the subject of Adam's "sin" and put the concept of sin into the context of moral law, which she believes He taught:

> Here there arises the confusing notion that Adam was overcome by Satan, whereas Jesus was not, and Jesus had to come to redeem men for the sin of Adam. But if we consider seriously that Eden was the Garden of Innocence, filled with a child-like unwisdom rather than wisdom, and governed by a primitive code which was lawlessness by comparison with succeeding moral codes, we can see how Adam himself, by *laying down the first moral law for mankind also made man capable of sin.*
>
> The very establishment of any law suggests that it was formulated to correct definite deficiencies. If the law is not obeyed, the deficiencies themselves become the "sin" which is punishable in a physical sense by capital punishment and in a spiritual sense by a continuing low state of moral consciousness. Paul certainly was aware of this, for in explaining the law in Christian times, he said: "For until the law sin was in the world: but sin is not imputed where there is no law."[19] (Romans 5:13, KJV)

How logical it seems that the emergence of moral law would be the mystical key to the legend of Adam, Eve, the serpent, and the Tree of Knowledge.

Apparently Adam revealed to the people of His time the knowledge of good and evil and the concept of moral law. Eve, who represented the human self as well as the soul of man, would suffer severe pain as she made decisions based on divine law. She would be under the domination of the animal nature of Adam because he would initially be stronger, but she would always yearn for spiritual knowledge and to draw closer to God. Mankind was thus challenged, and that would be hard work, explained Marsella:

> This great prize was not, however, to be achieved without labor, and this interesting tidbit, omitted from Genesis, has caused Christians to believe that they have been unjustly plunged into a spiritual struggle for their souls' salvation, whereas certain of the Hebrew thinkers of old were well aware of the fact that man would have to win wisdom through a voluntary conquest of the baser aspects of his nature before he could hack his way through the final branches of the Tree of Knowledge and attain to a permanent spiritual enlightenment. Such a concept of gradual spiritual attainment is neither illogical nor unjust, unless we would feel ourselves cheated because we were not born with full sets of teeth, perfect balance, and an innate knowledge of Latin, Greek, and calculus.[20]

Marsella also correlated the days of creation with the cycles associated with the Manifestations of God:

> According to Hebraic mysticism the "days of creation" are each approximately a thousand years long, constituting what is known throughout their literature as a Lord's Day, a dispensation, a small cycle within a larger one, an era, or a *world*, over which a priest-prophet such as Adam, Noah, or Moses holds undisputed sway.[21]

Hebrew mysticism likens each day of the Genesis creation story to 1,000 years, thus creating a cycle of 6,000 years, the end of which is the deadline for the Messiah to appear. The seventh day, or seventh millennium, corresponds with the Sabbath, a universal time not only of rest and peace but, in the Bahá'í view, of consolidation of the achievements of the previous six millennia and the embrace of the Universal Manifestation.

REFLECTIONS OF WILLIAM BARNES

Another writer who reflected on the story of Adam was William Barnes, who approached the creation, fall, and redemption of humanity within the context of the advancement of human consciousness. He identified the "fall" of Adam as a psychic break from the old state of awareness that was necessary for the birth of a new spiritual consciousness. He identified four stages along this road to redemption:

> It begins in Eden; that is, symbolically, any **unconscious state of psychic unity**—where unconscious means people are not aware of the psychological forces holding them together. There occurs what is traditionally termed a fall, or breaking of the unity into its component parts and their successive temporal appearance. This is the birth of consciousness, for consciousness always implies a separation or awareness of difference. From this perspective, the fall is not a loss of anything except innocence and ignorance. Spiritually, the fall stems from an increase of knowledge, a breakthrough toward a new unity causing a breakdown of established unity. It is the start of an advance.
>
> When this separating tendency reaches its full extent, *a reversal suddenly occurs and the third stage, that of apocalypse, happens*. An apocalypse is the revealing of the hidden and complete form of Reality by the burning away of the partial and imperfect perceptions of reality that the "fall" gives us. We must undergo this fiery unifying ordeal if our true state and nature are to be manifest. *Finally, redemption occurs, which is the regaining of Eden but with consciousness.*

Re-entering Eden transformed means our vision of Eden is transformed. That is, the mind perceives the real Eden burning within and shining through every form of a cooled surface of wilderness, a perception symbolized in its specialized form in the biblical burning bush and in its generalized form in Buddha's Fire Sermon.

Regained Eden is a new, more psychologically complete unity of consciousness, one in which the human perceptual powers are restored in new form, where humanity recognizes its true self.[22] (emphasis added)

Barnes saw the Prophet Adam as presiding over a "primordial historical stage of the spiritual conception of humankind—the birth of consciousness, which always implies a separation."[23]

Next, Barnes considered the two creations in Genesis—the general and the special. He saw creation as one phenomenon with two aspects. The general creation is bottom up, following the evolutionary development of life on Earth, with humans appearing last. In this scenario, the essence of man comes from the natural world, and his spirituality grows slowly. The secondary revelations of individual Prophets, or progressive revelation, are the province of the general creation. But even though the general creation is bottom up, transformation resulting from the various Dispensations of the Prophets is top down, starting with humanity. Each secondary revelation is a power that recreates all things, beginning with those souls who recognize the Revelation of their day and working down toward the physical earth itself. The secondary revelations push the animal, vegetable, and mineral kingdoms to find their potential and to more fully manifest the original unity of creation by forming and reforming in more complex patterns. Bahá'u'lláh asserted:

In every age and cycle He hath, through the splendorous light shed by the Manifestations of His wondrous Essence, recreated all things, so that whatsoever reflecteth in the heavens and on the earth the signs of His glory may not be deprived of the outpourings of His mercy, nor despair of the showers of His favors.[24]

The special creation is top down, beginning in light with man created as a living soul when God breathed into his nostrils the breath of life. Man came from dust, but he was created not as the highest of the animals but as a soul that would try to raise itself clear of nature, out of the lower world and into our true original condition. Barnes explains the dynamic this way:

> The special creation of God is also imaginatively higher because, here, rebirth is not merely putting offspring into the treadmill of birth and death, as in nature. Spiritually, rebirth is a lifting movement raising us clear of nature, a resurrection out of the lower world (into which we have plunged) into our true original condition; that is, not from hell or a lower world back into this one called earth, but from this world perceived in its real form. Christianity calls this movement salvation or redemption, the buying back of one's spiritual self at the price of one's natural life.[25]

The two creations are thus mirror images of man, split between his two natures, the animal and the spiritual. They move, metaphorically, in parallel opposition. These contrasting movements are greatly complex with the result that, as 'Abdu'l-Bahá stated, *"In no other species in the world of existence can such difference, distinction, contrast and contradiction be seen as in man."*[26]

Barnes suggested that the final implication of considering the single creation as a double revelation is that at the end of time mentioned by Daniel, which was the close of the Prophetic Cycle in 1844, the secondary prophetic revelations will be perceived as linked to and emanating from the same source. Together they will form a cycle of human development universal in its unfoldment. All divine revelations, the universal and the secondary, preexisted in eternity or in what could be called sacred time as opposed to historical time. In other words, the secondary revelations were those of the Prophets of the Adamic Cycle, and Bahá'u'lláh, as the Supreme Manifestation of the Universal Cycle, initiated the union of the universal and secondary revelations for which the general and special creations of Genesis stand as allegories.

THE GIFTS OF ṬÁHIRIH

No reflection on Adam is complete without reading the poem, "Adam's Wish," written by Ṭáhirih (born Fátimih Baraghání in 1814), a woman famous in Persia for her sacrificial efforts toward the emancipation of women. She was one of the eighteen disciples of the Báb, who were referred to as "Letters of the Living," and the only woman among them. He gave her the name Ṭáhirih, the Pure One. Having been born into a wealthy family, she was given that most rare of advantages for women of nineteenth century Persia—an education. As a child, she was recognized as a prodigy who exhibited an innate capacity to interpret some of the most enigmatic passages in the Qur'an and the hadith (traditions attributed to Muḥammad and his companions). She was a leading Islamic scholar of her day.

Ṭáhirih did not have the freedom to travel that men took for granted, and she never met the Báb in person. But she taught and served His Cause nobly and without reservation, stretching and even breaking the strictures placed on her by Islamic society. She was martyred in 1852. Dressed as a bride for the occasion, Ṭáhirih was strangled with her scarf, and her body was thrown down a well. The loss to the world of her spiritual brilliance and supreme intellect is still incomprehensible.

The poetry of Ṭáhirih often took the form of philosophical and religious treatises. John S. Hatcher and Amrollah Hemmat note in their book, *Adam's Wish: Unknown Poetry of Ṭáhirih*, that the tone of conviction and authority found in her writing indicates that she was a special figure in religious history. "One senses that she possessed a knowledge, capacity, and station that set her above even some of the most astute and dedicated followers of the Bábí movement. Indeed, some passages possess something of the dynamic tone and power usually associated with the utterances of the Prophets themselves."[27]

Hatcher and Hemmat summarize Ṭáhirih's three interpretations of Adam in her poetry. The first is the signifier of the Will of God that manifests through the emanation of the reality of the Manifestations of God, a creative process that provides humanity with free will. The second is the historical Adam as a distinct and unique Manifestation of God with His own specific purpose and mission. The third sees Adam as a "return" in the age of the Báb's dispensation, a return in the sense that the Báb incarnated the same attributes, character, and as did the historical Adam. Her poetry presents that the Báb, as a Manifestation of God, incarnated the same attributes, character, and actions as did Adam.

The mystical scope of Ṭáhirih's poetry about Adam is beyond the purpose of this volume. Therefore, only one example of her poetry is given below, a teaser if you will. Ṭáhirih gives a unique perspective on Adam's "fall," as the following verses show:

> Indeed, the truth was instigated by Adam from rays
> [emitted] from the face of the fa'ál* of the new
> creation.**
> Adam arose from His place to bring forth the nation of
> the Knower!***
> From that illuminable light shone forth the concept
> of "Ḥadd."****
> With the dawning of the Bayán,***** He observed from
> His station mere nothingness become manifest.
> Sobbing in remorse,****** He became wondrously reborn
> so that heavenly streams poured forth from Him.[28]

*fa'ál : a "doer" or a "very active agent"
** This passage refers both to the mythological allusion of Adam as the beginning of creation and to the fact that with the appearance of each new Manifestation, all things are made new.

59

*** Táhirih seems to give her own interpretation of this phrase [Knower]. Adam was the reality of Muḥammad as the Manifestation of God. This reality, which was the acting primordial "acting agent" for the creation of the universe, arose to manifest action and knowledge, and through that action, the world of limitations was created. This action of manifesting knowledge and action by Adam has taken place again at this age through the revelation of the Báb.

**** The "limited" necessarily pertains to all revelations—that humankind can understand and utilize only a certain amount of new information in a single age or dispensation.

***** Probably Adam foresaw how in the future the Báb would, through the revelation of the Bayán, manifest total selflessness— as opposed to the temptation to exalt the self as exemplified in the Adamic myth.

****** The repentance of Adam and His shedding of tears is symbolic of aligning one's will with the Will of God and wishing what God wishes.

The purpose of each Manifestations of God has been to educate humanity so that, progressively, humankind can become capable of demonstrating the attributes and perfections of God. Hatcher and Hemmat state:

> All of the Manifestations desired the redemption of humankind from the darkness of the material world and their return to that original paradisiacal and spiritual state of their souls. Therefore, according to the Qur'an, because all the Manifestations of God possessed this same desire, They have all repented and all have desired to return to the original paradisiacal purity of the spiritual world.[29]

Adam's wish was that the kingdom of God be replicated on Earth. Adam's "sin" was that, like all the Prophets, He devoutly wished that the process of humanity's spiritual development could occur more speedily.

But God has His Will for each prophetic age. "Adam's desire and His subsequent expulsion and descent are therefore repeated in the sense that prior to the Day of God—the time of maturity of humankind—it is premature and presumptuous for one to desire the full manifestation of God's glory." [30]

Chapter 5

NOAH AND HIS FLOOD

Myths are metaphors that convey truth about the
indescribable through powerful images and experiences.

WILLIAM P. COLLINS[1]

NOAH, IT SEEMS, CAME from a highly distinguished family, said to be
descended from Adam. According to the fifth chapter of Genesis, Adam
lived 930 years, His son Seth 912, his son Enosh 905, his son Kenan
(Cainan, KJV) 910, his son Mahalalel 895, his son Jared 962, his son
Enoch 365, his son Methuselah 969, his son Lamech 777, and his son
Noah 950. *"He [Lamech] named him Noah and said, 'He will comfort us in the labor*
and painful toil of our hands caused by the ground the LORD has cursed.'" (Gen. 5:29)

Much conjecture has been made about the long lives of the patriarchs. The Sumerian King List states that Sumerian kings descended from
the heavens and gave the early kings longevities of thousands of years to
extoll their greatness. Some scholars have drawn a parallel between this
ancient custom and the supernumerary years given to the patriarchs of
the generations of Adam. However, Shoghi Effendi noted, "The ages of
the Prophets as specified in the Bible were based on a different calcula-
tion than the one used at present."[2] He also commented, "The years of
Noah are not years as we count them, and as our teachings do not state
that this reference to years means His dispensation, we cannot interpret
it this way."[3]

According to Genesis, Noah was a ninth-generation descendant of Adam and a great-grandson of Enoch, who was said to have walked with God but then was no more because God took him (Gen. 5:24). Other than this genealogy, Genesis gives no markers as to when or where Noah lived. There are traditions, however, to the effect that this family retained divine knowledge passed down from Adam to his descendants that was above and beyond what He gave to the people. For example, the book of Enoch, one of the apocryphal books attributed to various Jewish writers from perhaps the third century BCE to the first century CE, was claimed to have been divinely revealed, but it was excluded from the Hebrew canon. That book states that Enoch told his son Methuselah, the grandfather of Noah: *"And now, my son Methuselah, all these things I am recounting to thee and writing down for thee! and I have revealed to thee everything, and given thee books concerning all these: so preserve, my son Methuselah, the books from thy father's hand, and (see) that thou deliver them to the generations of the world."*[4]

Noah is best known for the flood that reputedly killed all living creatures, except those on the ark. Legends of global floods are common in many cultures, especially among people living in flood-prone areas such as river deltas. As with all alluvial plains, the lands between the Tigris and Euphrates Rivers experienced frequent floods, but archeological evidence shows that these floods were local and none of them converged for widespread flooding of the whole Mesopotamian area. However, distant memories of a catastrophic flood in the Middle East in about 5600 BCE could well have set the scene for Enlil's flood in *The Epic of Gilgamesh* and Noah's flood in Genesis.

THE HISTORICAL EPIC FLOOD

Two geophysicists at Columbia University's Lamont-Doherty Earth Observatory, William B. F. Ryan and Walter C. Pitman, published compelling scientific evidence for a catastrophic flood north of Mesopotamia in their book, *Noah's Flood: The New Scientific Discoveries about the Event That Changed History*. The authors conducted oceanographic explorations of the Black Sea using sound waves and coring devices to probe the sea floor. They obtained cores of lakebed sediment containing clear evidence that this inland body of saltwater had once been a freshwater lake lying hundreds of feet below the level of the world's rising oceans after the last ice age, the Pleistocene glaciation, which began about 1.5 million years ago and ended about 12,500 BCE. Massive amounts of water were locked up in glaciers at the height of the last ice age, when ocean levels were about four hundred feet lower than they are today, exposing much land that is now under water. Indeed, one could walk across land bridges from France to England, from Morocco to Spain, from Sicily to Italy, from New Guinea to Australia, and from Siberia to Alaska. As the earth gradually warmed, the ice melted and ocean levels rose about 400 feet over several thousand years. Eventually, pressure from the rising Atlantic Ocean caused water to push violently through the Straights of Gibraltar into the Mediterranean Sea. In turn, pressure in the Mediterranean pushed saltwater forcefully through the Aegean Sea and into the Sea of Marmara. But this massive surge of water did not stop there. It continued east across the Bosporus ledge, a twenty-mile strip of land between the Sea of Marmara and the Black Sea in today's Turkey, gouging out a channel from 280 to 425 feet deep. The saltwater poured into the Black Sea—with the unimaginable force of two hundred Niagara Falls—flooding the beaches and filling the rivers, chasing all life before it. This force of pummeling water carved out the Bosporus Straight, which is now a significant waterway separating European Turkey from Asian Turkey and connecting the Sea of Marmara with the Black Sea.

Ryan and Pitman used sophisticated dating techniques that confirmed the date of 5600 BCE for this catastrophic event. The freshwater Black Sea and the surrounding land had been an oasis of life for Neolithic farms and villages, but in the face of the flood, the people had to flee for their lives in all directions. The water level in the Black Sea rose several feet per day, eventually cresting at several hundred feet and submerging more than 60,000 square miles of surrounding land, a thirty percent expansion in size. The foundations of Neolithic structures have been found on the lakebed.

The deafening roar of the water crashing through the Bosporus must have been audible for miles. Within one year, the freshwater flora and fauna of the Black Sea were replaced by those in the saltwater pouring in from the Mediterranean Sea. The recognition of this swift change shattered the scientific belief that geological processes are always gradual. Ryan and Pitman gave a graphic depiction of this event and its legacy:

> The flood myth lives on for a number of reasons. First, it is surely a true story of the permanent destruction of a land and its people and a culture suddenly and catastrophically inundated, of farmers uprooted from their hard-won fields, their villages permanently destroyed. They had to flee with what little they could carry, old and young, straggling along day after day. They had to flee and at the same time obtain food from the land by hunting and gathering, skills they had long forgotten. Some, perhaps many, probably died of exhaustion. For those who had lived near the Bosporus at the western end of the lake, the sight and sound of the flume must have filled their hearts with terror and horror, "like the bellowing of a bull, like a wild ass screaming ... Earth shook, her foundations trembled, the sun darkened, lightning flashed, thunder pealed, and a deafening voice, the like of which was never heard before, rolled across mountain and plain."* So the tragedy was indelibly implanted in their oral history.
>
> Over the thousands of years since, with war, invasion, migrations, and other calamities, the legend disappeared from the folk memory of many. However, to those who fled to Mesopotamia and whose progeny are still there, the flood lived on for thousands of years, its telling and memory dramatically reinforced by the floods of the Tigris and Euphrates.[5]
>
> * Cited in R. Graves and R. Patai, *Hebrew Myth: The Book of Genesis*, 1986, 112.

The memory of this epic flood might have been refreshed by the constant floods in the alluvial plains of the Tigris and Euphrates delta. It certainly presented a superb framework for a divine allegory.

NOAH'S ARK EMBARKS

The Genesis account of Noah's flood can be seen as the climax of a sequence that begins with the creation of the world and humanity, continues with the threat to eliminate humanity and start over with Noah's descendants, and concludes with the renewal of God's promise for human life in the first known covenant with the one God. Interestingly, Genesis represents God as one deity, not a pantheon, albeit an anthropomorphic deity who can change His mind. Since the prehistoric legends and traditions of the Jews were first written down in the middle of the last millennium BCE, it appears that the monotheism of Abraham and Moses was adopted in the flood story.

Some Jews and Christians believe in a literal interpretation of Noah and the flood, but there is no archeological or geological evidence for such an event. Others relegate it to the status of an enchanting Sunday school story with bucolic scenes of Noah leading the animals onto the ark two by two, releasing the dove, and receiving a new Covenant with God signified by a rainbow. However, it appears that the Genesis account of Noah is a weighty discourse involving the coming of a Prophet of God; the rejection of His Revelation by most of the people; and a new Covenant with God, or Ark of the Covenant, that provided a new level of spirituality for those who embraced it and spiritual loss for those who did not.

A word of caution is timely before delving further into the Bahá'í perspective about Noah. 'Abdu'l-Bahá said: *"All the texts and teachings of the holy Testaments have intrinsic spiritual meanings. They are not to be taken literally."*[6] Referring to the Noah story, Shoghi Effendi wrote: "The Bahá'í Teachings state that the Ark and the flood were not actual physical events. Rather, the Ark is a symbol of the divine Covenant in every Age, and 'drowning' means being occupied with the things of this world instead of the things of God. Concerning the biblical flood story, the Ark and Flood we believe are symbolical."[7]

First, let's note that the Genesis story of Noah follows events in *The Epic of Gilgamesh* closely enough that most scholars believe that it was derived from this epic poem. Indeed, Victor H. Matthews and Don C. Benjamin, authors of *Old Testament Parallels*, commented that the stories of Adam and Eve and of Noah's flood are parallel to the saga of Gilgamesh, in which Endiku is parallel to Adam, Utnapishtim (who piloted Gilgamesh's boat) to Noah, and Dilmun, the land at the mouth of the rivers, to Eden.[8]

This borrowing does not, however, dilute the symbolic, spiritual significances found in both legends. We have no evidence that *The Epic of Gilgamesh* was inspired by Adam's Dispensation. However, the epic's symbology, especially that of Enkidu finding his human self and later searching for the meaning of his life and, unsuccessfully, the path to immortality (not covered in this book), portrays a spiritual journey. The poem relates how the survivors of the flood disembarked from their ark and offered food sacrifices to the gods, who had become famished during the humans' absence. The grateful gods now had a new appreciation for humans and offered a new covenant. The gods promised that they would never again try to wipe out humans, and the humans agreed to continue serving the gods.

Genesis introduces us to Noah with commentary about His character: *"Noah was a righteous man, blameless among the people of his time, and he walked faithfully with God"* (6:9). Bahá'u'lláh used the example of Noah when speaking of the divine Luminaries and Their successive returns: *"For instance, consider that among the Prophets was Noah. When He was invested with the robe of Prophethood, and was moved by the Spirit of God to arise and proclaim His Cause, whoever believed in Him and acknowledged His Faith was endowed with the grace of a new life."*[9] Before His calling, though, Noah seemed to have lived a life normal for His times, as described by Bahá'u'lláh:

> *Of him it could be truly said that he was reborn and revived, inasmuch as previous to his belief in God and his acceptance of His Manifestation, he had set his affections on the things of the world, such as attachment to*

earthly goods, to wife, children, food, drink, and the like, so much so that in the day-time and in the night season his one concern had been to amass riches and procure for himself the means of enjoyment and pleasure. Aside from these things, before his partaking of the reviving waters of faith, he had been so wedded to the traditions of his forefathers, and so passionately devoted to the observance of their customs and laws, that he would have preferred to suffer death rather than violate one letter of those superstitious forms and manners current amongst his people. Even as the people have cried: "Verily we found our fathers with a faith, and verily, in their footsteps we follow." [10]*

  *Qur'an 43:22

After accepting His mission, though, Noah suffered so grievously at the hands of the unbelievers because of His Revelation that He despaired and beseeched God to remove them. Bahá'u'lláh wrote:

How frequently they denied Him, how malevolently they hinted their suspicion against Him! Thus it hath been revealed: "And as often as a company of His people passed by Him, they derided Him. To them He said: `Though ye scoff at us now, we will scoff at you hereafter even as ye scoff at us. In the end ye shall know.'" Long afterward, He several times promised victory to His companions and fixed the hour thereof. But when the hour struck, the divine promise was not fulfilled. This caused a few among the small number of His followers to turn away from Him, and to this testify the records of the best-known books. These you must certainly have perused; if not, undoubtedly you will. Finally, as stated in books and traditions, there remained with Him only forty or seventy-two of His followers. At last from the depth of His being He cried aloud: "Lord! Leave not upon the land a single dweller from among the unbelievers."** [11]*

  *Qur'an 11:38
  **Qur'an 71:26

The Bahá'í Writings seem not to address the nature of Noah's mission or His teachings. Therefore we'll examine the symbology.

Massive bodies of water can signify a new Revelation that sweeps away the old and acts as a cleansing: *"Praise and glory beseem the Lord of Names and the Creator of the heavens, He, the waves of Whose ocean of Revelation surge before the eyes of the peoples of the world."*[12]

An ark is a large boat that enables safe travel on the seas and can be a symbol for safety and security. *The Epic of Gilgamesh* and the Genesis story of Noah both feature arks. Utnapishtim captained the ark of the great flood sent by the gods to destroy humanity and, in return, was granted immortality. Noah captained His ark of the great flood caused by God. Then God gave mankind the first recorded divine covenant, signified by a rainbow.

Each Dispensation presents a new covenant with God, an ark. A covenant is a binding agreement between God and man whereby God requires certain behavior of people and, in return, confers certain blessings. This covenant is amended and renewed with each new Revelation to reflect different circumstances and new expectations. The inhabitants of Noah's Ark were people who accepted His Revelation and were sheltered in the Ark of His Covenant from the persecutions heaped upon them so that they could survive to teach this new faith. Noah's Ark settled on a mountain as the flood receded.

Mountains can symbolize God, constancy, eternity, and higher spirituality. Moses encountered God on a mountain: *"The LORD descended to the top of Mount Sinai and called Moses to the top of the mountain."* (Exod. 19:20). The author of Psalm 36 compared the righteousness of God with the highest mountains: *"Your righteousness is like the highest mountains, your justice like the great deep"* (Psalm 36:6). Jesus experienced the Transfiguration on a mountain: *"After six days Jesus took with him Peter, James and John the brother of James, and led them up a high mountain by themselves. There he was transfigured before them"* (Matt. 17:1–2).

When Noah's people disembarked, they erected an altar to God and sacrificed animals and birds as burnt offerings. The aroma was pleasing to the Lord, who said to Noah and His sons:

"I now establish my covenant with you and with your descendants after you and with every living creature that was with you—the birds, the livestock

and all the wild animals, all those that came out of the ark with you—every living creature on earth. I establish my covenant with you: Never again will all life be destroyed by the waters of a flood; never again will there be a flood to destroy the earth." And God said, "This is the sign of the covenant I am making between me and you and every living creature with you, a covenant for all generations to come: I have set my rainbow in the clouds, and it will be the sign of the covenant between me and the earth. Whenever I bring clouds over the earth and the rainbow appears in the clouds, I will remember my covenant between me and you and all living creatures of every kind. Never again will the waters become a flood to destroy all life. Whenever the rainbow appears in the clouds, I will see it and remember the everlasting covenant between God and all living creatures of every kind on the earth." (Gen: 9:9–16)

Another source of information about the symbolic meanings of the ark is found in a glossary compiled for Messages of the Universal House of Justice 1963–1986:

The word "ark" means, literally, a boat or ship, something that affords protection and safety, or a chest or box. It is used in two senses in the Bible. In the first sense it refers to the Ark of Noah, which He was bidden to build of gopher wood to preserve life during the Flood. In the second sense it refers to the Ark of the Covenant, the sacred chest representing to the Hebrews God's presence among them. It was constructed to hold the Tablets of the Law in Moses' time and was later placed in the Holy of Holies in the Temple of Jerusalem. The Ark, as a symbol of God's Law and the Divine Covenant that is the salvation of the people in every age and Dispensation, appears in various ways in the Bahá'í writings. Bahá'u'lláh refers to His faithful followers as "the denizens of the Crimson Ark"; He refers to the Ark of the Cause and also to the Ark of His Laws. A well-known passage in which this term is used appears in the Tablet of Carmel: "Ere long will God sail His Ark upon thee, and will manifest the people of Baha who have been mentioned in the Book of Names."*[13]

* The Tablet of Carmel, Tablets of Bahá'u'lláh Revealed After the Kitáb-i-Aqdas, 4–5.

THE TOWER OF BABEL – ANOTHER SIGNIFICANT ALLEGORY

Immediately following the Noah epic and a genealogy of Noah's descendants, Genesis 11:1–9 presents the story of the tower of Babel, which is not only a timeless tale in its lessons but also seems to be especially pertinent today.

According to Genesis, the whole world had one language when people moved to the plain of Shinar (Mesopotamia). They started building a city with a tower that would reach to the heavens so that they could make a name for themselves and avoid being scattered over the face of the earth.

> But the LORD came down to see the city and the tower the people were building. The LORD said, "If as one people speaking the same language they have begun to do this, then nothing they plan to do will be impossible for them. Come, let us go down and confuse their language so they will not understand each other." So the LORD scattered them from there over all the earth, and they stopped building the city. That is why it was called Babel*—because there the LORD confused the language of the whole world. From there the LORD scattered them over the face of the whole earth. (Gen. 11:5–7)
>
> * NIV Bible Note: That is, Babylon; Babel sounds like the Hebrew for confused.

And so it happened that many languages replaced the one language, and the people were scattered over the face of the earth.

In both Persian and Akkadian, the word *báb* meant gate, and in Hebrew the word *El* meant "God," as in Bethel (house of God). Therefore, the name Babel meant the Gate of God. In Akkadian, *ilu* meant god, so Babel translated to Babylon.[14] The building of Babel, the gate of God, represented an attempt to circumvent God—to turn away from God—in attaining material greatness of might and power that could be imposed on the people and enslave them. As portrayed here, God has a sense of humor. He gave the city a name that would be a divine pun by substituting a similar-sounding word to enshrine the confusion of the language, which stopped the construction. Instead of establishing a city called, in Akkadian, the "Gate of God," it is now known by the Hebrew word Babel, from *balal*, meaning "to mix, mingle, confound, confuse."[15]

Nimrod was the great-grandson of Noah through Ham, who had not recognized his father's station (see chapter 6) and was associated with Babylon and other cities in Mesopotamia (10:6–10). Therefore, the tower of Babel is about people who do not recognize the Prophets and, rather, create their own version of heaven in materialistic terms.

The Babel story seems to be a corollary to the protection from humanity that was given to the Tree of Life, with *"cherubim and a flaming sword flashing back and forth to guard the way to the Tree of Life"* (3:24). As explained in Chapter 4, Jesus brought the fruits of this tree into His ministry. The Tree of Life is also understood as the station of the Universal Manifestation of the universal cycle, who is Bahá'u'lláh and who referred to Himself as the Tree of Life.

There would be no shortcuts, and to a certain extent, humanity would have to be protected from itself. The fruits of the Tree of Life would be extended progressively, in God's good time. And God's time for the inauguration of the Cycle of Fulfillment was 1844. Bahá'u'lláh called for the eventual selection of one of the world's languages as an auxiliary language to be globally taught. When this happens, humanity will have one common language in addition to innumerable mother tongues.

Wade Fransson, a biblical researcher, perceived that Babel was humanity's aborted attempt to ascend to heaven on its own terms "apart from submission to God, to appropriate the name 'the Gate of God,' which God had in fact reserved for another time…. God chose to call it what it was—confusion—and in confusing the language, to thwart the clarity of purpose, the power of their unity, which was being put to an evil purpose."[16] The result today is a "system of profit-driven materialism that is ultimately posing a threat to civilization and destroying the planet in the process. Its defenders praise this system for its ability to create the jobs, wealth, goods, and services that we all crave. But this system exists in a symbiotic relationship with humankind, in our role as caretakers of the planet; we are in a codependent, materialistic death embrace."[17]

Chapter 6

ABRAHAM, INTO THE FUTURE

The Founder of monotheism was Abraham; it is to
Him that this concept can be traced, and the belief
was current among the Children of Israel.

'ABDU'L-BAHÁ[1]

IN THE WAKE OF Noah's Dispensation, the winds of divine revelation started blowing across the Holy Land. These gusts and gales knocked over idols amid the proclamation of the One God, who promised Abraham the land of Canaan, that His offspring would be like the dust of the earth, and that He would be the father of many nations (Gen. 13:14–16, 15:17–21, 17:3–8). The essence of God's request from Abraham was faith, which at times was a desperate, soul-trying faith. His people struggled with idolatry and obedience to the Abrahamic Covenant for many centuries. Despite their backsliding, though, these ancient Israelites manifested two qualities essential to accomplishing their task: zealotry and an inner examination of their sins and shortcomings. Probably no other people of that time or since has linked their misfortunes to their own transgressions as the ancient Israelites did.

As we progress into the narratives of the patriarchs, let's remember that the Bible is true in substance but often not literally accurate and that symbolic texts might need authoritative interpretation. Early dates are problematical. Shoghi Effendi explained, "There are no dates in our teachings regarding the actual dates of the Prophets of the Adamic Cycle, so we cannot give any. Tentatively we can accept what historians may consider accurate. Naturally the dates referring to Muhammad, the Báb and Bahá'u'lláh we are sure of."[2] In the case of Abraham, the consensus among biblical scholars is that He lived between 2100 and 2000 BCE, although a time closer to 1800 BCE is sometimes suggested.

The saga of Abraham,[3] a Prophet of God and the first of the Hebrew patriarchs, is one of the most studied epics in the Hebrew Bible. The book of Genesis states that Abraham was descended from Shem, son of Noah. Most biblical scholars agree that Abraham was born in or near Ur in Sumer, sometime in the early second millennium BCE. He grew up in polytheistic Mesopotamia. His ministry would shatter the mindset of Mesopotamian religion and raise many deep theological questions.

Genesis states that Abraham fathered not one but two peoples, the Hebrews and the Arabs. Over 4,000 years, Abraham's descendants founded five monotheistic religions—Judaism, Christianity, Islam, the Bábí Faith, and the Bahá'í Faith. The scriptures of the first three faiths proclaim the advent of the Prophets of the fourth and fifth, the Bábí Faith and the Bahá'í Faith.[4] All five faiths from the Abrahamic heritage now have shrines and holy places in the Holy Land. They all arose in the Middle East.

Memories of Adam survived in mythic, symbolic accounts, and the situation of Abraham is much the same. Genesis devotes more than fourteen chapters (11:26 to 25:10) to Abraham, but these accounts were not committed to writing until more than a millennium after His lifetime. The accuracy of portions of their rendering seem to be confirmed by the Bahá'í Writings and the Qur'an. The contexts within which spiritual truths are conveyed, however, cannot always be considered "true" because, simply put, Prophets do not come to revise beliefs about past history. Denying folk legends has never been their stock in trade. They spoke within the general knowledge of the people so that They could be understood rather than risk blinding the people to new spiritual teachings through confusion and ire brought about by challenging their traditional history. In 1998 the Universal House of Justice summarized the situation and added a challenge for Bahá'ís:

> Although, in conveying His Revelation, the Manifestation uses the language and culture of the country into which He is born, He is not confined to using terminology with the same connotations as those given to it by His predecessors or contemporaries; He delivers His message in a form which His audience, both immediate and in centuries to come, is capable of grasping. It is for Bahá'í scholars to elaborate, over a period of time, methodologies which will enable them to perform their work with this understanding. This is a challenging task, but not one which should be beyond the scope of Bahá'ís who are learned in the Teachings as well as competent in their scientific disciplines.[5]

Considering all this, let's proceed with the Dispensation of Abraham. Bahá'u'lláh introduced Abraham as a young man before His exile from His city of birth:

> *Later, the beauty of the countenance of the Friend of God* appeared from behind the veil, and another standard of divine guidance was hoisted. He invited the people of the earth to the light of righteousness. The more passionately He exhorted them, the fiercer waxed the envy and waywardness of the people, except those who wholly detached themselves from all save God, and ascended on the wings of certainty to the station which God hath exalted beyond the comprehension of men. It is well known what a host of enemies besieged Him, until at last the fires of envy and rebellion were kindled against Him. And after the episode of the fire came to pass, He, the lamp of God amongst men, was, as recorded in all books and chronicles, expelled from His city.*[6]
> *Abraham

The episode of the fire is explained in the Qur'an, which states that Abraham had been a questioning youth who mocked and exposed the powerlessness of the Mesopotamian gods. *"Worship ye what ye carve, when God hath created you, and that ye make?"* (Qur'an 37:97). His father, who made and sold wooden idols for a living, was understandably not amused. When Abraham continued His relentless ridicule of the idols with his father and townspeople, the outrage escalated to the point where Abraham's father turned Him over to the authorities. True to character, Abraham even argued with Emperor Nimrod and challenged him:

> *When Abraham said, "My Lord is He who maketh alive and cause to die,"*
> *He [Nimrod] said, "It is I who make alive and cause to die!" Abraham*
> *said, "Since God bringeth the sun from the East, do thou, then, bring it from*
> *the West." The infidel was confounded; for God guideth not the evil doers.*
> (Qur'an 2:258)

Confounded and lacking any coherent response to this challenge, Nimrod sentenced Abraham to death in a burning furnace, the episode of the fire that is mentioned by both Muḥammad and Bahá'u'lláh. Into the fire went Abraham:

> *They said: "Burn him, and come to the succour of your gods: if ye will*
> *do anything at all."*
> *We said, "O fire! be thou cold, and to Abraham a safety!"*
> *And they sought to lay a plot against him, but we made them the*
> *sufferers.*
> *And we brought him and Lot in safety to the land which we have blessed*
> *for all human beings.* (Qur'an 21:68–71)

The Qur'an states that Abraham offered a prayer while being taken to the fire, a prayer that indicated He knew that He would not be killed: *"And he said, 'Verily, I repair to my Lord who will guide me: O Lord give me a son, of the righteous.' We announced to him a youth of meekness."* (Qur'an 37:97–99).

INTO EXILE

Having failed to silence or kill Abraham, Nimrod exiled Him. Abraham left Ur in Sumer for Haran in northern Mesopotamia with His father

Terah, His nephew Lot, and their households and herds. There is no mention of what Terah, the idol maker, thought about accompanying his wayward son and of reaping the bitter harvest of exile that his son had sown. According to Genesis, Abraham received the first message from God while He was in Haran:

> The LORD had said to Abram, "Go from your country, your people and
> your father's household to the land I will show you.
> I will make you into a great nation, and I will bless you; I will make
> your name great, and you will be a blessing.
> I will bless those who bless you, and whoever curses you I will curse; and
> all peoples on earth will be blessed through you."
> So Abram went, as the LORD had told him. (Gen. 12:1–4)

Abraham ventured into a new future propelled by His faith in the promises of God. Thomas Cahill explained the implications of this new consciousness:

> So, "wayyelekh Avram" ("Abram went")—two of the boldest words in all literature. They signal a complete departure from everything that has gone before in the long evolution of culture and sensibility. Out of Sumer, civilized repository of the predictable, comes a man who does not know where he is going but goes forth into the unknown wilderness under the prompting of his god. Out of Mesopotamia, home of canny, self-serving merchants who use their gods to ensure prosperity and favor, comes a wealthy caravan with no material goal. Out of ancient humanity, which from the dim beginnings of its consciousness has read its eternal verities in the stars, comes a party traveling by no known compass. Out of the human race, which knows in its bones that all its striving must end in death, comes a leader who says he has been given an impossible promise. Out of mortal imagination comes a dream of something new, something better, something yet to happen, something—in the future.[7]

First Abraham went to the area that is now Aleppo, Syria, with His family, herds, and retainers and then to the land of Canaan to the south, which had been settled by a son of Ham, the son of Noah who had *not* recognized His father's station as a Prophet. Genesis relates that one day, Noah planted a vineyard and *"became drunk and lay uncovered inside his tent"* (9:21). Frances Worthington, an American scholar, explained that Noah was not growing grapes but was nurturing the seeds of a new Revelation. Working in this vineyard represented Noah communing with God. His seeming drunkenness was the revelatory mode in which He was becoming divinely clothed. Two of His sons, Shem and Japheth, recognized their father's station and what was happening. They covered their father with a garment of respect.[8] But his third son, Ham, did not recognize his father's station and thought that He was literally drunk when he saw His naked body. Worthington commented:

> Noah's other son, Ham, is appalled by what his father is doing. He does not understand that his father has drunk the wine of a new revelation from God. And he rejects the notion that Noah has been commanded to strip off His old clothes—His old traditions—in order to embark on a spiritual mission requiring different attitudes and behavior. Ham wants everything to stay as it is.
>
> Ham's rejection of his father's astonishing wine and heavenly clothing is continued by two of Ham's descendants: a son named Canaan and a grandson called (aha!) Nimrod.[9]

Instead of cursing Ham, Noah cursed Ham's son, Canaan. It seems strange that Canaan received the curse rather than his father. Maybe Canaan was an even sorrier specimen than Ham. At any rate, Genesis states that Canaan established himself in the eastern Mediterranean area named after him.

God sends His Prophets to places where people are wallowing in a moral abyss. Abraham was sent to the land of Canaan, where polytheism was practiced to the point of child sacrifice to appease the gods.

He arrived at Shechem in today's north central West Bank. Abraham and Lot prospered to such an extent that the land could not support both of them, so Lot took his herds, tents, and household and settled in the east, on the plain of Jordan near the ancient city of Sodom, believed to have been near the Dead Sea. According to Genesis, it was then that God told Abraham that all the land he could see was given to him and his offspring forever and that his offspring would be as uncountable as the dust.

Abraham moved a short distance south to Hebron, where he pitched his tents and built an altar to the Lord. His adventures show that He was not a solitary herdsman but a tribal chieftain with hundreds of people in His encampments. Abraham was a shrewd businessman and consummate communicator who earned respect and recognition. He was a warrior chief as well as a spiritual teacher. For example, Abraham and His fighting men, in alliance with various other tribal leaders, rescued Lot from captivity against four named kings in Elam.

As Abraham continued to prosper, from time to time God reminded Him of the Covenant. But Abraham was not getting any younger. What he needed was a son or his estate would go to his cousin Eliezer in Damascus. God was patient with Abraham: *"He took him outside and said, 'Look up at the sky and count the stars—if indeed you can count them.' Then he said to him, So shall your offspring be'"* (15:5).

Abraham was understandably not convinced and asked for proof. So the Lord told Him to get a heifer, a goat, and a ram, each three years old, and a dove and a pigeon. This was done, and the three large animals were cut in half and their halves placed facing each other:

> *When the sun had set and darkness had fallen, a smoking firepot with a blazing torch appeared and passed between the pieces. On that day the LORD made a covenant with Abram and said, "To your descendants I give this land, from the Wadi of Egypt to the great river, the Euphrates—the land of the Kenites, Kenizzites, Admonites, Hittites, Perizzites, Rephaites, Amorites, Canaanites, Girgashites and Jebusites."*
> (Gen. 15:17–21)

This ritual seems weird to us, not to mention gory, but this was how a contract could be sealed at a time without lawyers or written accords. The two parties would walk between the halves of the animals, making sure that they stepped in the blood to acknowledge that if the contract were broken, the offending party would suffer the same fate as these animals—far worse than any summary judgment from a court today! However, this contract with Abraham seems one-sided since only one party, the Lord, symbolized as the lighted lamp, was active. He passed between the pieces as Abraham watched.

Years passed, and still no son was born to Abraham and Sarah, so she gave Abraham her servant girl, Hagar. Soon Hagar was pregnant, and she made the mistake of getting haughty with Sarah, who mistreated Hagar until she ran away. But that was not God's plan. An angel of the Lord appeared to Hagar in the desert and counseled her to return to Sarah and submit to her. The angel added, *"I will increase your descendants so much that they will be too numerous to count"* (16:10). Hagar was told that she would give birth to a son and was to name him Ishmael.

Genesis relates that when Abraham was ninety-nine years old, the Lord appeared to Him to talk again about the Covenant and the destiny of His descendants:

> *Abram fell facedown, and God said to him, "As for me, this is my covenant with you: You will be the father of many nations. No longer will you be called Abram; your name will be Abraham, for I have made you a father of many nations. I will make you very fruitful; I will make nations of you, and kings will come from you. I will establish my covenant as an everlasting covenant between me and you and your descendants after you for the generations to come, to be your God and the God of your descendants after you. The whole land of Canaan, where you now reside as a foreigner, I will give as an everlasting possession to you and your descendants after you; and I will be their God." (17:3–8)*

Abraham was confounded. Was this mockery? Sarah was now ninety years old. He pleaded for Ishmael to live under God's blessing. But

THE COMING OF THE GLORY

no. Sarah would bear a son who would be called Isaac, and God would establish a covenant with him as an everlasting covenant for his descendants after him. Ishmael would also be blessed as the father of twelve rulers, and his people would become a great nation. *"But my covenant I will establish with Isaac, whom Sarah will bear to you by this time next year"* (17:21).

Isaac was born within the year.

DIVINE SACRIFICE

Most readers are familiar with the account of Abraham and the events of His near sacrifice of Isaac in Genesis 22:1–19. This episode has perplexed, even agonized, religious believers and theologians for 4,000 years. How could God ever command such an atrocity? But Abraham had obeyed with a heavy heart, and at the last minute, as the sacrificial knife was poised above the bound Isaac, an angel of the Lord intervened and said:

> *"I swear by myself, declares the LORD, that because you have done this and have not withheld your son, your only son, I will surely bless you and make your descendants as numerous as the stars in the sky and as the sand on the seashore. Your descendants will take possession of the cities of their enemies, and through your offspring all nations on earth will be blessed, because you have obeyed me."* (22:15–18)

A nearby ram was caught in a thicket and was offered as the sacrifice instead.

THE QUR'ANIC VERSION

The Qur'an states that it was Ishmael whom Abraham was directed to sacrifice, not Isaac. Ishmael was only a boy when his father received the directive from God. However, Ishmael demonstrated a surprising level of spiritual maturity and obedience. When Abraham asked him what he thought about being sacrificed, Ishmael answered, *"My father, do what thou art bidden; of the patient, if God please, shalt thou find me"* (Qur'an

37:102). Ishmael was indeed the son of righteousness and meekness that Abraham had been promised back in Ur!

The practice of human sacrifice, even that of children, was the norm in the ancient Middle East. As such, Abraham would have been familiar with the custom. The staying of Abraham's sacrificial knife was the first known divine teaching against human sacrifice. Later, the Mosaic Dispensation would explicitly forbid it. There is, however, another framework of reference for this event. Bahá'u'lláh put the divine purpose of the sacrifice of Abraham's son into another perspective—the spiritual concept of sacrifice as a ransom:

> *That which thou hast heard concerning Abraham, the Friend of the All-Merciful, is the truth, and no doubt is there about it. The Voice of God commanded Him to offer up Ishmael as a sacrifice, so that His steadfastness in the Faith of God and His detachment from all else but Him may be demonstrated unto men. The purpose of God, moreover, was to sacrifice him as a ransom for the sins and iniquities of all the peoples of the earth. This same honor, Jesus, the Son of Mary, besought the one true God, exalted be His name and glory, to confer upon Him.*[10]

It is a core Christian belief that Jesus took on the sins of mankind and effected its forgiveness through His martyrdom. Bahá'u'lláh confirmed the foundational importance of Jesus's sacrifice but added a new layer of meaning when he wrote, *"Know thou that when the Son of Man [Jesus] yielded up His breath to God, the whole creation wept with a great weeping. By sacrificing Himself, however, a fresh capacity was infused into all created things."*[11] Rather than the sacrifice of Jesus being only for personal salvation, its wider purpose was to advance the spiritual progress of all creation.

Sacrifice as a ransom for the spiritual welfare of humanity was also realized in the heart-wrenching death of Mírzá Mihdí, a son of Bahá'u'lláh and the younger brother of 'Abdu'l-Bahá.[12] This tragedy struck in the early days of the Holy Family's incarceration in Akka, as described by Shoghi Effendi:

To the galling weight of these tribulations was now added the bitter grief of a sudden tragedy—the premature loss of the noble, the pious Mírzá Mihdí, the Purest Branch, 'Abdu'l-Bahá's twenty-two year old brother, an amanuensis [scribe] of Bahá'u'lláh and a companion of His exile from the days when, as a child, he was brought from Ṭihrán to Baghdád to join his Father after His return from Sulaymáníyyih. He was pacing the roof of the barracks in the twilight one evening, wrapped in his customary devotions, when he fell through the unguarded skylight onto a wooden crate, standing on the floor beneath, which pierced his ribs and caused, twenty-two hours later, his death, on the 23rd of Rabí'u'l-Avval 1287 A.H. (June 23, 1870). His dying supplication to a grieving Father was that his life might be accepted as a ransom for those who were prevented from attaining the presence of their Beloved.[13]

Bahá'u'lláh gave Mírzá Mihdí the option to be healed. However, the son asked that his life be accepted as a sacrifice so that the stringent conditions of his father's imprisonment would be lessened and the Bahá'ís would be able to gain access to Him. The Holy Family had been held in the prison city of Akka for two years under stark conditions that prohibited visitors from seeing Bahá'u'lláh, who was kept in total isolation.

In a poignant prayer revealed by Bahá'u'lláh in memory of His son—a prayer that exalts his death to the rank of those great acts of atonement associated with Abraham's intended sacrifice of His son, the crucifixion of Jesus Christ, and the martyrdom of the Imám Ḥusayn—we read Shoghi Effendi's account of Bahá'u'lláh's prayers: *"I have, O my Lord, offered up that which Thou hast given Me, that Thy servants may be quickened, and all that dwell on earth be united."*[14] And these prophetic words were addressed to His martyred son: *"Thou art the Trust of God and His Treasure in this Land. Erelong will God reveal through thee that which He hath desired."*[15] Three months after Mírzá Mihdí's sacrificial death, the ban on visitors to Bahá'u'lláh was lifted.

ABRAHAM, INTO THE FUTURE

A FORERUNNER OF MUHAMMAD

Genesis continues the story of Ishmael after his expulsion with his mother from the encampment of Abraham, their suffering in the desert, and Hagar's assurance from an angel that God would make Ishmael into a great nation. Her eyes were opened to see a well of water, and God was with the boy as he grew up in the desert and became an archer. He is reported to have returned to Canaan to attend the burial of Abraham seven decades after His exile. Tribal ties were strong regardless of squabbles, and His daughter married His nephew Esau. The male descendants of Ishmael are listed as twelve sons who all became tribal chiefs and settled over a wide area, from the Persian Gulf to the border of Egypt.

Worthington gives much symbolic insight into the life of Ishmael. She notes that Hagar had come from polytheistic Egypt and probably did not understand Abraham's station. Hagar believed that she and Ishmael would die of thirst, a metaphor for spiritual confusion; instead, she was shown the well of spiritual life. Ishmael's role as an archer could refer to his character as a saintly man who could shoot the arrows of knowledge into the hearts and souls of the idolatrous inhabitants of the wilderness of ignorance. And the settlement of Hagar and Ishmael in the wilderness of Paran is seen by both Islam and the Bahá'í Faith as a prophecy of the advent of Muḥammad, who would descend from Ishmael.[16]

According to the Qur'an, Abraham did not abandon Hagar and Ishmael but provided for them and visited them several times. On His last visit, He and Ishmael were directed by God to build the very first house of worship dedicated to the One God in a small sanctuary near the well of Zamzam. This piece of land was then an isolated, desolate spot, but over the centuries, it developed into the town of Mecca. This first house of God was built in the form of a cube, with its four corners corresponding to the four points of the compass. Abraham and Ishmael were directed to place a rock in the eastern corner to point the direction to which worshippers should face for prayers. This first place of worship dedicated to the One God became known as the *Kaaba*, the cube. This most holy site has been a place of pilgrimage for Muslims since the early days of Islam.

Abrahamic monotheism was thus planted in Mecca by Abraham and Ishmael. However, in time, the One God to whom the cubic house of worship had been dedicated was forgotten. Idols were brought into the Kaaba, and polytheistic worship took over. The Prophet Muḥammad appeared in Mecca about 2,500 years later. He destroyed the idols in the Kaaba and reclaimed that house of worship for the One God.

FROM CIRCULAR TO FORWARD MOTION

In addition to everything else Abraham accomplished, He was instrumental in changing humanity's concept of time. In Middle Eastern belief, time was cyclical—a wheel that went nowhere except around and around in its own track. In that recurrent world, there were neither beginnings nor endings. Everything was repeated, and individual acts and decisions were limited in effect because the gods were in charge. Personal destiny was at their mercy, and that was that. Adam probably cracked the edges of cyclical time as part of inaugurating His cycle, while Abraham smashed the crystallization of repetitive time and set Judaism on a linear timeline. Abraham did the unthinkable when he packed up His household and strode into a "future" by believing the implausible promises He had been given by God.

Abraham left the land and the mindset of belief in deities who created man to do the work so that they could run the world the way it had always been run. He turned a new page in the understanding of the divine. The One God of the Israelites could not be manipulated, cajoled, or controlled through human rituals. Instead, He made inexplicable statements and strange demands, and He fulfilled His promises. Because God could not be understood through human reasoning, obedience to Him was based on the new concept of faith that robbed life of predictability.

The Abrahamic Dispensation was the instrument through which a fundamentally new understanding emerged of the nature of God and His relationship with man. It would take many centuries for the ancient Israelites to overcome the temptation of idols, and they would be taken "kicking and screaming," one could say, into the future.

'Abdu'l-Bahá paid a monumental tribute to Abraham in 1912 during a talk at Temple Emmau-El in San Francisco:

Among the great Prophets was Abraham, Who, being an iconoclast and a Herald of the oneness of God, was banished from His native land. He founded a family upon which the blessing of God descended, and it was owing to this religious basis and ordination that the Abrahamic house progressed and advanced. Through the divine benediction noteworthy and luminous prophets issued from His lineage. There appeared Isaac, Ishmael, Jacob, Joseph, Moses, Aaron, David and Solomon. The Holy Land was conquered by the power of the Covenant of God with Abraham, and the glory of the Solomonic wisdom and sovereignty dawned. All this was due to the religion of God which this blessed lineage established and upheld. It is evident that throughout the history of Abraham and His posterity this was the source of their honor, advancement and civilization. Even today the descendants of His household and lineage are found throughout the world.[17]

The legacy of Abraham was even more than His foundational Dispensation. The lineages of five succeeding Manifestations of God have been traced to Abraham—Moses and Jesus through Sarah, Muḥammad and the Báb through Hagar, and Bahá'u'lláh through Sarah on His father's side and Keturah on his mother's side. (Abraham married Keturah after Sarah's death, and they had six sons.) These descents are theologically and symbolically important because they are yet another illustration of the unity of the Holy Land Prophets who contributed to God's unfolding plan.

Chapter 7

JOSEPH, AN ALLEGORY
OF DIVINE BEAUTY

O My Brother! Until thou enter the Egypt of love, thou shalt
never come to the Joseph of the Beauty of the Friend; and until,
like Jacob, thou forsake thine outward eyes, thou shalt never open
the eye of thine inward being; and until thou burn with the fire
of love, thou shalt never commune with the Lover of Longing.

BAHÁ'U'LLÁH[1]

JOSEPH, RECORDED IN GENESIS as the son of Jacob, grandson of Isaac, and great-grandson of Abraham, is of major importance in the Hebrew Bible, the Qur'an, and the Bahá'í Faith. As with most if not all the Pentateuch,[2] the saga of Joseph was probably not written down until the seventh century and then the exilic period, and no claim can be made concerning its historic accuracy. However, Joseph is recognized in the Bahá'í Writings as a lesser prophet and regarded with reverence.

The well-known account of Joseph is told in about 300 verses in Genesis. He was born to Jacob's favorite wife Rachel, who also gave birth to Benjamin, her second son and his twelfth. Jacob loved Joseph more than his other sons, which set the stage for the sibling rivalry of the ages. When Joseph was seventeen, Jacob gave him a coat of many colors in a show of favoritism that worsened matters among the brothers. Then Joseph had two dreams that he described to the family with youthful naiveté and enthusiasm. In one dream, he saw his brothers' sheaves of wheat stand around his sheaf and make obeisance to it. In the other, he saw the sun, the moon, and eleven stars make obeisance to him. His brothers did not take this well.

When next the brothers went away to feed the flocks, Joseph was sent by Jacob to check on their welfare. When he found them, they cast him into a pit and then sold him for twenty pieces of silver to Midianites on their way to Egypt, where he was sold to Potiphar, an officer of the pharaoh and a captain of the guard. They dipped Joseph's coat of many colors in goat blood and returned it to their father with the claim that a beast had killed him. Jacob was inconsolable in his grief.

Joseph did well in Potiphar's household. He was considered a goodly person and was made a trusted overseer. When Potiphar's wife tried to seduce him, Joseph fled her presence, losing his shirt to her in the process. Although innocent, Joseph was imprisoned. In prison, he earned a reputation for interpreting prisoners' dreams. For example, a royal cupbearer dreamed of a vine with three branches with ripened grapes, which he squeezed into the pharaoh's cup and gave to him. Joseph told him that in three days he would be restored to his position at court. A baker dreamed of three baskets on his head, the top one with baked goods for the pharaoh, but birds picked at it. Joseph saw that in three days the baker would be executed by order of the pharaoh; his head would be put on a pole, and birds would eat his flesh. Both dreams came true.

His reputation as an interpreter of dreams spread to the court, and the pharaoh sent for Joseph to interpret his troubling dreams. He had dreamed of seven sleek, fat cows grazing by the Nile as seven ugly and gaunt cows came out of the Nile and ate them. He then saw seven healthy heads of grain growing on a stalk and seven other heads of thin and scorched grain sprouting and swallowing the good grain. Joseph explained that there would be seven years of good crops followed by seven years of famine. As a result, the pharaoh appointed Joseph to manage and store each year's harvest to prepare for the famine. Joseph thus became the most powerful man in the kingdom after the pharaoh's son and heir.

Joseph prepared Egypt well. When the famine came, people arrived from far away to buy corn, including the sons of Jacob from Canaan. Joseph was twenty years older by this time, and his brothers did not recognize him. He recognized them but used an interpreter to keep his identity secret. Upon questioning, the brothers said that Benjamin, the youngest, had been left behind with his father, who was still alive. To get Benjamin to Egypt, Joseph set in motion a plan that would force the brothers to bring him back with them. Their departure set in motion, Joseph turned his back and wept.

The brothers set off with bags of grain, but they soon learned that their money had been put back in the sacks. Upon arriving home, they told Jacob their story. In time, the grain ran low, and the brothers knew that they could not return to Egypt without Benjamin. Over Jacob's protestations, Judah guaranteed Benjamin's safety. They left bearing gifts and double the silver to repay what had been returned to them. Joseph warmly received and hosted them, but they still didn't know him. Deeply moved by seeing his brother Benjamin, Joseph again wept.

When it was time for the brothers to leave, they received full sacks of food, and each man's silver was again put in his sack. Along with his silver, Benjamin's sack included Joseph's silver cup. Joseph's men were sent to catch up with the caravan and accuse the brothers of theft, which they denied, but the cup was found in Benjamin's sack nonetheless. Joseph's men decided that he would become a slave, and the brothers returned to the city in grief. Upon their arrival, Joseph only questioned Judah about his father and requested that he also be brought to Egypt while Benjamin was left behind. Judah gave a heart-wrenching account of his father's love for Benjamin and offered to trade places with him.

The dam burst. Weeping, Joseph revealed himself to his brothers. He begged them not to be distressed with guilt for selling him but to accept his forgiveness, because it had been part of God's plan that he be sent ahead of them to Egypt to save their lives and preserve for them a remnant on the earth. This reunion for all time was punctuated by tears and praises.

Joseph asked that they bring Jacob to him. They would then live nearby in Egypt with their children and grandchildren and their flocks and herds, and he would provide for them during the remaining five years of famine. Joseph's departing words were *"Don't quarrel on the way!"* (Gen. 45:24).

So the brothers returned home and told Jacob, *"Joseph is still alive! In fact, he is ruler of all Egypt"* (45:26). A little hyperbole there, but the donkeys laden with food and silver made the point.

On the subsequent trip to Egypt, Jacob was reassured in a vision that God would go with him, that Joseph's hand would close his eyes at death, and that God would bring His people back to Canaan. Thus Jacob was reunited with his son Joseph, the extended family was settled on choice land, and, in time, Jacob died and Joseph took his body to the cave of Machpelah in Canaan, the resting place of Sarah, Isaac, Rebekah, and Jacob's wife Leah.

JOSEPH IN THE QUR'AN

The Qur'an devotes a whole sura, or chapter, of 111 verses to Joseph. This version follows the biblical one but with details that more vividly portray the allegory, although both versions present spiritual and metaphorical truths. The Qur'anic additions enhance the central motifs.

The Qur'an shows how Jacob handled the news of Joseph's reported death with inner sight: *"And they brought his shirt with false blood upon it. He said, 'Nay, but yourselves have managed this affair. But patience is seemly: and the help of God is to be implored that I may bear what you tell me'"* (Qur'an 12:18).

When Joseph rejected the advances of Potiphar's wife and they both made for the door, she tore his shirt. And who was at the door but her husband! A quick explanation was definitely in order:

> *"What," said she, "shall be the recompense of him who would do evil to thy family, but a prison or a sore punishment?"*
>
> *He said, "She solicited me to evil." And a witness out of her own family witnessed: "If his shirt be rent in front she speaketh truth, and he is a liar:*

But if his shirt be rent behind, she lieth and he is true."

And when his lord saw his shirt torn behind, he said, "This is one of your devices! Verily your devices are great!" (12:25–28)

Word of the incident traveled about the city. In the Qur'an, Potiphar is called Aziz, which denotes a high-ranking official or a powerful and respected person:

And in the city, the women said, "The wife of the Prince [Aziz] hath solicited her servant: he hath fired her with his love: but we clearly see her manifest error."

And when she heard of their cabal, she sent to them and got ready a banquet for them, and gave each one of them a knife, and said, "Joseph shew thyself to them." And when they saw him they were amazed at him, and cut their hands, and said, "God keep us! This is no man! This is no other than a noble angel!" (12:30–31)

The gossip had also reached the court:

And the King [Pharaoh] said, "Bring him to me." And when the messenger came to Joseph he said, "Go back to thy lord, and ask him what meant the women who cut their hands, for my lord well knoweth the snare they laid."

Then said the Prince to the women, "What was your purpose when ye solicited Joseph?" They said, "God keep us! we know not any ill of him." The wife of the Prince said, "Now doth the truth appear. It was I who would have led him into unlawful love, and he is one of the truthful." (12:50–51)

Jacob released Benjamin to his sons with not only a pledge from them for his safety but also with trust in God:

He said, "I will not send him with you but on your oath before God that ye will, indeed, bring him back to me, unless hindrances encompass you." And when they had given him their pledge, he said, "God is witness of what we say."

And he said, "O, my sons! Enter not by one gate, but enter by different gates. Yet can I not help you against aught decreed by God: judgment belongeth to God alone. In Him put I my trust, and in Him let the trusting trust." (12:66–67)

The Qur'an adds another episode about Joseph's shirt:

"Go ye with this my shirt and throw it on my father's face, and he shall recover his sight: and bring me all your family."

And when the caravan was departed, their father said, "I surely perceive the smell of Joseph: think ye that I dote?"

They said, "By God, it is thy old mistake."

And when the bearer of good tidings came, he cast it on his face, and Jacob's eyesight returned.

Then he said, "Did I not tell you that I knew from God what ye knew not?"

They said, "Our father, ask pardon for our crimes for us, for we have indeed been sinners."

He said, "I will ask you pardon of my Lord, for he is Gracious, Merciful." (12:93–98)

Joseph's youthful dreams were fulfilled:

And when they came unto Joseph he took his parents* to him, and said, "Enter ye Egypt, if God will, secure."

And he raised his parents to the seat of state, and they fell down bowing themselves unto him. Then said he, "O my father, this is the meaning of my dream of old. My Lord hath now made it true, and he hath surely been gracious to me, since he took me forth from the prison, and hath brought you up out of the desert, after that Satan had stirred up strife between me and my brethren; for my Lord is gracious to whom He will; for He is the Knowing, the Wise." (12:100–101)

* Joseph's mother was long dead (Gen. 35:17–18). Perhaps it was another wife, Bilhah, Joseph's stepmother and the mother of two of Jacob's sons, who was meant.

The Sura of Joseph ends by emphasizing the spiritual timelessness of the story and its confirmation of previous scriptures:

> *"Certainly in their histories is an example for men of understanding. This is no new tale of fiction, but a confirmation of previous scriptures, and an explanation of all things, and guidance and mercy to those who believe."* (12:111)

The Qur'an gives deep insight into Jacob's spiritual stature. Jacob had not grieved endlessly because he believed that Joseph had been murdered. Rather, Jacob was a symbol for patience, knowing the crime his sons had committed but realizing a higher purpose to the situation. After all, this was the Jacob who, in his younger years, had wrestled an angel of God to a draw! Jacob believed that he saw God face to face and yet his life had been spared. Instead of merely accepting his life, Jacob demanded and received from the angel a blessing, which was that his name would now be Israel because he had struggled with God and humans and had overcome. This time Jacob *earned* his blessing as compared with his youthful theft of his father Isaac's blessing meant for Esau!

The story of Joseph is an allegory of tragedy and transcendence, betrayal followed by forgiveness and reconciliation. It can also be approached as a parable of the spiritual journey, the quest of the seeker for God's spiritual sustenance, and the state of being spiritually lost and then finding that nourishment through the Prophet of God for his day. In addition, the narrative's events illustrate what happens when the message is opposed by those who feel threatened, usually the religious authorities of the day.

The symbology of the Joseph story is a vast reservoir for contemplation. Joseph's shirts, which may have been knee-length tunics or full-length cloaks, are primary symbols, first of a father's love and then the brothers' betrayal. The coat of many colors is a reminder that all colors are diffused from white, the color of purity. While his brothers undoubtedly wore drab grays and browns, Joseph's purity was signified by this multi-colored coat, but they could only see colors, not the oneness of the light falling upon it. The torn shirt in Egypt proved Joseph's innocence and led to his appointment to a high position in the land. A shirt with his scent upon it opened his father's spiritual eyes and became a symbol of spiritual reunion. This much-mentioned shirt could also be a metaphor for Joseph's own spiritual journey and struggles as well as healing, spiritual understanding, holiness, and faith.

Bahá'u'lláh often referred to the fragrance of Joseph, sometimes as a metaphor for the recognition of a Manifestation of God: *"This is the Day whereon every sweet smelling thing hath derived its fragrance from the smell of My garment—a garment that hath shed its perfume upon the whole of creation."*[3]

Many aspects of the Joseph story seem to depict the life and mission of each Prophet of God. The famine refers to the spiritual famine of a people and the full granaries the spiritual sustenance brought by a Prophet. The cupbearer could portray the person who accepts the new Manifestation of God and the baker one who does not and dies spiritually. The agony of Jacob's separation from Joseph is sometimes seen as a metaphor for the separation of the soul from God until he recognizes the Prophet of God for his time. Jacob's blindness alludes to figuratively closing his eyes to the world and opening them to the wisdom of the inner level.

The inner beauty of Joseph so startled the women that they cut their hands in consternation. Such beauty is spiritual beauty that confounds. It also represents the celestial beauty of a Manifestation of God. Bahá'u'lláh was often referred to as the Blessed Beauty.

The betrayal by Joseph's brothers enacted the treacheries that all Prophets of God experience as Their missions are met with rejection and bitter betrayal. Often Their own families do not recognize Their station.

Bahá'u'lláh was relentlessly opposed by a half-brother who caused almost insurmountable problems for the new religious community. Bahá'u'lláh wrote of the futility of such resistance:

> *Say: O people! Dust fill your mouths, and ashes blind your eyes, for having bartered away the Divine Joseph for the most paltry of prices. Oh, the misery*

that resteth upon you, ye that are far astray! Have ye imagined in your hearts that ye possess the power to outstrip Him and His Cause? Far from it! To this He, Himself, the All-Powerful, the Most Exalted, the Most Great, doth testify. [4]

Bahá'u'lláh also made sweeping references to the symbology of Joseph:

Cleanse thy heart from every blasphemous whispering and evil allusion thou hast heard in the past, that thou mayest inhale the sweet savours of eternity from the Joseph of faithfulness, gain admittance into the celestial Egypt, and perceive the fragrances of enlightenment from this resplendent and luminous Tablet, a Tablet wherein the Pen hath inscribed the ancient mysteries of the names of His lord, the Exalted, the Most High. Perchance thou mayest be recorded in the holy Tablets among them that are well assured. [5]

The section above is only a glimpse of the motifs of Joseph. In particular, they include the events of May 22, 1844, when the Báb revealed His identity to His first disciple and started writing his celebrated commentary on the Sura of Joseph, the Qayyúmu'l-Asmá' (The Self-Subsisting Lord of All Names). In this work of 9,300 verses in 111 chapters—one for each in the Qur'anic Sura of Joseph—He announced His station and forecast the vicissitudes of the ministry of the true Joseph, Bahá'u'lláh, and what He would endure at the hands of one who was at once His archenemy and blood brother. For an in-depth exploration of the symbology of the Joseph story presented by the Báb in the Qayyúmu'l-Asmá', I refer you to the book, *Gate of the Heart*, by the Nader Saiedi, who is a foremost scholar on the writings of the Báb.

Articles listed in the endnotes provide much material for further exploration.[6]

Chapter 8

A COLLAPSE AND A CALL

O my Lord! O my Lord! This is a lamp lighted by the fire of
Thy love and ablaze with the flame which is ignited in the
tree of Thy mercy. O my Lord! Increase his enkindlement,
heat and flame, with the fire which is kindled in the Sinai
of Thy Manifestation. Verily, Thou art the Confirmer,
the Assister, the Powerful, the Generous, the Loving.

'ABDU'L-BAHÁ[1]

NOTHING OCCURS IN A VACUUM. There is always cause and effect. Likewise, the advent of Prophets of God is not happenstance but events carefully timed in accordance with necessity.

Civilization developed throughout the Middle East and reached heights previously unrealized as technological and cultural advances took place within empires that controlled vast territories. These empires rose and fell as each one conquered, taxed vassals, and controlled lucrative trade routes until being defeated by another empire in turn. They fought each other and then traded with each other. An international economy developed with strengths and weaknesses like those of today. International relations were also similar, with warfare interspersed with commercial and diplomatic negotiations and the interests of merchants vying with those of emperors. Parallel to empire building was hyper-domestication that exponentially increased societal stratification and conflict.

99

Why should we care about the squabbles of these ancient powers? Because the movement of armies in the Middle East often meant tromping through the biblical land of Canaan, which had significant geopolitical importance in the second millennium BCE thanks to the major trade routes running through it. Sea trade stretched from the Far East through the Indian Ocean to the ports in the southern Arabian Peninsula, where goods were offloaded onto caravans traveling to Egypt, the Levant,[2] and beyond. Whoever controlled these fabled routes collected the fees and taxes and had the upper hand in diplomatic negotiations. The Egyptian, Hittite, and Assyrian spheres of interest converged in Canaan by the fifteenth century.

International trade brought extraordinary wealth to the upper classes. A fascinating time capsule depicting the extent of these riches was unearthed from a ship that sank near the city of Uluburun, off the southern coast of Anatolia, Turkey, in about 1300 BCE. Researchers conducted an excavation in a series of 22,400 dives between 1984 and 1994, recovering seventeen tons of artifacts that represented a microcosm of international trade and illuminated how interconnected empires were at that time.

The primary freight was ten tons of Cypriot copper and one ton of tin, which was as valuable in the Late Bronze Age as oil is today. A partial list of the excavated cargo included gold and silver ingots, jewelry, raw glass, logs of African ebony, and incense and spices from the Far East. Seeds have been identified for olives, almonds, pine nuts, figs, pome-granates, and fruits. The ship also carried exotic items such as an ivory elephant tusk, hippopotamus teeth, ostrich eggshells, and thousands of opercula, the spirals of sea snail shells that were used as decorative items on clothing. Textiles and other perishable items were probably on board, but they would not have survived the thousands of years in the water. This stunning diversity represented numerous cultures: Canaanite, Mycenaean, Cypriot, Egyptian, Nubian, Baltic, northern Balkan, Old Babylonian, Kassite, Assyrian, Central Asian, and possibly south Italian or Sicilian.[3]

A COLLAPSE

By the early thirteenth century BCE, the Middle East had reached a previ-ously unknown level of wealth and prosperity thanks to a flourishing network of empires and a sophisticated infrastructure to support them. This all began to collapse starting about 1250 BCE. The year 1177 BCE is generally used by historians and archeologists as the benchmark for the demise of the empires and the end of the Late Bronze Age. An excellent source of information on the collapse of the Late Bronze Age and its empires in the Middle East is the book, *1177 BC: The Year Civilization Collapsed*, by Eric H. Cline.

Cline refers to the events of the decades between 1250 and 1177 as a "perfect storm of calamities," a rolling process whereby the interconnectedness between cultures and empires facilitated a domino effect of disasters that ultimately destroyed the world as it had been known. Several contributing factors intertwined with and exacerbated each other. Cline wrote that thanks to recent research by archeological seismologists, it is now clear that the Aegean and Eastern Mediterranean region experienced a series of earthquakes that began about 1225 and lasted for a period as long as fifty years. Destruction by earthquake is noticeably different from devastation by war. The archeological markers for earthquakes are collapsed, patched, or reinforced walls, crushed skeletons, toppled columns lying parallel to each other, slipped keystones in archways and doorways, and walls leaning at impossible angles.

Meanwhile, climate change cooled the water of the Mediterranean Sea, which in turn caused a decrease in rainfall that turned the fertile Levant and other Mediterranean areas into semi-arid deserts. Frantic letters from the Hittites to the pharaoh of Egypt begged for massive shipments of grain. For example, in the mid-thirteenth century a Hittite queen wrote to Pharaoh Rameses II (1279–1213), "I have no grain in my lands." An inscription dated to his successor, Merneptah (1213–1203), states that he had "caused grain to be taken in ships, to keep alive this land of Hatti." [4]

The long drought and cold spell are dated from about 1250 to 1100 BCE in the eastern Mediterranean region. A study of pollen samples taken from the sediment of the Sea of Galilee confirmed the severe climate change. [5] Pollen is organic matter with high endurance that had been driven into the sea by wind and streams for millennia to become

101

embedded in the underwater sediment. Sixty-foot core samples from the sea's sediment allowed for the extraction of fossil pollen grains at intervals of forty years during the last 9,000 years. Data from the sediment cores were used to reconstruct past climate changes and human effect on the vegetation of the Mediterranean zone of the southern Levant.

The final blow was the incursions of the Sea Peoples, as they were called by the Egyptians, whom the Hebrews called the Philistines. Their origin is unknown, but they seem to have been ethnic European peoples who were driven east by droughts. They came by land and sea, first as raiders and then as settlers with their families and belongings. Their attacks started in the early twelfth century and lasted for decades. By 1180 the Sea Peoples had caused the disintegration of the Hittite empire and destroyed major cities on the Levantine coast. In southern Canaan, they established a pentapolis of settlements—Ashdod, Ashkelon, and Gaza on the coast and Ekron and Gath a few miles inland in the Judean hills. As is often the case, these marauders were not as culturally advanced as the people they raided, and their predations caused a plummeting of levels of civilization. The Egyptians managed to defeat the Sea Peoples in the Nile Delta in 1177, but this effort so weakened the Egyptian kingdom that it never reemerged as a major power. Most important to the Hebrews is that the Egyptians had to withdraw from Canaan.

Empires are built not only on conquests but, just as importantly, on trade. The invasions of the Sea Peoples not only disrupted but cut international trade routes, thereby severing the cohesion and codependence that had promoted and sustained the Near Eastern empires. Archeological, geological, and historical studies have provided evidence of the droughts, famines, earthquakes, migrations, and internal rebellions that all contributed to the end of the Bronze Age.

The book of Judges seems to confirm the reduced circumstances in Canaan when it gives background to the story of Deborah in the twelfth century: *"In the days of Shamgar son of Anath, in the days of Jael, the highways were abandoned; travelers took to winding paths"* (Judg. 5:6).

Noah Wiener, an editor with the Biblical Archeological Society in Washington, D.C., succinctly noted how this decline created the opportunity for the Hebrews to return to Canaan. "The Bronze Age collapse was swift and sudden, ushering in a so-called 'Dark Ages' of decreased literacy, population and technology in much of the Eastern Mediterranean. The power vacuum and increased migration surely played a role in the emergence of the biblical Israelites and classical Greeks." [6]

A CALL

Genesis states that Joseph's family moved to Egypt and prospered there. That was not at all unusual. Emigration from Canaan to the fertile Egyptian delta region, where the Nile River mitigated the effects of droughts, had been common for centuries, and there may have been many Canaanites living in Lower Egypt by Joseph's time. This large immigrant population, loosely called the Hyksos, had become strong enough that by 1720 BCE it became an independent force in the eastern Nile delta. By 1650 the Hyksos had taken over and ruled lower and middle Egypt. They were defeated by the Egyptians in 1520. The slavery of the Hebrews might have dated from that time, along with the servitude of other defeated Hyksos peoples. Moses would probably proclaim His message to a polyglot of people as well as to the small number of Hebrews who had retained their identity.

According to the book of Exodus, the call came to Moses in midlife on a day when He was tending the flocks of Jethro by Mount Horeb. He saw a bush on fire that was not being consumed, and He went to investigate this strange sight. Bahá'u'lláh described this mystical encounter with the Holy Spirit:

*Moses entered the holy vale, situate in the wilderness of Sinai, and there beheld the vision of the **King of glory** from the "Tree that belongeth neither to the East nor to the West."* There He heard the soul-stirring Voice of the Spirit speaking from out of the kindled Fire, bidding Him to shed upon Pharaonic souls the light of divine guidance; so that, liberating them from the shadows of the valley of self and desire, He might enable them to attain the meads of heavenly delight, and delivering them through the*

103

Salsabíl of renunciation, from the bewilderment of remoteness, cause them to enter the peaceful city of the divine presence."[7]
*Qur'an 24:35

The Tree that belonged neither to the East nor the West is an allegory for the Tree of Life, which is the Word of God that each Manifestation of God brings in His Dispensation. *The King of glory* might allude to Bahá'u'lláh. The Burning Bush is laden with many meanings. The heat of fire can be a metaphor for suffering. Fire is also a symbol for the purification of the soul and the burning away of dross, which is generally an emotionally and spiritually painful process. Metaphorical fire produces the heat of love. The Burning Bush was symbolic of God's presence in the heart of Moses.[8] It was also a symbol for the Holy Spirit.

Allegory is often used for the Holy Spirit because this is a mystery mostly beyond human understanding. The Holy Spirit appeared to all the Manifestations of God yet in different forms—the Sacred Fire (Zoroaster), the Burning Bush (Moses), the Dove (Jesus), the angel Gabriel (Muḥammad), and the Maiden (Bahá'u'lláh).

The Báb made many references to the Burning Bush and Sinai in His Commentary on the Sura of Joseph, the Qayyúmu'l-Asmá'. The Báb wrote the first chapter of this monumental work on that memorable evening of May 22, 1844, when He met with Mullá Ḥusayn, His first disciple. In this chapter, He proclaimed His station and referred to Himself as the flame of the supernal lamp that lay concealed in the Burning Bush.

I am the Mystic Fane which the Hand of Omnipotence hath reared. I am the Lamp which the Finger of God hath lit within its niche and caused to shine with deathless splendor. I am the Flame of that supernal Light that glowed upon Sinai in the gladsome Spot, and lay concealed in the midst of the Burning Bush.[9]

The Báb made several references in the Qayyúmu'l-Asmá' to Himself and the Burning Bush, including, *"Indeed We conversed with Moses by the leave of God from the midst of the Burning Bush in the Sinai and revealed an infinitesimal glimmer of Thy Light upon the Mystic Mount and its dwellers, whereupon the Mount shook to its foundations and was crushed into dust ... "*[10] and *"Give ear unto God's holy Voice proclaimed by this Arabian Youth Whom the Almighty has graciously chosen for His Own Self. He is indeed none other than the True One, Whom God hath entrusted with this Mission from the midst of the Burning Bush."*[11]

Layer upon layer are the mystical and spiritual meanings of the above verses. Saiedi commented on the fire symbology and the voice in the Burning Bush:

> Most directly, however, the fire symbol is a reference to divine revelation and the Logos, as expressed in the call of God that emanates from the Burning Bush. The Burning Bush unites in a mystical symbol the three motifs of fire, the tree, and the voice of God.
>
> The Burning Bush, of course, belongs to the story of Moses, and it is one of the most significant features of the Báb's self-definition in all His writings. In the Qayyúmu'l-Asmá' the voice of God that spoke to Moses through the Burning Bush is in fact the Báb: "O People of effacement!" the Báb writes, "Hearken ye unto My Call, appearing out of the Point of Confirmation, from this Arabian Youth Who hath addressed, by the leave of God, Moses upon Mount Sinai."[12]

Saiedi asserted that the Báb was the "Gate through which God spoke to Moses, that Moses in fact attained the presence of God *through the mediation of the Báb.*"[13]

Bahá'u'lláh also alluded to His having been a voice in the Burning Bush, as follows:

> *Say: This, verily, is the heaven in which the Mother Book is treasured, could ye but comprehend it. He it is Who hath caused the Rock to shout, and the Burning Bush to lift up its voice, upon the Mount rising above the Holy Land, and proclaim: "The Kingdom is God's, the sovereign Lord of all, the All-Powerful, the Loving!"*[14]

105

Shoghi Effendi states below that Bahá'u'lláh is not an intermediary between other Manifestations and God but confirms that He did converse with Moses in the Burning Bush:

> Bahá'u'lláh is not the intermediary between other Manifestations and God. Each has His own relation to the Primal Source. But in the sense that Bahá'u'lláh is the greatest Manifestation to yet appear, the One who consummates the Revelation of Moses, He was the One Moses conversed with in the Burning Bush. In other words, Bahá'u'lláh identifies the glory of the God-Head on that occasion with Himself. No distinction can be made amongst the Prophets in the sense that They all proceed from one Source and are of one essence. But Their stations and functions in this world are different.[15]

Since the Prophets of God were preexistent, they were involved in aspects of creation and the development of human spirituality for eons of time. Human language is inadequate to convey the subtleties of the meanings of what the Báb and Bahá'u'lláh wrote. Ponder on their mysteries.

MOSES GOES

The book of Exodus portrays Moses reacting to His call with overwhelming fear. First awed, then alarmed, and finally desperate in His feelings of inadequacy to fulfill this mission, Moses agreed to go to Pharaoh and bring the Hebrews back to the "land of milk and honey" but only when armed with a rod that had divine powers and accompanied by His brother Aaron as spokesman. Moses's purported response raises the question about when Prophets of God become aware in their earthly lives of the essential nature of Their being or when they have an inner knowledge on some level of Their eventual missions. 'Abdu'l-Bahá spoke of all the Manifestations of God when He explained, *"From the beginning, that sanctified Reality is undoubtedly aware of the secret of existence, and from childhood the signs of greatness are clearly manifested in Him. How then could He fail, in spite of such bounties and perfections, to be conscious of His own station?*[16] The consciousness of their identities as Prophets seems to be only partially submerged until the call of the Holy Spirit comes.

Armed with the power of God, Moses set forth to lead His people from spiritual slavery in Egypt to a new life in the Promised Land, to release them from the cyclical mindset and idolatry of Egypt and lead them into a divinely ordained future. He succeeded in leading His followers from abject spiritual slavery into a mindset prepared to receive a new revelation from God. The people joined Him, grumbling and complaining, on a spiritual journey for all time.

Chapter 9

A SPIRITUAL EXODUS

All down the ages the prophets of God have been sent into the
world to serve the cause of truth—Moses brought the law of
truth, and all the prophets of Israel after him sought to spread it.

'ABDU'L-BAHÁ[1]

THE BOOK OF EXODUS contains no details that make it possible to date the most famous migration in history. No pharaoh is named, and no Egyptian records have been discovered that mention the Hebrews in Egypt. However, something of great magnitude happened. 'Abdu'l-Bahá wrote that the Exodus *"was both spiritual and physical."*[2] Its spiritual significance cannot be understated.

The Hebrew migration from Egypt is generally dated from the mid- to late thirteenth century, which would coincide with the collapse of the Middle Eastern empires and the Canaanite kingdoms. The weakening of Egypt after defeating the Sea Peoples could have enabled the Hebrews to slip out of Egypt, while a power vacuum in Canaan could have made Hebrew immigration possible.

As we progress with the mission of Moses, it is important to remember that no historical or archeological evidence for the Exodus, either in Egypt or in Sinai, has been found. Most archeologists, such as Israel Finkelstein and Neil Asher Silberman, are adamant about this. They state that except for the Egyptian forts along the northern coast, not a single campsite or sign of occupation from the time of Ramesses II and his immediate predecessors and successors has ever been identified in Sinai:

> And it has not been for lack of trying. Repeated archeological surveys in all regions of the peninsula, including the mountainous area around the traditional site of Mount Sinai ... have yielded only negative evidence: not a single sherd, no structure, not a single house, no trace of an ancient encampment. One may argue that a relatively small band of wandering Israelites cannot be expected to leave material remains behind. But modern archeological techniques are quite capable of tracing even the very meager remains of hunter-gatherers and pastoral nomads all over the world. Indeed, the archeological record from the Sinai Peninsula discloses evidence for pastoral activity in such eras as the third millennium BCE and the Hellenistic and Byzantine periods. There is simply no such evidence at the supposed time of the Exodus in the thirteenth century BCE.[3]

Yet the Exodus is the central event of the Hebrew Bible, and more space is devoted to the mission of Moses than any other subject. Does the lack of historical and archeological data for the biblical Exodus mean that this story is to be interpreted only as a legend? Most biblical scholars do accept that something monumental happened to generate this national epic. Carol Redmount, an archeologist who specializes in Egyptian antiquities, was one of them:

> To some, the lack of a secure historical grounding for the biblical Exodus narrative merely reflects its nonhistorical nature. According to this view, there was no historical Exodus and the story is to be interpreted as a legend or myth of origins. To others, still in the majority among scholars, the ultimate historicity of the Exodus narrative is indisputable. The details of the story may have become clouded or obscured through the transmission

process, but a historical core is mandated by that major tenet of faith that permeates the Bible: God acts in history.[4]

Indeed, God has always acted in history, and Moses was the Prophet of God to bring a divine Revelation at a propitious time, the time of the collapse. Bahá'u'lláh wrote of this momentous event:

> *And when His [Abraham's] day was ended, there came the turn of Moses. Armed with the rod of celestial dominion, adorned with the white hand of divine knowledge, and proceeding from the Párán of the love of God, and wielding the serpent of power and everlasting majesty, He shone forth from the Sinai of light upon the world. He summoned all the peoples and kindreds of the earth to the kingdom of eternity, and invited them to partake of the fruit of the tree of faithfulness. Surely you are aware of the fierce opposition of Pharaoh and his people, and the stone of idle fancy which the hands of the infidels cast upon that blessed Tree.*[5]

SYMBOLOGY OF THE EXODUS

The saga of the Exodus is high drama of the struggle of a Prophet with the forces that oppose Him, told with rich symbolism, such as the plagues, a shape-shifting rod, and the parting of the sea.

Pharaoh represents the enemy, single or collective, of every Manifestation of God. The pharaonic enemy resists the light of a new Dispensation and clings to the status quo. The Hebrew pharaonic souls were not anxious to be released from their spiritual slavery. Their bondage was figurative as well as literal. Sometimes the freedom to accept new truths can seem more oppressive than the shackles of darkness. Pharaoh's struggle with Moses portrays the struggle every person faces—whether to cling to outmoded traditions and dogmas or to recognize the Manifestation of God for his day. 'Abdu'l-Bahá identified the core element of this drama as the insistent self:

> *How can the darkness hope to overcome the light, how can a magician's cords hold fast "a serpent plain for all to see"? "Then lo! It swallowed up*

111

*their lying wonders."** Alas for them! They have deluded themselves with a fable, and to indulge their appetites they have done away with their own selves. They gave up everlasting glory in exchange for human pride, and they sacrificed greatness in both worlds to the demands of the insistent self. This is that of which We have forewarned you. Erelong shall ye behold the foolish in manifest loss.*[6]

* Qur'an 26:31; 26:44; this reference is to Moses's rod and the enchanters.

According to the Exodus narrative, each time the pharaoh refused Moses's pleas to "let my people go," Moses escalated His negotiations with the threat of another plague.[7] These plagues were symbolic of human shortcomings that afflicted the Egyptians and those who deny the Manifestation for their day. They remain with us today.

The first plague was the turning of the Nile River into blood. The Nile was the source of Egypt's life, but it represented ages-old traditions. 'Abdu'l-Bahá commented, *"Thus the sovereignty, wealth, and power of Pharaoh and of his people, which were the source of that nation's life, became, as a result of their opposition, denial, and pride, the very cause of its death, ruin, destruction, degradation and wretchedness."*[8]

The scriptural scholar JoAnn Borovicka remarked on the plague of darkness and the general meanings of all the plagues, then and now:

> The plague of darkness takes on fresh meaning when one considers Bahá'u'lláh's teaching that God's purpose in sending His Prophets unto men is "first is to liberate the children of men from the darkness of ignorance, and guide them to the light of true understanding."*
>
> Reflection … demonstrates the value of focusing on inner meanings. Instead of one-time frogs, flies, gnats, darkness, lightening, thunder, and hail that may or may not have caused mayhem three thousand years ago, these afflictions become powerful symbols in an easy-to-remember story that reminds us of the ultimate futility of falsehood and dismay,

the dangers of the violation of the Covenant, the inevitability of doubts and temptations, and the suffering caused by ignorance. There is no need to argue about whether or not the plagues happened three thousand years ago—these are things that plague us today.[9]

* *Gleanings from the Writings of Bahá'u'lláh*, no. 34.5, 79–80.

'Abdu'l-Bahá used the symbology of frogs and flies when he referred to people who were like the Pharisees who persecuted Jesus. *"Verily, the eagle soareth high in the supreme apex while the flies rumble in the lowest rubbish."*[10] The meanings of the other plagues become obvious upon reflection.

The metaphors continue as 'Abdu'l-Bahá explained the spiritual connotations of the crossing of the Red Sea:

> *The crossing of the Red Sea has a spiritual meaning. It was a spiritual journey, through and above the sea of corruption and iniquity of the Pharaoh and his people, or army. By the help of God through Moses, the Israelites were able to cross this sea safely and reach the Promised Land (spiritual state) while Pharaoh and his people were drowned in their own corruption. The Egyptian History recorded even trifling events. Had such a wonderful thing happened as the partings of the physical sea it would also have been recorded.*[11]

The biblical Exodus was a repudiation of Egyptian polytheism and superstitious delusions and an embrace of faith in an unseen God and His Covenant with Moses. The wilderness of the Sinai was a spiritual wilderness representative of the spiritual condition of the people when a Prophet appears. The spiritual feeding of Moses's followers was described as manna, which was ingested for forty years. The flowing water struck from the rock by Moses's staff would have been the continual flow of divine teachings for the Hebrews.

Forty years is used symbolically throughout the Bible, often meaning a period of trials and testing.[12] Moses lived forty years in Egypt and forty years in the desert before starting His ministry. Moses also spent forty days alone on two separate occasions—first to receive the Ten Commandments, which He subsequently smashed in anger when He saw the golden calf and the people dancing around it, and second to again receive the Ten Commandments on stone tablets together with various directives of divine covenantal law.

Abraham went into a future of the unknown. Moses led His people into the future of a society based on core spiritual law and extensive codes of conduct.

THE DECALOGUES AND CODES

Moses melded into His role of divine lawgiver within three months after the arrival in Sinai when, as recorded in the Hebrew Bible, He received the Ten Commandments on Mount Sinai. For the Hebrews, this was the first known divinely revealed code of spiritual law. Called the Decalogues, the Ten Commandments appear in three places (Exod. 20:1–17, 34:1–26, Deut. 5:1–21) in varying forms. The first reads:

> *And God spoke all these words:*
> *"I am the LORD your God, who brought you out of Egypt, out of the land of slavery.*
> *"You shall have no other gods before me.*
> *"You shall not make for yourself an image in the form of anything in heaven above or on the earth beneath or in the waters below. You shall not bow down to them or worship them; for I, the LORD your God, am a jealous God, punishing the children for the sin of the parents to the third and fourth generation of those who hate me, but showing love to a thousand generations of those who love me and keep my commandments.*
> *"You shall not misuse the name of the LORD your God, for the LORD will not hold anyone guiltless who misuses his name.*
> *"Remember the Sabbath day by keeping it holy. Six days you shall labor and do all your work, but the seventh day is a sabbath to the LORD your God. On it you shall not do any work, neither you, nor your son or daughter, nor your male or female servant, nor your animals, nor any foreigner residing in your towns. For in six days the Lord made the heavens and the earth, the sea,*

and all that is in them, but he rested on the seventh day. Therefore the LORD blessed the Sabbath day and made it holy.

"Honor your father and your mother, so that you may live long in the land the LORD your God is giving you.

"You shall not murder.

"You shall not commit adultery.

"You shall not steal.

"You shall not give false testimony against your neighbor.

"You shall not covet your neighbor's house. You shall not covet your neighbor's wife, or his male or female servant, his ox or donkey, or anything that belongs to your neighbor."

(Exod. 20:1–17)

The source is stated plainly: *"I am the LORD your God, who brought you out of Egypt, out of the land of slavery"* (Exod. 20:2). Thus was the imperative for obedience. The Commandments were of absolute certainty, totally beyond dispute and negotiation.

The first three Commandments emphasize the exclusive claim that God has on the lives of people, and the remaining seven are essential requirements for a community to live together in trust and security. The fourth Commandment, to keep the Sabbath holy, was an absolute break with previous law codes of the Middle East. It was the first recorded recognition that people need regular respite—time to rest, contemplate, and study—in order to live fully. It may well have been the first social welfare law on the books.

In addition to the Ten Commandments, extensive laws governing conduct were given—the Covenant Code (Exod. 20:19–23:33), the Holiness Code (Lev. 17–26), and the Deuteronomic Code (Deut. 12–26). The Covenant Code immediately follows the first presentation of the Ten Commandments and covers domestic relations, treatment of servants and slaves, personal injuries, property rights, social responsibilities, justice and mercy, and observance of three annual religious festivals. The Middle East had many law codes designed for the smooth functioning of society and the protection of social, economic, and political rights, although they were weighted with the lightest penalties for the higher classes and free-born men and progressively stronger penalties for freed men and slaves.

These codes, such as the Code of Hammurabi,[13] with its 282 laws, focused on the organization of society and the preservation of the social hierarchy. The Code of Hammurabi, named after the king who ruled from 1792 to 1750 BCE, was undoubtedly based on previous codes. The god Marduk is mentioned but not as the revealer of this Code. The epilogue states, "Hammurabi is a ruler, who is as a father to his subjects, who holds the words of Marduk in reverence, who has achieved conquest for Marduk over the north and south, who rejoices the heart of Marduk, his lord, who has bestowed benefits for ever and ever on his subjects, and has established order in the land."[14] Neither Marduk nor any other god is mentioned as the source of the Code.

Most of the Code's provisions dealt with domestic matters, merchants and mercantilism, and farming. Written between the lines was that no social chaos could be tolerated, because humans had been created to serve the gods, not to disturb their peace.

The Code was pragmatic, with many provisions for literal and parallel retribution. For example, if a man raped his neighbor's wife, then his own wife would be raped. If he caused the death of someone's child, then his own child would be killed. Alternative punishments could be harsh and often disproportionate to the crime. Striking the body of another free-born man higher in rank would cost sixty blows with an ox-whip in public, but if the victim was of equal status, the perpetrator would pay one gold mina (a little more or less than 30 ounces of gold at any given time). If a man put out the eye of a slave or broke his bones, he would pay one-half of the slave's value to his owner. Many punishments were disproportionate to the crime, such as death for false accusation of a crime, thievery by lower-class individuals, harboring fugitive slaves, or harming the property or person of a captain. One could be marked on the brow for slandering a wife or a temple priestess. A tongue could be cut out of the son of a mistress or prostitute who told his adoptive parents that they were not his parents. The breasts of a wet nurse could be cut off if she nursed another child, unknown to the parents, and the first child died in her hands. Hands could be amputated when a son struck his father, when a barber cut out the brand of a slave without the owner's permission, or when a surgeon lost a patient under the knife. And on and on in like vein.

But there were also provisions for making victims whole, either in kind or in coin. Inadvertent wounding of another meant paying the doctor bills or half a mina if the victim died. If house walls were toppling before completion, the builder had to make the walls solid using his own means.

The Code is important because it not only preceded Mosaic Law but demonstrated parallels with it. This is not surprising, because the way of life—farming, herding, and basic commerce—had not changed much for hundreds of years. There is a demarcation, though, between previous Middle Eastern codes of law and Mosaic Law. Since Mosaic Law came from God, infractions not only violated the social order but were also sins! *What was once illegal was now also immoral.*

The Mosaic Law codes were influenced by other codes of the time, but for the most part, they were gentler. Compensation in varying degrees, in coin or kind, was the usual punishment for various infractions. The provisions for brandings and mutilations allowed by previous Middle East codes were absent from Mosaic Law.

Yes, there are the famously quoted *"eye for eye, tooth for tooth, hand for hand, foot for foot, burn for burn, wound for wound, bruise for bruise"* (Exod. 21:24), *"fracture for fracture, eye for eye, tooth for tooth"* (Lev. 24:20), and *"Show no pity: life for life, eye for eye, tooth for tooth, hand for hand, foot for foot"* (Deut. 19:21). 'Abdu'l-Bahá gave perspective on this harshness on May 7, 1912, in an address to an audience in Pittsburgh, Pennsylvania, when He stated that the divine Prophets not only taught the essential and eternal spiritual realities but also decreed material laws according to the exigencies of the time and the capacity of the people:

> *For instance, in the day of Moses Ten Commandments in regard to murder were revealed by Him. These commandments were in accordance with the*

requirements of that day and time. Other laws embodying drastic punish-
ments were enacted by Moses—an eye for an eye, a tooth for a tooth. The
penalty for theft was amputation of the hand. These laws and penalties
were applicable to the degree of the Israelitish people of that period, who
dwelt in the wilderness and desert under conditions where severity was
necessary and justifiable. But in the time of Jesus Christ this kind of law
was not expedient; therefore, Christ abrogated and superseded the commands
of Moses.[15]

Some aspects seem cruel by our standards, but it is important to remember that there were no prisons, no rehabilitation centers, and no mental health counseling. The community had to be protected from immorality and criminality, especially in this new and fragile situation when divine law began to guide personal and community life. The welfare of family and community took precedence over what we call individual rights, which is a recent concept in human history. Death was the penalty for many offenses—deliberate homicide, attacking or cursing one's parents, kidnapping, various sexual offenses, sorcery, ownership of a known dangerous animal that killed someone, blasphemy, child sacrifice, pagan worship and enticing others to follow other gods, false prophecy in the name of the Lord, and desecration of the Sabbath.

Human slavery is also abhorrent to us. However, neither Jesus nor Muḥammad abrogated it. Bahá'u'lláh was the first Prophet to forbid slavery.[16] Nevertheless, the Mosaic Code had humanitarian rules about the treatment of slaves. An owner who destroyed a slave's eye or knocked out a tooth had to let the slave go free. Beating a slave to death was punishable by death. Fellow Israelites were not to be sold into slavery for any reason but were to be hired as workers.

Sanctity of life was foremost. Persons were valued over property. Most unusual was the equality of all people before the law. Nowhere in the Pentateuch is it found that the social status of the perpetrator or the victim changes the decreed obligation or punishment. The rights of the poor and the powerless were stressed repeatedly, as Cahill observed:

The constant bias is in favor not of the powerful and their possessions but of the powerlessness and their poverty; and there is even a frequent enjoinder to sympathy: "A sojourner you are not to oppress: you yourselves know (well) the feelings of the sojourner, for sojourners were you in the land of Egypt."

This bias toward the underdog is unique not only in ancient law but in the whole history of law. However faint our sense of justice may be, insofar as it operates at all it is still a Jewish sense of justice.[17]

Mosaic Law emphasized justice as protection for the poor and less fortunate and as a social equalizer. Local judges and officials were to be appointed in every town with the mandate to judge fairly. *"Do not pervert justice or show partiality. Do not accept a bribe, for a bribe blinds the eyes of the wise and twists the words of the innocent. Follow justice and justice alone, so that you may live and possess the land the LORD your God is giving you"* (Deut. 16:18–20).

Before the days of forensic science, there was built-in protection for defendants—two or more witnesses were required, not one. If a witness was proved to be maliciously false, what he had meant to do to another would be done to him. A distinction was made between murder and manslaughter. Three cities of refuge were to be designated in Canaan, places where persons that committed manslaughter could seek sanctuary and save their lives, free from pursuit and blood revenge.

Many provisions were made for the poor. Whether a Hebrew or a sojourner, a poor man was to be hired upon his need and paid his wages each day before sunset. The gleanings from the harvests were to belong to the poor, not salvaged by the owner. And every seventh year, when the land was fallow after six years of crops, only the poor could harvest whatever grew.

Periodic debt release had long been a tradition in Mesopotamia, where the peasants supported the rich lifestyle of a temple-palace economy. Peasants were provided with land rentals, tools, draught animals, livestock, and water for irrigation so that they could support the temples and palaces as well as themselves. But during poor times, peasants accumulated debts to the state and money lenders. The inability to repay these debts could result in serfdom or slavery. The resulting demoralized countryside would not be productive and would jeopardize the welfare of society. It was recognized that extremes of wealth and poverty were detrimental to the common good, so measures were implemented to restore a more equitable balance. Eric Toussaint, an expert on Third World debt, wrote, "In order to ensure social peace and stability, and especially to prevent peasants' living conditions from deteriorating, the authorities periodically cancelled all debt [except between traders] and restored peasants' rights.... In all, historians have identified with certainty about thirty general debt cancellations in Mesopotamia from 2400 to 1400 BC. "[18] Thus were social stability and prosperity routinely restored. Whether this policy was pragmatic or altruistic, it provided merciful relief to the poor while benefitting society.

Mosaic Law provided for a periodic and general debt release every seven years and a promise that this anti-poverty measure would bring the blessings of the Lord. When a poor man needed a loan when a seventh year was near, his need was not to be put off but fulfilled. Hebrew slaves were to be freed with provisions, livestock, and equipment to start a new life, and the masters would be blessed in all they did.

The fifty-year Hebrew Jubilee Year was built upon this progressive foundation. Proclaimed as a year of liberty, when each person could return to his tribe and his property, the Jubilee Year was also a year of rest for the land. Little work was to be done, and one ate only what grew by itself in the fields. Land could not be sold because it really belonged to God; the Hebrews lived on it as foreigners and strangers. The poor were to be maintained, and entry into debt slavery by non-Hebrews was not only prohibited but substituted with paid servitude. Loans to the poor were to be interest free, and food was to be sold to them at no profit. Why this magnitude of generosity? Because *"I am the LORD your God, who brought you out of Egypt to give you the land of Canaan and to be your God"* (Lev. 25:38).

The Holiness Code found in Leviticus is most explicit—the purpose of Mosaic Law was for everyone to be holy. *"The LORD said to Moses,*

'Speak to the entire assembly of Israel and say to them: Be holy because I, the LORD your God, am holy'" (Lev. 19:1–2). Thirty-six admonitions were then given, including prohibitions against idolatry, theft and fraud, false witness, perverting justice, slander, life endangerment, divination and mediums, and making one's daughter a prostitute. Foreigners were to be treated as native-born for the Hebrews had been foreigners in Egypt. Admonitions ranged from respect for parents to observing the Sabbath and from the use of honest weights and measures to standing up in the presence of the aged. Moreover, Moses said, *"Do not seek revenge or bear a grudge against anyone among your people, but love your neighbor as yourself. I am the LORD"* (19:18).

The 613 *mitzvot* (commandments) in the Pentateuch covered all aspects of life. Living in accordance with these laws would have been an all-encompassing, focused effort that probably kept many Israelites out of trouble.

The bar was set high at justice and holiness. We will never know whether this bar was ever reached by individuals or tribes. We do know from the Hebrew Bible that failure to abide by Mosaic Law set the stage for the coming of the minor prophets of the kingdoms of Israel and Judah. These prophets condemned the corruption of their days while offering hope from Prophets to come. Knowledge of Mosaic Law is essential to understanding Israelite history and a society that gave rise to the prophets.

THE ROLE OF RITUAL SACRIFICE

We cannot leave this review of Mosaic Law without remarking on the practice of animal sacrifice. In the Middle East, it was believed that the gods were literally nourished by animal, fruit, and grain sacrifices. There had also been a progression from animal to human sacrifice, which had become endemic throughout the Middle East, including in the land of Canaan. The Israelites were living in its midst. Moses specifically prohibited human sacrifice: *"You must not worship the LORD your God in their way, because in worshiping their gods, they do all kinds of detestable things the LORD hates. They even burn their sons and daughters in the fire as sacrifices to their gods"* (Deut. 12:31). It seems that Moses tried to wean the Hebrews away from human sacrifice by putting an inordinate emphasis on animal sacrifice. The laws of ritual sacrifice were endless and exacting, extensive and intricate. The first seven chapters of Leviticus are devoted to the minutiae of all facets of these sacrifices. In Hebrew belief, these sacrifices did not literally feed God, but He did smell the burning sacrifice as a *"pleasing aroma"* (Lev. 1:13). Did God really enjoy all those animal sacrifices? Prominent biblical scholars Michael Coogan and Bruce Metzger commented on this:

> Taken as a whole, the Hebrew Bible manifests certain ambivalence toward sacrifice. In the Pentateuch, it is solemnly enjoined as a positive divine requirement, while other passages seem to articulate God's rejection of the practice as a whole (e.g., Amos 5:21–27; Isa. 1:10–20; Ps. 51:16–17). The latter formulations are best seen as hyperbolic reminders of the truth that cultic sacrifice is pleasing to God only when offered by one whose whole life is lived in accordance with God's will.[19]

BLESSINGS AND CURSES

Moses had educated and prepared His rebellious and stiff-necked people as best He could. Then it was time to release them to enter the Promised Land, their spiritual destination. His heart must have been heavy as He gave the farewell address for He knew that the children of Israel would not be faithful to His Covenant. His forebodings were verified after His address to the departing Hebrews when the Lord said to Him, *"You are going to rest with your ancestors, and these people will soon prostitute themselves to the foreign gods of the land they are entering. They will forsake me and break the covenant I made with them"* (Deut. 31:16).

Moses's final address contained encouragements and warnings that are often referred to as the blessings and curses. The blessings for obedience to the Covenant of Moses were sweeping (Deut. 28:1–14). The Israelites would be set high above the nations on the earth; they would be blessed in the city and the country and when they came in and went out; the fruits of the land, crops and livestock, would be blessed; the rains would come abundantly in season; the people would be protected from their enemies, who would be defenseless against the Israelites; and they would be the head, not the tail, and would be at the top, not the bottom. The Lord would establish them as His holy people if they kept His commands and walked in obedience to Him.

The curses for disobedience to the Covenant were likewise sweeping (28:15–68). The Israelites would be cursed in the cities and the country and when they came in and went out; crops and livestock would be destroyed; the Lord would send confusion and would rebuke everything the Israelites undertook; there would be plagues, heat, and drought; foreigners in their midst would rise above them; and they would be defeated and enslaved by enemies, scattered among the nations, where they would worship gods of wood and stone but find no rest.

The era of the judges, prophets, and kings lay ahead. Stresses between obedience to Mosaic Law and the corruption in Hebrew society would be graphic. The prophets who condemned unfaithfulness to the laws of Moses would also catch glimpses of the coming of the Glory, Bahá'u'lláh.

Chapter 10

JUDGES, PROPHETS, AND KINGS

Hear, Israel, and be careful to obey so that it may
go well with you and that you may increase greatly
in a land flowing with milk and honey, just as the
LORD, the God of your ancestors, promised you.

DEUTERONOMY 6:3

LED BY JOSHUA, THE Hebrews entered the land of Canaan, the much-promised land of milk and honey. While not without its challenges, the land was much better than the Sinai Peninsula. Fertility ranged from reasonably adequate in the north to poor and rocky in the south, with levels of rainfall decreasing from north to south. Thirty to forty inches of rain fell annually in the upper Galilee but only four to eight inches in the south. The summer months were hot and dry, with rains only from November through March. A lack of winter rain would trigger drought and famine.

The geography was varied, with fertile valleys, semi-arid deserts, marshes, and hills. The peaks in the central hill country rose to 3,000 feet, and those in the upper Galilee reached 4,000. The extremes in elevation ranged from Mount Hermon at 9,000 feet above sea level to the Sea of Galilee at 700 feet below sea level and the Dead Sea, just fifty-four miles south, more than 1,000 feet below sea level. The heartland of the country was Judea, Samaria, and the hills of Galilee, but its terrain was fragmented by hills and ravines.

The four international trade routes crossing Canaan had been an economic bonanza that helped to ameliorate the effects of a challenging climate and landscape, but they had collapsed by the time the Hebrews entered the land. The days of imperial governments providing law and security were over.

CONQUEST OR IMMIGRATION?

The Israelites entered this geographically challenging land fueled by their faith in Moses and His Dispensation. Did they conquer Canaan as the events in the books of Joshua and Judges portray?

Despite the biblical accounts, there is no archeological evidence that the Israelites conquered Canaan by force. Exhaustive land surveys and archeological excavations of Canaanite sites have resulted in virtually no evidence for such military destruction at that time.

William G. Dever, an eminent archeologist, examined the archeological reports of excavations of these sites and noted that they showed an utter lack of fortified cities.

> We must confront the fact that the external material evidence supports almost *nothing* of the biblical account of a large-scale, concerted Israelite military invasion of Canaan... Of the more than forty sites that the biblical texts claim were conquered, no more than two or three of those that have been archaeologically investigated are even potential candidates for such an Israelite destruction in the entire period ca. 1250–1150 BC.[1]

How did the "conquests" of Joshua gain so much traction in Israelite memory? It is important to remember that the Pentateuch and the nine succeeding books of the Hebrew Bible (Joshua, Judges, Ruth, 1 and 2 Samuel, 1 and 2 Kings, 1 and 2 Chronicles) were not put in final written form until several hundred years after the events they told, probably during the Exile. Scholars and scribes in the Babylonian Exile would have had strong motivation to promote a heroic past. So let's look at other alternatives for how the land of Canaan became Israelite.

The times were chaotic but not because of the Israelites. The collapse of the empires caused by climate change, earthquakes, disruption of the trade routes, and incursions of the Sea Peoples all contributed to the rolling up of the old order of Canaan. Egypt had withdrawn by 1160 BCE, the system of Canaanite city-states had disintegrated, and there had been a substantial decrease in population. Military conquest by anyone was unnecessary because the door was wide open to newcomers.

Peaceful infiltration is the most-cited hypothesis for the entry of the Israelites into Canaan. They gradually encroached as nomadic herdsmen settling in outlier areas and developing symbiotic relationships with towns. Labor shortages caused by population reduction would have given the new arrivals opportunities to integrate into both the agricultural countryside and the towns.

There is also the intriguing theory of a Canaanite peasant revolution assisting the newcomers. Most peasant revolts throughout history failed unless the right circumstances existed, such as the Black Death in fourteenth-century Europe that killed one-third to one-half of the population. The acute labor shortage caused by that plague enabled survivors to name their own terms for labor in agriculture and the trades.

Likewise, the right circumstances for peasant revolution existed in Canaan, which had most recently been a vassal to Egypt. The land had belonged to Egypt, which extracted tribute from the Canaanite kings, who in turn took it from the sweat of their serfs. When the Egyptians withdrew, the Canaanite kingdoms crumbled, and the population level fell precipitously. Surviving peasants could have voted with their feet and moved to the highlands to start new lives at a safe distance from any lingering authorities. The new immigrants with their ardent message of Moses offered the possibility of a better life to many Canaanites. As Finkelstein and Silberman put it, "The rise of early Israel was therefore a social revolution of the underprivileged against their feudal lords, energized by the arrival of a visionary new ideology."[2] Dever added, "The real insight and the continuing value of the peasant revolt model is that it draws attention for the first time to the largely *indigenous* origins

127

of the early Israelite peoples, which previous academics tended to resist but which virtually all scholars now accept." [3]

One aspect that goes unnoticed because it is not part of traditional archeological and historical education and training is that a newly revealed divine Dispensation releases energies that revolutionize society. The divine springtime of each Revelation quickens spiritual life in each being, and the Mosaic Dispensation was no exception. Knowingly or not, the ancient Israelites entered Canaan as missionaries and spread their beliefs and faith to a receptive population. The most probable prospects for this new faith would have been their Hebrew cousins, many times removed, whose ancestors remained in Canaan when Joseph's family moved to Egypt. Perhaps some memories of Abraham and His teachings remained and were stirred by the Israelites teaching their new religion to these distant kin. Also, the native Canaanites would have been unhappy with their gods at this point of cultural breakdown and would have been open to a new faith.

There is extensive archeological evidence for a rapid building of a dense network of highland settlements starting about 1200 BCE, propelled by a population explosion far surpassing the birth rate, thus suggesting an influx of peaceful immigrants. These settlements sprang up in both the upper and lower Galilee areas, in the hills of Samaria and Judah, and south to the Negev. Most of them were built on bedrock, indicating that they were original, and none were fortified. The number of settlements grew to about 250 by 900 BCE, with a population of 45,000. By the eighth century, they numbered about 500 with a population of 160,000. [4]

These settlers lived on the hillsides and developed terrace agriculture. They farmed and raised livestock in the valleys. Multitudes of sheep and goat bones have been found that indicate herding, but no pig bones, which strongly indicates that the inhabitants were Israelites.

One indication of a social revolution spurred by the arrival of the Israelites was the appearance of a distinctive house plan, the pillar-courtyard house that featured ground-level stables, storage rooms, a rock-cut cistern, an oven or hearth, and a courtyard. The second story had bedrooms and space for domestic work. Sometimes two or three homes were joined together in a sharing mode. Each living unit was designed for domestic self-sufficiency, with little need for outside trade. A strong family-oriented, self-sufficient socioeconomic unit replaced feudalism.

It appears that the establishment and cohesion of the people known as the Israelites happened rather quickly, which is typical of events and movements during a divine springtime.

THE JUDGES AND EARLY PROPHETS

According to the book of Judges, the Israelites lived in Canaan as a loose confederation of twelve tribes for almost 200 years, loosely governed by a series of fifteen judges who served as informal rulers, military leaders, and circuit judges. These judges were believed to have been chosen by God or, when a son succeeded the father, served through His grace. There was no central governmental administration or unified military. First loyalty was to the family and then to the village and tribe, with alliances made to handle external threats.

Although the Israelites converted many of the Canaanites, they were living among other Canaanites who worshipped the traditional gods and followed superstitious ways, including all sorts of divination. Moses was conservative in His mention of permitted forms of divination and divine communication, condemning most of those that were prevalent at that time. Only three methods were sanctioned in the Pentateuch: dreams, prophets, and the Urim and Thummim. Dreams and visions from a prophet were sanctioned (Num. 12:6) unless the prophet tried to entice people to follow false gods (Deut. 13:1–3). It is no longer known exactly what the Urim and Thummim were, but they seemed to be objects placed inside the breastplate of the high priest and used for divination (Exod. 28: 30). A verse in the book of I Samuel mentions all three: *"When Saul saw the Philistine army, he was afraid; terror filled his heart. He inquired of the LORD, but the LORD did not answer him by dreams or Urim or prophets"* (1 Sam. 28:5–6).

The loose theocracy of the judges, combined with a lack of central administration, did not deliver much security from enemies within and without. The book of Judges mentions several incidents of Israelite backsliding, divine punishment, repentance, and admonitions delivered by a prophet. For example, in one incident when the Israelites had done evil in the eyes of the Lord, God gave them over to the depredations of the Midianites. When the Israelites cried out to the Lord, He sent them a prophet who delivered the following message:

> "I brought you up out of Egypt, out of the land of slavery. I rescued you from the hand of the Egyptians. And I delivered you from the hand of all your oppressors; I drove them out before you and gave you their land. I said to you, 'I am the Lord your God; do not worship the gods of the Amorites, in whose land you live.' But you have not listened to me" (Judg. 6:8–10).

This theme of disobedience to God and His ensuing wrath with entreaties for repentance would be repeated over and over for centuries, becoming deafeningly familiar and generally ignored.

The book of Judges states that there were fifteen prophets, the fourteenth of whom was Eli. A prophet simply called a "man of God" visited Eli, the high priest and judge, whose two sons and heirs to the priesthood were corrupt and parentally undisciplined. Eli got quite a tongue-lashing and was told that he had honored his sons more than God and that they would not succeed him but would die prematurely on the same day. *"I will raise up for myself a faithful priest, who will do according to what is in my heart and mind"* (1 Sam. 2:35).

At the time, Eli was raising a small boy named Samuel who had been dedicated to the priesthood at an early age. Samuel was the first prophet whose call from God was recorded in the Hebrew Bible. The Lord called, *"Samuel! Samuel!* Then Samuel replied, *"Speak, for your servant is listening"* (3:10). The message Samuel received was the same given previously to the man of God, that God would judge the family of Eli because of the sins of Eli's sons. Upon adulthood, Samuel became the fifteenth and last judge of Israel, as well as a priest and a prophet. He had a long and eventful life, defeating the Philistines every so often and teaching the people. He also went on circuit every year to adjudicate disputes and then returned home to Ramah, where he also held court.

Unfortunately, Samuel had the same problem that Eli had—corrupt sons who were not fit to inherit his position. Therefore, when Samuel was old and the Ammonites were threatening Israel, the elders asked him for a king to lead them in battle. They wanted a king like other people had. And the Lord told Samuel that the people had not rejected him as a judge but as their king: *"As they have done from the day I brought them up out of Egypt until this day, forsaking me and serving other gods, so they are doing to you. Now listen to them; but warn them solemnly and let them know what the king who will reign over them will claim as his rights"* (8:8–9).

Samuel in turn warned the people that a king would take men for military service and other purposes. A king would take the best of the people, the land, the cattle and donkeys, and a tenth of the grain and vintage flocks. The people would become his slaves, and when that day came, they would cry out, but the Lord would not answer them.

But the people were adamant, so God instructed Samuel in how to find a candidate. A man named Saul had been scouring the countryside hunting for his father's lost donkeys when he sought out Samuel to ask where the donkeys were. Samuel told him that the donkeys had been found and invited him to a sacrificial feast. The next day, Samuel anointed Saul king of the Israelites. Saul walked home to Gibeah and received an auspicious welcome by a group of prophets. There is general agreement among biblical scholars that the transition from the period of the judges to the monarchy occurred about 1025 BCE.

THE SCHOOLS OF THE PROPHETS

There had always been practitioners of prophesy and divination in the Middle East. The more formal Israelite schools or guilds of the prophets originated after the death of Joshua and during the age of the judges who ruled on the village and tribal levels in the twelfth and eleventh centuries BCE. The origin of these schools is traditionally attributed to Samuel, but they may have been started earlier because their purpose was to educate and train young men to disseminate the Word of God, the Mosaic Dispensation, throughout the land. Moses had directed that parents teach their children the law and that every seventh year the people should assemble—men, women, children, and foreigners—to listen to the reading of the law. As most Israelites were illiterate, it was the function of the early prophets to travel from village to village to provide religious education. Literacy would not be common for Israelite men for several hundred years.

Students at these schools learned to read and write and studied music and poetry. We can assume that they were counseled to live as exhorted by Moses and attain a higher level of ethics than what the general population followed. These schools of the prophets preserved and copied the Word sent to Moses from whatever sources were available to them.

The students became preachers and teachers who were educated in the sacred scriptures and could communicate the contents to priests, kings, and the people. As time went on, the schools evolved to primarily train prophets to serve kings and priests. But the schools would also produce a few unaffiliated independent prophets that warned the kings and people of the wrath of God for their sins—and would also prophesy the coming of future Prophets of God.

Samuel was associated with the schools in Gibeah and Ramah and Elijah and Elisha with those at Bethel, Jericho, and Gilgal. Some of the schools were large, with dormitories and classrooms. For example, it is recorded that Elisha and a hundred men ate together in a dining hall. Some of the biblical prophets, like Elisha, were graduates of these schools, but others, like Amos, were not.

KING SAUL

Now we embark on the story of the first of the three kings of the united kingdom—Saul, David, and Solomon. The written record of Saul indicates that he had a checkered career as the first king of the Israelites. His reign did not start well. Samuel, in his farewell address to the people, reminded them of their sin in asking for a king *"even though the LORD your God was your king"* (1 Sam. 12:12). If both the king and the people followed God, all would be fine, he said. But if they did not, His hand would be against them. Samuel continued relentlessly: *"Now then, stand still and see this great thing the LORD is about to do before your eyes! Is it not wheat harvest now? I will call on the LORD to send thunder and rain. And you will realize what an evil thing you did in the eyes of the LORD when you asked for a king"* (12:16–17). The rain and thunder came, and the people were chastened. It had rained thoroughly on Saul's parade by the time Samuel reached the last item on the program, the presentation of Saul to the people as their king.

There are two major themes for King Saul's reign—his disobedience to God, which cost him his dynastic succession, and his altercations with David, whom Samuel anointed to succeed him. Early in his reign, Saul made a fatal error for his royal house when he disobeyed Samuel. When he and Samuel gathered the Israelites to fight the Philistines, Samuel told Saul to wait seven days for him to return to the camp. But Saul panicked when the Philistine chariots, charioteers, and soldiers, *"as numerous as the sand on the seashore,"* came into view and his own troops were *"quaking with fear"* (13:5, 8). Without waiting for Samuel to return, Saul sacrificed the burnt offering and the fellowship offering preparatory to beseeching God's favor. Samuel returned just as Saul completed the sacrifices and pronounced judgment on him: *"You have done a foolish thing. You have not kept the command the LORD your God gave you; if you had, he would have established your kingdom over Israel for all time. But now your kingdom will not endure; the LORD has sought out a man after his own heart and appointed him ruler of his people, because you have not kept the LORD's command"* (13:13–14).

The significance of this disobedience was that Saul had violated the strict division between the sacred and the secular. The priesthood had its duties and privileges that were never to be encroached upon by any king or non-Levite.

Samuel never saw Saul again, although he mourned for the wayward king. Instead, Samuel was guided to find a young shepherd son of Jesse of Bethlehem, David, whom he anointed as the next king. The rest of Saul's reign was intertwined with David, who was loyal to his king until his death. David alternately soothed Saul's madness with his harp and singing and evaded Saul during the king's attempts to kill him.

An intriguing account is given of three encounters that Saul's soldiers had with prophets while in hot pursuit of David. The first time Saul's men encountered a group of prophets prophesying with Samuel standing as their leader, they joined with the prophets. A second contingent of troops went after David, with the same result. And it happened a third time when the pursuers forgot their prey and fell in with the prophets.

Saul and his three sons were eventually killed in one of their interminable battles with the Philistines. In his desperation prior to the battle, Saul had sought out the deceased Samuel through the medium living at Endor. This led to a heart-wrenching encounter between a despairing Saul and an irritated Samuel. The message Saul received from Samuel was devastating: *"The LORD has done what he predicted through me. The LORD has torn the kingdom out of your hands and given it to one of your neighbors—to David. The LORD will deliver both Israel and you into the hands of the Philistines, and tomorrow you and your sons will be with me"* (28:17, 19).

David would also stumble, but his reign would be charmed compared with Saul's. And David would also be a prophet.

Chapter 11

A KINGDOM UNITED
AND DIVIDED

If a kingdom is divided against itself, that kingdom cannot stand.
If a house is divided against itself, that house cannot stand.

Mark 3:24–25

AS REPORTED IN THE book of 2 Samuel, David was thirty years old when he became king, and he reigned for forty years, seven from Hebron and thirty-three from the conquered village on a hill called Jerusalem. David might have come to power a few years before the turn of the ninth century BCE, but it is more likely to have been early in the ninth.

The reign of David was blessed indeed. Particularly unusual is the fact that before starting his reign, he was a bandit chieftain! David was the eighth son of Jesse of Bethlehem. Saul could not contain his jealousy of this upstart who slew Goliath and had been anointed by Samuel to succeed him, so David fled for his life. Denied sanctuary among the Philistines, David and his men escaped to the caves. Those who were in distress or in debt gathered around him. Finkelstein and Silberman gave a delightful account of David's career as a rebel leader:

> As a guerrilla force, David's men are quick and mobile. They come to the rescue of beleaguered villages, humiliate an arrogant local strongman, outsmart the ruler of a powerful neighboring

135

Philistine city, and evade the relentless pursuit of King Saul again and again. Extortion, seduction, deception, and righteous violence are David's methods. His story is filled with larger-than-life ironies, cosmic episodes, and entertaining events. It is a classical bandit tale of a type known all over the world, then and now, in which popular rebels—like Robin Hood, Jesse James, and Pancho Villa—use bravado and cunning to challenge the corrupt, brutal powers that be.[1]

Memories of such folk heroes tend to fade with time, but David's destiny was not only to succeed Saul as king but also to found the House of David that would endure as an earthly dynasty for roughly 400 years and then live on metaphorically.

As king, David defeated the Philistines, finally and for good, along with other enemies. He defeated the Jebusites and took their fortified city of Jerusalem, with its population of 500 to 700 across eleven or twelve acres,[2] as the seat of his government and power. Slowly, the centralized systems of monarchical administration evolved—taxation, diplomatic communications, a standing army, priestly administration, court organization, and more. The Israelites now controlled the international trade routes that ran through their land, and the duties and taxes poured into royal coffers. David rebuilt much of Jerusalem and a series of fortress cities for his army to protect the land.

The prophets no longer served as political leaders or warriors as in the years of the judges but as advisors and statesmen, although a few paved an independent course. Nathan, court advisor to David, fulfilled the role of an exemplary court prophet. Two incidents during Nathan's tenure illustrate fulfillment of that office at its best. The first concerned David's desire to build a temple: *"Here I am, living in a house of cedar, while the ark of God remains in a tent"* (2 Sam. 7:2). But it was not to be. Nathan mulled over the matter and then reported to David:

> *"The LORD declares to you that the LORD himself will establish a house for you: When your days are over and you rest with your ancestors, I will raise*

up your offspring to succeed you, your own flesh and blood, and I will estab-
lish his kingdom. He is the one who will build a house for my Name, and
I will establish the throne of his kingdom forever. I will be his father, and he
will be my son. When he does wrong, I will punish him with a rod wielded
by men, with floggings inflicted by human hands. But my love will never be
taken away from him, as I took it away from Saul, whom I removed from
before you. Your house and your kingdom will endure forever before me; your
throne will be established forever. (2 Sam. 7:11–16)

The House of David would also be a major theological stumbling block because most Israelites believed that it would endure forever, while several prophets warned that it would not. The Israelites interpreted this message literally, meaning that the House of David would never be defeated militarily. This belief in the invincibility of the Davidic monarchy deafened seventh-century Israelites to the warnings of the prophets that the Babylonians would conquer the southern kingdom of Judah, which was ruled by the House of David, just as the Assyrians had conquered the northern kingdom of Israel a century earlier. The House of David would indeed endure but not as hereditary royalty for an earthly realm. Instead, Jesus would descend from the House of David, but He would stress that His kingdom was the Kingdom of God. Bahá'u'lláh used the symbology of the throne of David when addressing the Jewish people:

The Most Great Law is come, and the Ancient Beauty ruleth upon the throne
of David. Thus hath My Pen spoken that which the histories of bygone
ages have related. At this time, however, David crieth aloud and saith: 'O
my loving Lord! Do Thou number me with such as have stood steadfast in
Thy Cause, O Thou through Whom the faces have been illumined, and the
footsteps have slipped!'[3]

The second event that illustrates Nathan's wisdom, honesty, and bravery was his confrontation with his sovereign over an unpleasant truth. David lusted for Bathsheba, the wife of Uriah, who was a trusted army officer. When she became pregnant with David's child, he ordered Uriah to the front lines of battle, where he was soon killed. Nathan told David the poignant story of the rich man who had many sheep and cattle and the poor man who had nothing except one ewe lamb whom he and his family treated as one of the family. *"Now a traveler came to the rich man, but the rich man refrained from taking one of his own sheep or cattle to prepare a meal for the traveler who had come to him. Instead, he took the ewe lamb that belonged to the poor man and prepared it for the one who had come to him"* (2 Sam. 12:4).

David was incensed. Who did this? He must die and pay for that lamb four times over because he had no pity. *"You are the man!"* (12:7). Nathan delivered the Lord's severe rebuke, which brought David to his knees in repentance and remorse. *"The LORD has taken away your sin. You are not going to die. But because by doing this you have shown utter contempt for the LORD, the son born to you will die"* (12:13–14). The baby born to David and Bathsheba subsequently died, but their second son, Solomon, would succeed David on the throne.

THE GOOD LIFE

The relatively small population of about 150,000 in the united kingdom during the tenth century was overwhelmingly rural. Just five percent of people lived in urban centers and twenty percent in towns.[4] Jerusalem was much smaller than we would imagine, with about 1,000 people in the tenth century, but it would grow to about 15,000 people by the eighth century.[5]

The rural nature of Israel is all-important to understanding the times and ethos. The land was dotted with hundreds of small agricultural settlements typically composed of extended family compounds and villages of from 100 to 250 people. The next village would have been within walking distance and kin based. This pattern would produce an extremely close-knit society based on family ties, commonly shared traditional values, and loyalty to the clan and to tribal sheiks rather than to any external authority. The rural life had been presented as the good life:

For the LORD your God is bringing you into a good land—a land with brooks, streams, and deep springs gushing out into the valleys and hills; a land with wheat and barley, vines and fig trees, pomegranates, olive oil and honey; a land where bread will not be scarce and you will lack nothing; a land where the rocks are iron and you can dig copper out of the hills. (Deut. 8:7–9)

The good life was probably better than nomadism, although agricultural life was hard and life expectancy short. Rural villages developed social and economic self-sufficiency, but they had few resources to fall back on when drought and famine came. Taxes were due to the growing central administration regardless of whether the rains came and nourished the land. Personal security lay with one's family and village. For better or worse, the intrinsic conservatism of isolated rural life would also have meant resistance to outside ideas and authority. Stability was the goal and tradition the means to achieve it.

Out in the countryside, there was probably little understanding of the concept of the state, although the tentacles of a royal administration were reaching out. Few people from the villages would have been to Jerusalem, let alone have seen the king. Rural people mostly relied on the Canaanite tradition of the "high places," altars built on hilltops, because they had little access to the Levitical priesthood and, later, to the Temple in Jerusalem. Worship at the high places was adamantly opposed by the Levitical priesthood. The hilltop altars and shrines in the Canaanite tradition were the places for rural worship and would be a contentious issue for hundreds of years.

THE REIGN OF SOLOMON

The book of 1 Kings narrates the reign of Solomon, who succeeded David and inherited an increasingly prosperous kingdom by the standards of the time. The centralized machinery of the state was gradually gaining ascendancy over the segmented tribal organization. The kingdom under Saul and David had been constantly at war, thus perpetuating their roles in mythic history as charismatic chieftains as well as kings. Fortunately for Solomon, his father stabilized the kingdom and set its boundaries. The reign of Solomon was relatively peaceful, and he is traditionally known for his wisdom. It is reported that early in Solomon's reign, the Lord appeared to him in a dream and told him to ask for whatever he wanted. Solomon responded by acknowledging His great kindness to David and expressing his inadequacy to carry out his duties. Then he asked for a discerning heart to govern and to distinguish between right and wrong. That was granted. As a bonus, Solomon received what he had not asked for—wealth and honor.

His wealth came from taxes on the people, tribute from conquered peoples, and duties from the renewed trade routes. His court grew so vast that he had twelve district governors throughout Israel who supplied provisions for the royal household. Solomon's need for daily provisions was immense, reported to be about five tons of flour, eleven tons of meal, ten head of stall-fed cattle, twenty pasture-fed cattle, and 100 sheep and goats. These provisions came primarily from the labor of the kingdom's rural farmers.

Solomon is best remembered for having built the first Temple. However, he first built a huge palace for himself and rebuilt the walls of Jerusalem and Fort Millo, a southern fortification of Jerusalem. His sumptuous palace, complete with a throne room covered from floor to ceiling with cedar wood from Lebanon and a throne covered with ivory overlaid with gold, took thirteen years to construct. Next, Solomon built a magnificent palace for a wife who was the pharaoh's daughter. He built cities for storage and for his horses and charioteers. Solomon also rebuilt the cities of Hazor, Megiddo, and Gezer as fortified defense sites and constructed several other fortresses.

Finally, Solomon built the Temple. For years, he had acquired vast quantities of cedar and juniper from King Hiram in Lebanon. It is written that the inner sanctuary of the temple was overlaid with gold and had a chain of gold. The cherubim in the inner sanctuary were lined with gold. The floors of both the inner and outer temple rooms were covered in gold. Descriptions of the bronze works and other furnishings for the temple are extensively recorded in 1 Kings.

The reigns of Saul, David, and Solomon could be considered the summer of the Mosaic Dispensation. But within this golden age of Israel were the seeds for the slide into its autumn. Solomon was not wise in all respects. His massive building projects strained the people with taxes and forced labor.

Like all kings of his time, Solomon had many marriages with foreign women for diplomatic reasons, and these wives brought their gods and idolatrous beliefs and superstitions with them. He acceded to their wishes by building temples for their polytheistic worship and sacrifices. Far worse, Solomon himself turned to the worship of Asherah, Molek, and other Canaanite gods:

> *As Solomon grew old, his wives turned his heart after other gods, and his heart was not fully devoted to the LORD his God, as the heart of David his father had been. He followed Ashtoreth, the goddess of the Sidonians, and Molek the detestable god of the Ammonites. So Solomon did evil in the eyes of the LORD; he did not follow the LORD completely, as David his father had done.*
>
> *On a hill east of Jerusalem, Solomon built a high place for Chemosh the detestable god of Moab, and for Molek the detestable god of the Ammonites. He did the same for all his foreign wives, who burned incense and offered sacrifices to their gods.* (1 Kings 11:4–8)

Back in the days before the Israelites entered the Promised Land, God warned them that any king they might have must be chosen by God from among the Israelites, never a foreigner. In addition: *"He must not take many wives, or his heart will be led astray. He must not accumulate large amounts of silver and gold"* (Deut. 17:17). God also gave explicit instructions for the spiritual welfare of each sovereign to ensure the continuity of the kingdom:

> *When he takes the throne of his kingdom, he is to write for himself on a scroll a copy of this law, taken from that of the Levitical priests. It is to be with him, and he is to read it all the days of his life so that he may learn to revere the LORD his God and follow carefully all the words of this law and*

these decrees and not consider himself better than his fellow Israelites and
turn from the law to the right or to the left. Then he and his descendants will
reign a long time over his kingdom in Israel. (Deut. 17:18–20)

This was excellent advice. Some biblical scholars believe that it was added during the exilic or postexilic times when Deuteronomy was put in final form.

It is reported that God decided to tear the kingdom away from Solomon and to give it to one of his subordinates but not during Solomon's lifetime. That would happen during the reign of Solomon's son Rehoboam. As with Samuel, who had been guided to find and anoint Saul and then David, a prophet named Ahijah was guided to find Jeroboam, who was a manager of labor battalions under Solomon but had been rebellious toward him. Jeroboam was promised that he would be king over Israel, and God would be with him if he did as he was commanded and walked in obedience to His decrees and commandments. In the short term, Jeroboam fled for his safety to Egypt to await Solomon's death, which occurred between 931 and 928 BCE. This estimated date of Solomon's death is the first reasonably accurate date given in biblical history.

Rehoboam succeeded Solomon, but he did not have an iota of his father's alleged wisdom. There was much resentment about Solomon's forced labor policies, and it is recorded that the whole assembly of Israel went to Rehoboam and said to him, *"Your father put a heavy yoke on us, but now lighten the harsh labor and the heavy yoke he put on us, and we will serve you"* (1 Kings 12:4). Unfortunately, Rehoboam rejected the advice of his elders to tread softly and instead hearkened to his young court friends, who urged him to push back. *"My father made your yoke heavy; I will make it even heavier. My father scourged you with whips; I will scourge you with scorpions"* (1 Kings 12:14).

Revolt ensued. The administrator of forced labor was stoned to death, and the kingdom split into two. Rehoboam ruled from Jerusalem as king of the southern kingdom of Judah, retaining control over only the tribes of Judah and Benjamin. Jeroboam became king of the northern kingdom of Israel and asserted control over the much larger, more populous, and wealthier region with the other ten tribes. This quick dissolution of the united monarchy demonstrated the inadequacies of Solomon's reign and vindicated Samuel's warnings about having a king.

Historically, though, the monarchy of Saul, David, and Solomon was an exceptional achievement. Canaan had been ruled by multiple Canaanite kinglets and chiefs, either as vassals under imperial powers or independently. The united monarchy of Israel was the first territorial state to encompass this land. It lasted less than a century, but it has been remembered through tears, nostalgia, and hope for three millennia. The kingdoms of Israel and Judah would share traditions, history, and ideologies, but the fall of the united monarchy was the end of Israel's golden age. Divided, they both inevitably fell: Israel to the Assyrians in 722 BCE and Judah to the Babylonians in 586 BCE.

The united kingdom was more than nostalgia. King David, the musician, singer, and psalmist, was also a prophet. 'Abdu'l-Bahá confirmed this when he responded to a question about how many kinds of prophets there were. His answer was twofold: Independent Prophets are lawgivers, the founders of new cycles, and bring a new book and a new revelation, while prophets who are not independent follow and reinforce the latest Dispensation. *"The universal Prophets Who have appeared independently include Abraham, Moses, Christ, Muḥammad, the Báb, and Bahá'u'lláh. The second kind, which consists of followers and promulgators, are like Solomon, David, Isaiah, Jeremiah and Ezekiel."*[6] He further explained that the universal Prophets establish new religions to *"recreate the souls, regenerate the morals of society, and promulgate a new way of life and a new standard of conduct"* and the second kind are followers who *"promulgate the religion of God, spread His Faith, and proclaim His Word."*[7]

By tradition, Psalms 72 and 127 are attributed to Solomon. Psalm 72 praises the all-encompassing justice and judgment of God, and Psalm 127 praises children as a heritage and reward from the Lord. The psalms attributed to David have deep emotions of praise and worship of God— and they also appear to contain veiled references to the coming of Jesus and Bahá'u'lláh.

Chapter 12

LEND AN EAR UNTO
THE SONG OF DAVID

*The interpretation of prophecy is notoriously difficult, and
on no subject do the opinions of the learned differ more
widely. This is not to be wondered at, for, according to
the revealed writings themselves, many of the prophecies
were given in such a form that they could not be fully
understood until the fulfillment came, and even then, only
by those who were pure in heart and free from prejudice.*

J. E. ESSLEMONT[1]

ACCORDING TO THE BLOG site Bible Overview, the book of Psalms is the
most read book of the Bible[2] and the most quoted by Jesus.[3] The psalms are
universally acknowledged as uplifting and hopeful for the future regardless
of how dire the present seems. Lamentations of distress are followed by
expressions of faith in God, weaving two disparate emotions into a tapestry
of inspiration. Few are the readers who cannot empathize with the depths
of human despair, hope, and poignancy that are expressed in the psalms.

We will never know how many of the psalms credited to David
were actually written by him. Some of those written during his time
were penned for the Temple choir and may not have been composed by
David himself. The *Sefer Tehillim* (The Book of Psalms), the traditional
Hebrew version of Psalms, has superscriptions for 100 of the 150 psalms

that ascribe the authorship to several persons—one psalm to Moses, ten to the sons of Korah (who lived in the time of Moses), seventy-three to David, two to Solomon, one each to Heman and Ethan (contemporaries of Solomon), and twelve to Asaph (who lived in the late sixth century BCE). The Septuagint (the Greek translation of the Hebrew Bible) credits an additional ten psalms to David. Sixteen psalms have other headings indicating their musical origins. The psalms can also be grouped by content—hymns of praise, elegies, and instruction.[4]

There is basic agreement among biblical scholars today that the authorship of the psalms is far more diverse than tradition allows, primarily because they were written across several centuries.

Some of the psalms are joyous in praise and celebration of God: *"Make a joyful noise unto the LORD, all ye lands. Serve the LORD with gladness: come before his presence with singing"* (Ps. 100:1–2, KJV). Anguish at social injustice and iniquity gushes forth: *"LORD, how long shall the wicked, how long shall the wicked triumph? How long shall they utter and speak hard things? and all the workers of iniquity boast themselves?"* (Ps. 94:3–4, KJV). Above all, faith in God is absolute: *"Truly my soul waiteth upon God: from him cometh my salvation. He only is my rock and my salvation; he is my defense; I shall not be greatly moved"* (62:1–2, KJV).

The psalms go beyond expressing grief and faith, despair and hope. Some are prophetic, although their prophecies are obvious only in retrospect. Let's examine Psalm 22, which is attributed to David.

PSALM 22

Psalm 22 is called "The Psalm of the Cross" by Christians. The crucifixion is described in accordance with its depiction in the Gospels, even with the casting of lots for His garments. This psalm, which was written centuries before the events it describes, not only presents Jesus's despair and suffering but also His inner thoughts that could not be discerned by observers. The first line presents the words recorded in Matthew 27:46 about His anguish.

My God, my God, why have you forsaken me?
Why are you so far from saving me,

so far from my cries of anguish?
My God, I cry out by day, but you do not answer,
   by night, but I find no rest.
Yet you are enthroned as the Holy One;
   you are the one Israel praises.
In you our ancestors put their trust;
   they trusted and you delivered them.
To you they cried out and were saved;
   in you they trusted and were not put to shame.

The psalm continues at length with His suffering and abasement and then describes the events of His crucifixion:

Dogs surround me,
   a pack of villains encircles me;
   they pierce my hands and my feet.
All my bones are on display;
   people stare and gloat over me.
They divide my clothes among them
   and cast lots for my garment.

Deliverance is asked:

But you, LORD, do not be far from me.
   You are my strength; come quickly to help me.
Deliver me from the sword, my precious life from the power of the dogs.
Rescue me from the mouth of the lions;
   save me from the horns of the wild oxen.

His deliverance will not be earthly but will eventually come from the faith of His followers:

From you comes the theme of my praise in the great assembly;
   before those who fear you I will fulfill my vows.

> *The poor will eat and be satisfied;*
>   *'those who seek the Lord will praise him—*
>   *may your hearts live forever!*
> *All the ends of the earth will remember and turn to the Lord,*
>   *and all the families of the nations will bow down before him,*
>   *for dominion belongs to the Lord and he rules over the nations.*
> *All the rich of the earth will feast and worship;*
>   *all who go down to the dust will kneel before him—*
>   *those who cannot keep themselves alive.*
> *Posterity will serve him; future generations will be told about the Lord.*
> *They will proclaim his righteousness, declaring to a people yet unborn:*
>   *He has done it!* (Psalm 22:1–5, 16–18, 19–21, 25–31)

Jesus's despair was not due to His own lack of faith but His disappointment with the people who acted like dogs and lions. He taught to the end, *"You who fear the Lord, praise him!"* And He made the promise that *"All the ends of the earth will remember and turn to the Lord, and all the families of the nations will bow down before him, for dominion belongs to the Lord and he rules over the nations."* Christianity had spread throughout the world by the nineteenth century. *"He has done it!"*

Psalms 24, 45, and 60 contain many allusions to Bahá'u'lláh. Psalms 24 and 60 are attributed to David, and Psalm 45 is attributed to the sons of Korah.

PSALM 24

This psalm is short, with only ten verses. Traditionally, Christians have seen this psalm as a foretelling of Christ, and perhaps a psalm could allude to more than one Manifestation of God. "However, the symbology used in this psalm strongly relates to Bahá'u'lláh."

> *The earth is the Lord's, and everything in it,*
>   *the world, and all who live in it;*
> *for he founded it on the seas*
>   *and established it on the waters.*

Who may ascend the mountain of the LORD?
  Who may stand in his holy place?
The one who has clean hands and a pure heart,
  who does not trust in an idol
  or swear by a false god.
They will receive blessing from the LORD
  and vindication from God their Savior.
Such is the generation of those who seek him,
  who seek your face, God of Jacob.
Lift up your heads, you gates;
  be lifted up, you ancient doors,
  that the King of glory may come in.
Who is this King of glory?
  The LORD strong and mighty,
  the LORD mighty in battle.
Lift up your heads, you gates;
  lift them up, you ancient doors,
  that the King of glory may come in.
Who is he, this King of glory?
  The LORD Almighty—
  he is the King of glory.
(Psalm 24:1–10)

As discussed previously, scriptural words can have many symbolic interpretations. The earth often expresses the dominion of God and the seas the many revelations of God upon which Bahá'u'lláh would launch the ark of His Covenant. In His Tablet of the Holy Mariner, Bahá'u'lláh cast Himself as the Holy Mariner as He cast His Dispensation upon the seas of previous ones:

> *He is the Gracious, the Well-Beloved!*
> *O Holy Mariner!*
> *Bid thine ark of eternity appear before the Celestial Concourse,*
> *Glorified be my Lord, the All-Glorious!*

149

Launch it upon the ancient sea, in His Name, the Most Wondrous,
Glorified be my Lord, the All-Glorious![5]

Exploring symbolism further, we discover that a mountain or hill of God may mean where a Prophet has trodden. Bahá'u'lláh walked on Mount Carmel in Haifa and designated the spot where the remains of the Báb were to be put to rest. The doors and the gates could refer to the prison city of Akka, where Bahá'u'lláh was sent into exile in 1868.

Shoghi Effendi addressed the question: Who is this King of Glory? "David, in his Psalms, had predicted: 'Lift up your heads, O ye gates; even lift them up, ye everlasting doors; and the King of Glory shall come in. Who is this King of Glory? The Lord of Hosts, He is the King of Glory.'"[6]

Among the titles of Bahá'u'lláh are the King of Glory, the Glory of God, the Lord of hosts, and the Lord of Lords. Shoghi Effendi wrote, "Of Him David had sung in his Psalms, acclaiming Him as the 'LORD of hosts' and the 'King of Glory.'"[7]

In the early 1870s, Bahá'u'lláh sent tablets to Napoleon III and Pope Pius IX in which He used the titles *King of Glory* and *Lord of Lords*. These tablets announced His station and set forth the responsibilities of rulers. He wrote to Napoleon III:

> **The King of Glory** *proclaimeth from the tabernacle of majesty and grandeur His call, saying: O people of the Gospel! They who were not in the Kingdom have now entered it, whilst We behold you, in this day, tarrying at the gate. Rend the veils asunder by the power of your Lord, the Almighty, the All-Bounteous, and enter, then, in My name My Kingdom.*[8]
> (emphasis added)

Pope Pius IX received the words:

> *O Pope! Rend the veils asunder. He Who is the* **Lord of Lords** *is come overshadowed with clouds, and the decree hath been fulfilled by God, the Almighty, the Unrestrained. Dispel the mists through the power of thy Lord, and ascend unto the Kingdom of His names and attributes. Thus hath*

the Pen of the Most High commanded thee at the behest of thy Lord, the Almighty, the All-Compelling[9] (emphasis added)

PSALM 60

This psalm is one of lament and supplication to God for deliverance at a time of calamity at the hands of the Edomites, a people who lived in the southeast and were inveterate enemies of the Israelites:

You have rejected us, God, and burst upon us;
  you have been angry—now restore us!
You have shaken the land and torn it open;
  mend its fractures, for it is quaking.
You have shown your people desperate times;
  you have given us wine that makes us stagger.
But for those who fear you, you have raised a banner
  to be unfurled against the bow.
Save us and help us with your right hand,
  that those you love may be delivered.

Past promises of God for deliverance and victories are given, and then David asks the stirring question, *"Who will bring me into the strong city?"*

Who will bring me into the strong city?
  Who will lead me into Edom?
Is it not you, God, you who have now rejected us
  and no longer go out with our armies?
Give us help from trouble,
  For human help is worthless.
With God we will gain the victory,
  And he will trample down our enemies.
(Psalm 60:1–5, 9–12)

What was the strong city, and why would David want to be led to it? Bahá'u'lláh solved this puzzle when He exhorted a person He was

151

addressing: *"Lend an ear unto the song of David. He saith: 'Who will bring me into the Strong City?' The Strong City is 'Akká, which hath been named the Most Great Prison, and which possesseth a fortress and mighty ramparts."*[10]

This psalm offers a good example of a prophetic phrase—the strong prison city of Akka—being layered into historical reality roughly twenty-seven centuries in the future. The psalm transcended this huge length of time and tapped into the imprisonment of Bahá'u'lláh in the Ottoman prison city of Akka in Palestine. This stretches credulity until it is remembered that our concept of time is not God's. Divine time combines past, present, and future. In fact, 'Abdu'l-Bahá mentioned this when He wrote:

> *[The] hidden mysteries of the days to come were revealed to the Prophets, who thus became acquainted with future events and who proclaimed them in turn. This knowledge and proclamation were not the cause of the occurrence of these events.*
>
> *Likewise, God's knowledge in the contingent world does not produce the forms of things. Rather, that knowledge is freed from the distinctions of past, present, and future, and is identical with the realization of all things without being the cause of that realization.*[11]

PSALM 45

The imagery found in Psalm 45 offers a prophetic look at Bahá'u'lláh and his wife, Ásíyih Khánum. The details, which again pertain to a time incredibly distant, stretch our understanding of the nature of time:

> *My heart is stirred by a noble theme*
> *   as I recite my verses for the king;*
> *   my tongue is the pen of a skillful writer.*
> *You are the most excellent of men*
> *   and your lips have been anointed with grace,*
> *   since God has blessed you forever.*
> *Gird your sword on your side, you mighty one;*
> *   clothe yourself with splendor and majesty.*

In your majesty ride forth victoriously
  in the cause of truth, humility and justice;
  let your right hand achieve awesome deeds.
Let your sharp arrows pierce the hearts of the king's enemies;
  let the nations fall beneath your feet.
Your throne, O God, will last for ever and ever;
  a scepter of justice will be the scepter of your kingdom.
You love righteousness and hate wickedness;
  therefore God, your God, has set you above your companions
  by anointing you with the oil of joy.
All your robes are fragrant with myrrh and aloes and cassia;
  from palaces adorned with ivory
  the music of the strings makes you glad.
Daughters of kings are among your honored women;
  at your right hand is the royal bride in gold of Ophir.
(Psalm 45:1–8)

These verses were given for the king. Who was this king? The symbolic words and phrases lead us to Mírzá Ḥusayn-ʿAlí Núrí, who would be later known as Bahá'u'lláh. He was born into nobility. His father, Mírzá ʿAbbás Buzurg, was a vizier in the court of the Persian shah, and Bahá'u'lláh could have received a similar appointment. Instead He declined court service and devoted the early years of His adulthood to caring for the poor and imperiled, which made Him the most excellent of men. His lips were anointed with grace, a key attribute of a Manifestation of God who brings a divine Revelation. The sword would be His tongue and pen, which were not silenced during His forty years of imprisonment. If one were to give the core words for the spiritual teachings of Bahá'u'lláh's revelation, they would certainly include truth, humility, and justice. The sharp arrows of His teachings pierced the hearts of His many enemies in the court and among the Muslim clergy who arose against Him. As for letting the nations fall, Bahá'u'lláh sent letters to the national and ecclesiastical rulers of His day and warned several of them about the demise of their kingdoms.

153

In line with this presented interpretation of Psalm 24, the throne would reference the station of *the king*, Bahá'u'lláh, whose Revelation would last forever. His garments had the scent of the wealth into which He had been born as well as symbolically of the Revelation that He would deliver. The scepter of justice captures what is perhaps the major moral teaching of Bahá'u'lláh:

> *The best beloved of all things in My sight is Justice; turn not away there-from if thou desirest Me, and neglect it not that I may confide in thee. By its aid thou shalt see with thine own eyes and not through the eyes of others, and shalt know of thine own knowledge and not the knowledge of thy neighbour. Ponder this in thy heart how it behoveth thee to be. Verily justice is My gift to thee and the sign of My loving kindness. Set it then before thine eyes.*[12]

This psalm continues with verses that seem to be addressed to Ásíyih Khánum, the wife of Bahá'u'lláh:

> *Listen, daughter, and pay careful attention:*
>   *Forget your people and your father's house.*
> *Let the king be enthralled by your beauty;*
>   *honor him, for he is your LORD.*
> *The city of Tyre will come with a gift,*
>   *people of wealth will seek your favor.*
> *All glorious is the princess within her chamber;*
>   *her gown is interwoven with gold.*
> *In embroidered garments she is led to the king;*
>   *her virgin companions follow her—*
>   *those brought to be with her.*
> *Led in with joy and gladness,*
>   *they enter the palace of the king.*
> *Your sons will take the place of your fathers;*
>   *you will make them princes throughout the land.*
> *I will perpetuate your memory through all generations;*
>   *therefore the nations will praise you for ever and ever.*
> (Psalm 45:9–17)

> * Ophir was a port on the Red Sea through which King
> Solomon received a cargo of gold, silver, sandalwood,
> precious stones, ivory, apes, and peacocks every three years.

The father of Ásíyih Khánum was also a court vizier of immense wealth. As the daughter of one of the wealthiest nobles in the land, she received such a trove of wedding gifts that it took forty mules to carry them to her husband's home. Her wardrobe was rich, and because of the stunning wealth of both families, she must have resembled the princess within her chamber with her wedding dress with woven gold. The buttons of her garments were gold inset with precious stones.[13]

Like her husband, Ásíyih Khánum eschewed court life and the pursuits of the idle rich. Instead, she served the needy and troubled women who came to her in distress. Their daughter, Bahíyyih Khánum, described her mother as "tall, slender, graceful, eyes of dark blue—a pearl, a flower amongst women"[14] and reminisced that her mother was called the "The Mother of Consolation"[15] because of her work assisting poor women; her husband was called "The Father of the Poor."[16]

This gentle life lasted only nine or ten years. The Revelation of the Báb swept through Persia. The Báb was executed by the authorities in 1850 CE, and many thousands of His followers were massacred. As a known follower of the Báb, Bahá'u'lláh was sent to a loathsome prison in 1852, the Síyáh-Chál, which He barely survived. Their home was pillaged and destroyed by a mob, and almost all their valuables were stolen. The tragedies that befell her husband and family forced Ásíyih Khánum to fight for survival for herself and her three children during Bahá'u'lláh's incarceration. She then went with her husband into exile. She recognized the station of her husband, Bahá'u'lláh, and shared the hardships of His exiles in Baghdad, Constantinople (Istanbul), Adrianople (Edirne), and finally in the prison city of Akka. This fine, noble lady of Persia was forced to detach herself from her people, from the memories of her father, and from her homeland. She dedicated herself to her husband's mission. Her expression of divine attributes was such that Bahá'u'lláh wrote in a tablet to her:

"Hear thou Me once again," He reassures her, "God is well-pleased with thee, as a token of His grace and a sign of His mercy. He hath made thee to be His companion in every one of His worlds, and hath nourished thee with His meeting and presence, so long as His Name, and His Remembrance, and His Kingdom, and His Empire shall endure."[17]

Two sons and one daughter of this marriage survived childhood, and these children became princes not of earthly royalty but of spiritual standing. Mírzá Mihdí, as discussed previously, offered his life as a sacrifice so that the isolation of Bahá'u'lláh could end and the world could have access to Him. 'Abdu'l-Bahá, called the Most Great Branch by His father and appointed to succeed Him, is often referred to as the perfect Exemplar of His father's teachings. Shoghi Effendi, the firstborn great-grandson of Bahá'u'lláh and Ásíyih Khánum, served as the successor of 'Abdu'l-Bahá as head of the Bahá'í Faith, with the title Guardian of the Faith, from 1921 until his passing in 1957.

Their daughter, Bahíyyih Khánum, declined marriage and devoted her life to serving her father. After His passing, she was a foremost source of help and consolation to her brother 'Abdu'l-Bahá and then to her grandnephew, Shoghi Effendi. She helped safeguard the Bahá'í Faith not only during the ministry of 'Abdu'l-Bahá but also at the critical juncture when Shoghi Effendi first assumed the duties of Guardian. She served Shoghi Effendi unswervingly until her passing in 1937. Bahíyyih Khánum, called the Greatest Holy Leaf by her father, is recognized as one of the preeminent women of the Bahá'í Dispensation.

Chapter 13

A STILL SMALL VOICE

When there is a prophet among you, I, the LORD, reveal
myself to them in visions, I speak to them in dreams.

NUMBERS 12:6

THE BOUNDARY BETWEEN THE kingdoms of Israel and Judah was ten
miles north of Jerusalem and ran west to the lands of the Philistines and
the Phoenicians on the Mediterranean coast. The northern border with
the Arameans of Damascus was unstable and defined by whether the
Arameans or the Israelites had won the latest battle. Eastern borders
reflected the skirmishes in the Transjordan with the Moabites and the
Ammonites, while the Edomites to the south were constant enemies. The
kingdom of Israel, during its furthest extent, encompassed the fertile
Jordan Valley and the Jezreel Valley and reached from the Mediterranean coast north of the Philistine cities through the Carmel range to the
borders of the Phoenician territory.

The biblical history of the northern kingdom that we read today
was mostly recorded in Judah after the Assyrian conquest of Israel. It
is important to note that this written history has a strong theological
bent—God permitted the conquest of Israel because of its evil, and
this was an object lesson for Judah. The summary of each reign given
in the books of 1 Kings and 2 Kings ends with an indictment, such as,
"[Abijah] committed all the sins his father had done before him; his heart was not

fully devoted to the LORD *his God, as the heart of David his forefather had been"* (1 Kings 15:3), *"[Nadab] did evil in the eyes of the* LORD*"* (1 Kings 15:26), and *"He followed the ways of the kings of Israel, as the house of Ahab had done, for he married a daughter of Ahab. He did evil in the eyes of the* LORD*"* (2 Kings 8:27). However, the religious establishment of Judah had motes in its own eyes. 'Abdu'l-Bahá summarized the spiritual situation of both kingdoms as follows:

> *After the Israelites had advanced along every level of civilization, and had achieved success in the highest possible degree, they began little by little to forget the root-principles of the Mosaic Law and Faith, to busy themselves with rites and ceremonials and to show unbecoming conduct. The strife between Rehoboam and Jeroboam led to centuries of warfare between their descendants, with the result that the tribes of Israel were scattered and disrupted. In brief, it was because they forgot the meaning of the Law of God that they became involved in ignorant fanaticism and blameworthy practices such as insurgence and sedition. Their divines, having concluded that all those essential qualifications of humankind set forth in the Holy Book were by then a dead letter, began to think only of furthering their own selfish interests, and afflicted the people by allowing them to sink into the lowest depths of heedlessness and ignorance.*[1]

The people in the northern kingdom were cut off from the Temple in Jerusalem. Therefore, Jeroboam set up two alternate worship sites early in his reign—one at Bethel near the border with Judah and the other at Dan in the north. Most unfortunately, he erected a golden calf at each site, thus merging idolatry with Mosaic worship. Jeroboam also established additional hilltop shrines called the "high places." As mentioned previously, the Canaanites had always had altars on hills for worship and rituals, including child sacrifice. Now these local shrines were not only legitimized but their numbers were increased. Rituals at the high places became the object of indignation and charges of apostasy on the part of the Levitical priests in Judah, who insisted that the only legitimate place for sacrificial worship was the Temple in Jerusalem. However, it was virtually impossible for country people to walk more than a day or two to Jerusalem, and most of them probably never did. Jeroboam, in Israel, appointed as priests non-Levites who would be loyal to him. This new priesthood, motivated to protect its jobs and privileges, became a prime adversary of the prophets Amos and Hosea in the northern kingdom.

The institution of the court prophets did not fare much better. Since the time of Joshua, the power of the judges and then of the kings in the united kingdom had been balanced by the prophets, whose status was established in the ideology and system of governance of that time. The prophets were sentries responsible for challenging the kings when they faltered in their duty to God and the people. By the time of the divided kingdom, however, the system of court prophets was riddled with sycophancy and corruption. Lone prophets such as Elijah, Elisha, and others strove to fulfill the essential purpose of the prophets—to deliver the words of God and to draw the rulers and the people back into a proper covenantal relationship with Him.

It had been understood since the time of Moses that the people were to be ruled by God, who was depicted in anthropomorphic terms and believed to be not only living intimately with His people but also expressing His pleasure or displeasure about their actions. When the people strayed and adopted Canaanite beliefs and idolatry, the prophets would turn up with harsh judgments. However, life was physically precarious, and most people found survival to be their first consideration. Pragmatic approaches were taken to securing that survival. Dever observed:

> In a harsh environment at the mercy of the elements, surrounded by hostile foes, most people sought to placate the gods and seek their favor as best they could. And in a predominantly rural and agricultural society that meant giving back, as a token to the gods, what they had been provided: the surplus of the flocks, the produce of the fields, and perhaps even progeny. Only these

offerings could secure "plenty," without which the human family and its heritage could not survive.[2]

The Mosaic teachings were merged with Canaanite polytheism and idol worship. Fertility cults were prevalent along with the worship of Asherah, a Canaanite goddess. She was a fertility and mother goddess who was called the Queen of Heaven. Worship of Asherah usually consisted of food and drink offerings. The worship of Baal was a more serious matter. Since he was both a storm god and a fertility god, appeasing him necessitated child sacrifice.

The rural areas suffered not only from bad crops and poverty but from marauding armies. Just five years into Jeroboam's reign, the pillaging army of Pharaoh Shishak marched through the two kingdoms and reached Jerusalem, plundering the palaces and the Temple. A triumphal inscription found in the great temple of Karnak in Upper Egypt listed the 150 towns and villages that were devastated in this campaign. Even though the Egyptian army returned home, it left behind scenes of destruction that were uncovered by archeologists. This devastation had one positive result for the new Israelite kingdom though. The Egyptian incursion dealt a death blow to the vestiges of the Canaanite city-state system. This collapse made possible the expansion of the northern kingdom into new areas.

Conflict between the kingdoms was constant. In the ninth century, Israel and Judah were often at war with each other and with other neighbors. Then the Assyrian incursions started about 740 BCE. It would not have mattered much to a farmer which army trampled his fields. Armies on the move requisitioned grain and livestock as they passed through and often abused civilians through rape, plunder, death, and destruction.

Despite these rampaging armies, and sometimes because of them, officials from Samaria, the capital city of Israel, would not have been popular visitors in a pastoral society where traditions of tribalism prevailed. Villagers seldom met the king's officials except for purposes that disrupted or impoverished the people—the collection of taxes and the conscription of men for the military or for labor on royal building projects.

THE PROPHET ELIJAH

Enter into this sorry state of affairs Elijah of the northern kingdom. Elijah was an independent preaching prophet of the ninth century during the reign of Ahab of Israel (c. 874–853 BCE). He confronted and advised kings of their various misdeeds, but the public was his main audience. Elijah preached to the man on the street to repent and to renew his covenant with the God of Moses. 'Abdu'l-Bahá deftly described the divine sending of Elijah:

> *The high ethical standards and spiritual perfections ceased to exist. Conditions and morals became corrupt, religion was debased and the perfect principles of the Mosaic Law were obscured in superstition and polytheism. War and strife arose among the tribes and their unity was destroyed. The followers of Jeroboam declared themselves rightful and valid in kingly succession, and the supporters of Rehoboam made the same claim. Finally the tribes were torn asunder by hostility and hatred, the glory of Israel was eclipsed and so complete was the degradation that a golden calf was set up as an object of worship in the city of Tyre. Thereupon God sent Elijah the prophet who redeemed the people, renewed the law of God and established an era of new life for Israel.*[3]

Ahab, the second king of the Omri dynasty in Israel, and his Phoenician queen, Jezebel, provided the dramatic and adversarial setting for the major part of Elijah's ministry. Theirs was a diplomatic marriage, and Ahab indulged his wife's devotion to the god Baal: *"He set up an altar for Baal in the temple of Baal that he built in Samaria. Ahab also made an Asherah pole and did more to arouse the anger of the LORD, the God of Israel, than did all the kings of Israel before him"* (1 Kings 16:32–33). Asherah trees or poles stood near Canaanite religious sites to honor the goddess Asherah, also known as Astarte, consort of the major god El.

The prophet Elijah told Ahab, *"As the LORD, the God of Israel, lives, whom I serve, there will be neither dew nor rain in the next few years except at my word"* (17:1). Drought in the face of Baal, the mighty storm god of fertility and natural forces? The irony could not have been lost on Ahab, outraged as

161

he was. Elijah wisely fled to the wilderness east of the Jordan, where he was reportedly fed by ravens, and then he went to the region of Sidon in today's Lebanon. He lived there quietly for three years as the drought persisted. In the meantime, Jezebel had been killing the prophets of God. Elijah was directed by God, *"Go and present yourself to Ahab, and I will send rain on the land"* (18:1).

So Elijah duly presented himself to Ahab, who responded:

"Is that you, you troubler of Israel?"

"I have not made trouble for Israel," Elijah retorted. *"But you and your father's family have. You have abandoned the LORD's commands and have followed the Baals. Now summon the people from all over Israel to meet me on Mount Carmel. And bring the four hundred and fifty prophets of Baal and the four hundred prophets of Asherah, who eat at Jezebel's table."* (18:17–19)

Game on. These prophets and the people consequently assembled on Mount Carmel, where Elijah issued the challenge. *"How long will you waver between two opinions? If the LORD is God, follow him; but if Baal is God, follow him"* (18:21). This was an ultimatum whose bell has rung through the ages.

The contest that ensued was as clearly between a divine presence and a false god as a contest could get. Either Baal would light the sacrifice on his altar or God would light the sacrifice on His. Winner take all. The court prophets of Baal went first. They danced around their altar laden with a bull prepared for sacrifice to Baal. Nothing happened. Baal's prophets slashed themselves with swords and spears and frantically prophesied until the time for the evening sacrifice. Still nothing happened. Elijah taunted them that their god was asleep, or busy, or traveling. Time up.

The story continues. Elijah cut up a bull and arranged it on the altar, drenching it with water from the nearby Kishon River. Elijah prayed:

"LORD, the God of Abraham, Isaac and Israel, let it be known today that you are God in Israel and that I am your servant and have done all these things at your command. Answer me, LORD, answer me, so these people will know that you, LORD, are God, and that you are turning their hearts back again." (18:36–37)

God sent the fire that burned the sacrifice, the wood, the stones, and the soil, and it also licked up the water in a trench. The people fell prostrate and cried, *"The LORD—he is God! The LORD—he is God!"* (18:39). Elijah commanded the seizure and slaughter of the prophets of Baal in the Kishon Valley. The rains started, and the drought was over. One might reasonably think that the case against Baal and Asherah was closed, but the book of 1 Kings and subsequent books report that Elijah's victory only put a temporary dent in their worship.

The confrontation with the prophets of Baal is the last public miracle reported in the Hebrew Bible. Elijah, and Elisha after him, continued performing private miracles for individuals, but the people would no longer be exhorted to follow God through large demonstrations of a fearsome, supernormal nature. This was just as well because the results of such displays are short-lived and seldom infuse faith and piety. The worship of Baal and other Canaanite deities lasted for at least another 300 years, even though it was intermittently forbidden by a couple of reformist kings.

Elijah fled to Mount Horeb (also known as Mount Sinai) to escape the wrath of Jezebel, and there he had an experience that exemplified a new level of hearing the Divine. When Moses ascended Mount Horeb to receive the Ten Commandments, the scene was described as thunder and lightning, a thick cloud over the mountain, and a trumpet blast, all preparatory to the Lord descending through smoke onto the mountain in fire. This scene was reminiscent of the storm gods of Middle Eastern idolatry, a mode familiar to the early Israelites.

When Elijah ascended Mount Horeb, the voice of God was portrayed in a strikingly different mode. The narrative of Elijah's encounter with God starts with a Moses-like experience of strong wind, earthquake, and fire, but God is not in them.

And he [the LORD] said, Go forth, and stand upon the mount [Horeb] before the LORD. And, behold, the LORD passed by, and a great and strong wind rent the mountains, and brake in pieces the rocks before the LORD; but the LORD was not in the wind: and after the wind an earthquake; but the LORD was not in the earthquake: And after the earthquake a fire; but the LORD was not in the fire: and after the fire a still small voice. (1 Kings 19:11–12, KJV)

Elijah heard the voice of God on an inner, private level. This was a major departure from the Middle Eastern tradition of storm gods and miracle workers. Previous Mosaic prophets undoubtedly heard the *still small voice,* but here Elijah made the demarcation between the old and a new understanding of God and how He communicated with His people. The classical prophets would now receive divine guidance and communication in this quiet manner, even though their messages were often proclaimed loudly, even stridently, to king and country.

Elijah poured out his problems to God—how the Israelites had rejected His covenant, torn down His altars, and put all His prophets to death except him. And he was running for his life. The Lord told Elijah to go to the Desert of Damascus and there appoint Hazael king over Aram, Jesu king over Israel, and Elisha to succeed him as prophet.

Ahab had not seen the last of that gadfly Elijah, whose duty it was to confront the ruler with his sins. Elijah appeared when Ahab had the owner of a vineyard murdered so that he could obtain the property. *"So you have found me, my enemy!"* (1 Kings 21:20) was Ahab's challenge.

"I have found you," he answered, "because you have sold yourself to do evil in the eyes of the LORD. He says, 'I am going to bring disaster on you. I will wipe out your descendants and cut off from Ahab every last male in Israel— slave or free. I will make your house like that of Jeroboam son of Nebat and that of Baasha son of Ahijah, because you have aroused my anger and have caused Israel to sin.'" (21:20–22)

Astonishingly, Ahab repented deeply, so God postponed the fulfillment of His prophecy to the days of Ahab's son, Jehoram. Elijah outlived

Ahab and alternately assisted and confronted his two sons and heirs, Ahaziah and Jehoram. As predicted, the dynasty of Ahab ended abruptly. Ahaziah died within a year or two of injuries from a fall, and his brother Jehoram was murdered after eleven years by Jehu, an army officer who became the next king.

As amazing as these experiences of the prophets seem to us, they were evidently commonplace in ancient Israel. As the biblical scholar Edward F. Campbell, Jr. commented:

> Being confronted with prophets surprises neither king nor the people. In the stories of the prophets whom the DH* sets in the ninth-century BCE, notably Elijah, Elisha, and Micaiah, these men appear as lone actors—especially in conflicts with other prophetic actors saying the opposite. It is inappropriate to describe the prophets as isolated eccentrics and malcontents operating as free agents. Rather, they are part of a social phenomenon, the bands and groups of prophets, such as those whom Jezebel tries to kill off as well as those who eat at her table. Even the seven thousand who have not bowed the knee to Baal appear as a part of a support system, about whom perhaps Elijah has forgotten. Regularly Elijah and Elisha use members of their prophetic groups to carry out their prophetic tasks.[4]
>
> * DH refers to the Deuteronomistic History, a source identified by early biblical criticism that underlies much of the Hebrew Bible. It can also refer to the seventh-century scribes who recorded and edited the early religious history of Israel in accordance with major tenets of the book of Deuteronomy that served their own theological beliefs and agendas.

THE RETURN OF ELIJAH

It is written that Elijah bypassed physical death on Earth when he was taken by a celestial chariot while walking with Elisha: *"As they were walking along and talking together, suddenly a chariot of fire and horses of fire appeared and separated the two of them, and Elijah went up to heaven in a whirlwind"*

(2 Kings 2:11). This event generated much commentary over the centuries. Malachi, the last of the classical prophets, foretold that Elijah would come again: *"See, I will send the prophet Elijah to you before that great and dreadful day of the LORD comes"* (Mal. 4:5).

The Jews expected Elijah to literally and physically descend from heaven, possibly in the same fiery chariot in which he had left, before the coming of the Messiah. One reason they did not recognize Jesus as the Messiah was that they expected a literal return of Elijah. In addition, both John the Baptist and Jesus denied that they were Elijah. The apparent nonappearance of Elijah was confusing to the disciples. Then Peter, James, and John witnessed the Transfiguration, the appearance of Moses and Elijah with Jesus. As they afterward descended the mountain, the disciples asked Jesus why the teachers of the law said that Elijah must come first. Jesus replied:

> *"To be sure, Elijah comes and will restore all things. But I tell you, Elijah has already come, and they did not recognize him, but have done to him everything they wished. In the same way the Son of Man is going to suffer at their hands. Then the disciples understood that he was talking to them about John the Baptist."* (Matt. 17:11–13)

When 'Abdu'l-Bahá was asked why John the Baptist denied being Elijah, He responded:

> *The reason is that we consider here not the individuality of the person but the reality of his perfections—that is to say, the very same perfections that Elias [Elijah] possessed were realized in John the Baptist as well. Thus, John the Baptist was the promised Elias. What is being considered here is not the essence but the attributes.*[5]

Shoghi Effendi spoke of the Báb as the return of Elijah. He made the following comments on the deeply significant occasion of the internment of the mortal remains of the Báb on Mount Carmel in 1909 CE:

With the transference of the remains of the Báb—Whose advent marks the return of the prophet Elijah—to Mt. Carmel, and their interment in that holy mountain, not far from the cave of that Prophet Himself, the Plan so glorious envisaged by Bahá'u'lláh, in the evening of His life, had been at last executed, and the arduous labors associated with the early and tumultuous years of the ministry of the appointed Center of His Covenant ['Abdu'l-Bahá] crowned with immortal success." [6]

According to tradition, Elijah had a close association with Mount Carmel. It is believed that Elijah meditated on Mount Carmel before his encounter with the prophets of Baal and that he started a school of prophets on that mountain. He lived in one or more caves on its northwest slope in present-day Haifa. Today there are two caves in Haifa that are associated with Elijah. One is located at the foot of the mountain and is used for Jewish prayer, and the other is located a short distance higher on the mountain under the Stella Maris Church, next to the Stella Maris monastery, which is the world headquarters of the Carmelite order of monks. Both caves are within walking distance of the Shrine of the Báb.

Epilogue

PROPHETS OF THE EARLY centuries of the Mosaic Dispensation, both those who are well known and those who have been forgotten in the mists of time, guided the Israelites in renewing the law and spirit of Moses, the Prophet of God for that time. The greatest of the early prophets was undoubtedly Elijah, who had the same attributes as John the Baptist and had been given the task of renewing Israel. Then the scene went dark for about 100 years until the appearance of the prophets Amos and Hosea in the mid- to late-eighth century BCE, a time of ascending literacy when the words of the prophets could be more easily recorded and remembered.

Volumes 2 and 3 of *The Coming of the Glory* continue the survey of Israelite history and, more important, examine the deeds, warnings, and prophecies of the twelve classical prophets—First, Second, and Third Isaiah; Daniel, Micah, Zephaniah, Nahum, Habakkuk, Jeremiah, Ezekiel, Obadiah, Haggai, First and Second Zechariah; Joel, and Malachi. The known period of these prophets stretched from Amos and Hosea in the eighth century to Malachi in the late fifth.

These prophets mercilessly and unceasingly chastised the rulers and the people for their sins and warned of grim catastrophes to come. But they also gave messages of divine encouragement and the assurance of the coming of future Prophets of God: Jesus and the one who would be called the Glory of God, Bahá'u'lláh.

169

Appendix A

OBSERVATIONS OF E. G. BROWNE

IN APRIL 1890 PROFESSOR Edward Granville Browne met Bahá'u'lláh in four successive interviews. Of his first meeting, he wrote:

> I can never forget, though I cannot describe it. Those piercing eyes seemed to read one's very soul; power and authority sat on that ample brow ... No need to ask in whose presence I stood, as I bowed myself before one who is the object of a devotion and love which kings might envy and emperors sigh for in vain ... Here did I spend five most memorable days, during which I enjoyed unparalleled and unhoped-for opportunities of holding intercourse with those who are the fountain-heads of that mighty and wondrous spirit, which works with invisible but ever-increasing force for the transformation and quickening of a people who slumber in a sleep like unto death. It was, in truth, a strange and moving experience, but one whereof I despair of conveying any save the feeblest impression.[1]

Appendix B

SHOGHI EFFENDI SUMMARIZES THE PRINCIPLES OF THE FAITH AS GIVEN BY 'ABDU'L-BAHÁ

IT WAS IN THE course of these epoch-making journeys and before large and representative audiences, at times exceeding a thousand people, that 'Abdu'l-Bahá expounded, with brilliant simplicity, with persuasiveness and force, and for the first time in His ministry, those basic and distinguishing principles of His Father's Faith, which together with the laws and ordinances revealed in the Kitáb-i-Aqdas constitute the bed-rock of God's latest Revelation to mankind. The independent search after truth, unfettered by superstition or tradition; the oneness of the entire human race, the pivotal principle and fundamental doctrine of the Faith; the basic unity of all religions; the condemnation of all forms of prejudice, whether religious, racial, class or national; the harmony which must exist between religion and science; the equality of men and women, the two wings on which the bird of humankind is able to soar; the introduction of compulsory education; the adoption of a universal auxiliary language; the abolition of the extremes of wealth and poverty; the institution of a world tribunal for the adjudication of disputes between nations; the exaltation of work, performed in the spirit of service, to the rank of worship; the glorification of justice as the ruling principle in human society, and of religion as a bulwark for the protection of all peoples and nations; and the establishment of a permanent and universal peace as the supreme goal of all mankind—these stand out as the essential elements of that Divine polity which He proclaimed to leaders of public thought as well as to the masses at large in the course of these missionary journeys.[1]

Notes

FOREWORD

1   Bahá'u'lláh, *Gleanings from the Writings of Bahá'u'lláh*, no. 27, 65.
2   Bahá'u'lláh, *The Hidden Words*, Part 1 from the Arabic, no. 3.
3   *Gleanings*, no. 13, 24.
4   Ibid.
5   Ibid., no. 87, 172.

PREFACE

1   *Lithic* means "relating to or being a stone tool" (*Merriam-Webster's Collegiate Dictionary*). The Stone Age (known to scholars as the Paleolithic era) marks the period in human prehistory dating from about 2.7 million to 12,000 BCE. Within this period, the Lower Paleolithic ran from about 2.7 million to about 300,000 BCE and featured the earliest human-like skills, such as fashioning crude stone tools. The Middle Paleolithic, or Middle Stone Age, ran from about 300,000 to 45,000 BCE and witnessed the evolution of Neanderthals (the first anatomically modern Homo sapiens) and some of the first glimmers of modern behaviors, such as making sophisticated stone tools, caring for the elderly, and symbolic or ritual behavior. The upper Paleolithic, or Late Stone Age, spanned about 45,000 to 10,000 BCE and was characterized by cave art and the crafting of a wide range of tools from stone, bone, ivory, and antlers.

2   An archeological system divides the span of mankind into three early eras: the Stone Age, Bronze Age, and Iron Age. The Neolithic

175

Period (New Stone Age) preceded the Bronze Age. The Neolithic period in the Middle East lasted from about 10,000 to 3,300 BCE. During this period, people still used stone tools, but they also domesticated plants and animals and lived in villages.

3 "The Word Bahá: Quintessence of the Greatest Name," *Bahá'í Studies Review* 3:1, note no. 7, 1993. Lambden received his PhD in religious studies from the University of Newcastle upon Tyne. His work exhibits a special interest in the Bible and the Qur'an and their relationship to Bábí and Bahá'í Arabic and Persian primary scriptural texts and doctrinal teachings. He is currently a research scholar at the University of California, Merced.

4 Rodwell renumbered the Qur'anic chapters to put them in chronological order. A quick reference between the Qur'an's usual numbering and Rodwell's is available from https://www.sacred-texts.com/isl/qr/index.htm.

INTRODUCTION

1 The Báb, *Selections from the Writings of the Báb*, no. 3:34, 136–37.

2 Shoghi Effendi in the Introduction to *The Dawn-breakers: Nabíl's Narrative of the Early Days of the Bahá'í Revelation* by Nabíl-i-A'zam, xxix.

3 Bahá'í International Community, *A Statement on Bahá'u'lláh*, note no. 5.

4 Nabíl-i-A'zam, *The Dawn-Breakers: Nabíl's Narrative of the Early Days of the Bahá'í Revelation*, 315–16.

5 The complete account of the events surrounding the trial and execution of the Báb is described in *The Dawn-Breakers*, 500–26.

6 "Considered alone, Bahá is a verbal-noun meaning radiant 'glory', 'splendor', 'light', 'brilliancy', 'beauty', 'excellence', 'goodliness', 'divine majesty' - there are other shades of meaning also." Lambden, "The Word Bahá: Quintessence of the Greatest Name," *Bahá'í Studies Review*, 3:1.

7 Adib Taherzadeh, *The Revelation of Bahá'u'lláh*, vol. 1, 297.

8   Adib Taherzadeh commented: "Many times the Báb alluded to
    the 'year nine' as the date for the coming of 'Him Whom God
    shall make manifest'. The Báb's mission began in the year 1260
    A.H. (A.D. 1844). The 'year nine' was 1297 A.H., which started
    the middle of October 1852, when Bahá'u'lláh had already been
    imprisoned for two months in the Síyáh-Chál of Ṭihrán, the scene
    of His transcendent Revelation." *The Revelation of Bahá'u'lláh*, vol. 1,
    298–99.

9   Bahá'u'lláh, cited by Shoghi Effendi, *God Passes By*, 109.

10 Taherzadeh wrote: "On the other hand, the Báb also referred
    to the year nineteen, a year coinciding with the Declaration of
    Bahá'u'lláh in Baghdád, which occurred at the end of nineteen
    lunar years from the inception of the Bahá'í Era." *The Revelation of
    Bahá'u'lláh*, vol. 1, 299.

11 These tablets are published in *The Summons of the Lord of Hosts*.

12 Ibid., "Súriy-i-Mulúk" ("Súrih to the Kings"), no. 68, 213.

13 Bahá'u'lláh, *Gleanings from the Writings of Bahá'u'lláh*, no. 45, 99–100.
    The Ancient Beauty is one of the titles of Bahá'u'lláh.

14 *The Revelation of Bahá'u'lláh*, vol. 3, 420.

15 'Abdu'l-Bahá, *Tablets of 'Abdu'l-Bahá*, vol. 2, 430. The Blessed Perfec-
    tion is one of the titles of Bahá'u'lláh.

16 Shoghi Effendi wrote *God Passes By*, along with many of his
    commentaries and letters published as *The Advent of Divine Justice*,
    Citadel of Faith, *The Promised Day Is Come*, *Unfolding Destiny*, and *The
    World Order of Bahá'u'lláh*. He translated *The Dawn-breakers*, *The
    Hidden Words*, and assorted writings of Bahá'u'lláh and compiled
    them into *Gleanings from the Writings of Bahá'u'lláh* and *Prayers and
    Meditations of Bahá'u'lláh*.

17 Letters dated October 1, 2010, from the Research Department
    to the Universal House of Justice, and June 6, 2013, from the
    Universal House of Justice to an individual, found in "Texts, Sacred,
    Numbers, and Classifications by/on Behalf of the Universal House
    of Justice."

18 Ibid.

19 Bahá'u'lláh, "Tarazat" ("Ornaments"), *Tablets of Bahá'u'lláh Revealed after the Kitáb-i-Aqdas*, 33.

20 Letters dated October 1, 2010, from the Research Department to the Universal House of Justice, and June 6, 2013, from the Universal House of Justice to an individual, "Texts, Sacred, Numbers, and Classifications by/on Behalf of the Universal House of Justice."

21 Ibid.

22 Ibid., cited in a letter dated August 9, 1984, from the Universal House of Justice to an individual.

23 Mírzá Abu'l-Faḍl Gulpáygání, *Miracles and Metaphors*, 9.

24 Ibid.

25 'Abdu'l-Bahá, *Some Answered Questions*, no. 41.4–5, 183.

26 *Gleanings*, no. 10.2, 13.

27 The Báb, *Selections from the Writings of the Báb*, 125.

CHAPTER 1. ANIMISM AND ATONEMENT

1 Thomas Cahill, *The Gifts of the Jews*, 8.

2 Abdu'l-Bahá, *Some Answered Questions*, no. 47.11, 212.

3 Ibid., no. 38.5, 173.

4 Bahá'u'lláh, "Tablet of Maqsúd," *Tablets of Bahá'u'lláh Revealed After the Kitáb-i-Aqdas*, 161–62.

5 Bahá'u'lláh, *Gleanings from the Writings of Bahá'u'lláh*, no. 87, 174. The term "Dayspring" can be taken figuratively as equivalent to a fountain or source and can be used to mean a Manifestation of God. (From a letter written on behalf of Shoghi Effendi to an individual, February 19, 1935, *Lights of Guidance*, no. 1582, 480)

6 Patrick Symmes, "Turkey: Archeological Dig Reshaping Human History." *Newsweek*, February 17, 2010. Symmes is a correspondent and travel writer for several magazines. A former Harper's Fellow at the UC Berkeley School of Journalism, his works have been anthologized by Best American Science Writing and Best American Travel Writing eleven times.

7 "Turkey: Archeological Dig Reshaping Human History."

8 Ibid.

9   Andrew Curry, "Göbekli Tepe: The World's First Temple?" *Smith-sonian Magazine*, November 2008. Curry is a journalist and free-lance foreign correspondent who covers science, history, politics, and culture.

10   "Turkey: Archeological Dig Reshaping Human History."

11   Sandra Scham, "The World's Oldest Temple." *Archeology*, 61:6, November/December 2008. Scham is a specialist in artifacts of the Near East from the Neolithic through the Byzantine periods and has long been active in educational exchange and teaching about Near Eastern Archaeology. She has been on the archeological faculties of Catholic University of America, the University of Maryland, and Jerusalem University College. Scham is *Archaeology's* Washington, D.C., correspondent and a fellow of the American Association for the Advancement of Science.

12   "Turkey: Archeological Dig Reshaping Human History."

13   'Abdu'l-Bahá, *The Promulgation of Universal Peace*, 463.

14   Mark Nesbitt, "Where Was Einkorn Wheat Domesticated?" *Trends in Plant Science*, vol. 3, March 1998. Nesbitt is an ethnobotanist associated with the British Institute of Archaeology at Ankara who researched the long-term development of einkorn wheat in southwest Asia. See also Manfred Heun, et al., "Site of Einkorn Wheat Domestication Identified by DNA Fingerprinting," *Science*, 14 November 1997: Vol. 278, no. 5341, 1312-14. 1312. Heun is a professor at the Norwegian University of Life Sciences. He wrote that phylogenic analysis (evolutionary history of a genetically related group of organisms) through DNA testing of einkorn wheat indicated that the domestication of this grain originated near the Karadag Mountains of southeast Turkey.

15   Steven Mithen, cited by David Lewis-Williams and David Pearce, *Inside the Neolithic Mind*, 33.

16   Lewis Binford, cited by Michael G. Dever, *Who Were the Early Israelites and Where Did They Come From?*, 74. Binford (1931–2011) was a professor of archeology at the University of New Mexico and Southern Methodist University. His great contribution to

archeology was his effort to bring an anthropological perspective to
archeology, an approach that became known as the "New Archaeology" and "processual archaeology."

17 Karl W. Luckert, *Stone Age Religion at Göbekli Tepe: From Hunting to
Domestication, Warfare and Religion*, 23.

18 Ibid., 105.

CHAPTER 2. AUROCHS AND ANCESTORS

1 Jack R. Harlan, *Crops and Man*, 1992. Cited by Jacob L. Weisdorf,
2003. "From Foraging to Farming: Explaining the Neolithic Revolution," Institute of Economics, University of Copenhagen.

2 Alan H. Simmons, *The Neolithic Revolution in the Near East: Transforming the Human Landscape*, ix. Simmons's research focuses on the
origins and consequences of food production, archeological ethics,
Near Eastern and Mediterranean prehistory, lithic analyses, and
interdisciplinary research. He has participated in more than eighty
excavation projects in the Near East and North America and has
received a number of awards for his research, most recently the
P. E. MacAllister Field Archaeology Award for outstanding career
contributions to Near Eastern and eastern Mediterranean Archaeology from the American Schools of Oriental Research. Simmons
has published more than 170 articles, monographs, reviews, chapters, and technical reports and has spoken widely on his work.

3 Marshall Sahlins, "The Original Affluent Society," an extract from
his book *Stone Age Economics*. After his retirement as Distinguished
Professor at the University of Nevada, Las Vegas, Sahlins was
appointed that university's Charles F. Gray Distinguished Service
Professor Emeritus of Anthropology and Social Sciences. He has
participated in more than eighty excavation projects in the Near
East and North America and has received many awards for his
research, most recently the P. E. MacAllister Field Archaeology
Award for outstanding career contributions to Near Eastern and
Eastern Mediterranean Archaeology from the American Schools
of Oriental Research.

4   David Lewis-Williams and David Pearce, *Inside the Neolithic Mind*,
    20. Lewis-Williams is professor emeritus of cognitive archeology
    at the University of Witwatersrand (WITS) in South Africa and
    the founder of the Rock Art Research Institute at WITS. The
    Institute is internationally recognized for its high level of achieve-
    ment in research publications and the breadth of rock art research
    resources it has developed. David Pearce is an associate professor at
    WITS and director of the Institute's School of Geography, Arche-
    ology, and Environmental Studies. His primary research interest is
    cognitive archeology.

5   Deborah Rogers, "Inequality: Why Egalitarian Societies Died
    Out," *New Scientist*, Issue 2875, July 28, 2012. Rogers is affiliated
    with Stanford University's Institute for Research in the Social
    Sciences and directs the Initiative for Equality.

6   Karl W. Luckert, *Stone Age Religion at Göbekli Tepe: From Hunting to
    Domestication, Warfare and Religion*, 158–59.

7   Thomas Standage, *An Edible History of Humanity*, 16–18.

8   Spencer Wells, *Pandora's Seed: The Unforeseen Cost of Civilization*, Table
    1, 23. Cited from data published in "Health As a Crucial Factor in
    the Change from Hunting to Developed Farming in the Eastern
    Mediterranean" by J. Lawrence Angel, *Paleopathology at the Origins
    of Agriculture*, edited by Mark Nathan Cohen and George J. Armel-
    agos, 51–74, Chart 54–55. Cohen is the Distinguished Professor of
    Anthropology at the State University of New York at Plattsburgh.
    He was awarded a Guggenheim Fellowship in recognition of this
    book's impact. Armelagos is the Goodrich C. White professor of
    anthropology at Emory University and a recipient of the Viking
    Fund Medal.

9   *Pandora's Seed*, Table 1, 23. Cited from data published in "Health
    As a Crucial Factor in the Change from Hunting to Developed
    Farming in the Eastern Mediterranean" by J. Lawrence Angel,
    Paleopathology at the Origins of Agriculture, edited by Mark Nathan
    Cohen and George J. Armelagos, 51–74.

10 Ibid.

11 'Abdu'l-Bahá, *Some Answered Questions*, no. 52.2, 231.

12 *Inside the Neolithic Mind*, 111. Pages 102 to 122 cover the architectural and artistic symbolism of Çatalhöyük.

13 Ian Hodder, *Religion at Work in a Neolithic Society*, 3. Since 2002, Hodder has been the Dunlevie Family Professor of Anthropology Stanford University. He was awarded the Oscar Montelius Medal by the Swedish Society of Antiquaries and the Huxley Memorial Medal by the Royal Anthropological Institute. He was a Guggenheim Fellow and holds Honorary Doctorates from Bristol and Leiden Universities.

14 *Religion at Work in a Neolithic Society*, 3.

CHAPTER 3. GODS AND GODDESSES

1 Erich H. Cline, *From Eden to Exile*, 60.

2 Gwendolyn Leick, *Mesopotamia: The Invention of the City*, 6.

3 Robert N. Bellah, *Religion in Human Evolution*, 215. Bellah cites Andrew Sherratt, "Plough and Pastoralism: Aspects of the Secondary Products Revolution," *Pattern of the Past: Studies in Honour of David Clarke* by Ian Hodder, Glynn Isaac, and Norman Hammond, 261–305. Bellah was the Elliott Professor of Sociology Emeritus at the University of California, Berkeley until his death in 2013. He received the American Academy of Religion Martin E. Marty Award for the Public Understanding of Religion in 2007.

4 Ibid., 216.

5 Shoghi Effendi, *Citadel of Faith*, 80.

6 'Abdu'l-Bahá, *The Promulgation of Universal Peace*, 10.

7 John Bottéro, *Religion in Ancient Mesopotamia*, 45. Bottéro was a professor of Oriental History at the École Pratique des Hautes Études in Paris until his passing in 2007.

8 *Religion in Human Evolution*, 220.

9 *Religion in Ancient Mesopotamia*, 165.

10 Ibid., 169–70.

11 Ibid., 106–07.

12 Ibid., 107.

13 *The Gifts of the Jews*, 94.

14 *Mesopotamia: The Invention of the City*, 93–98.

CHAPTER 4. ADAM, EVE, AND EDEN

1   The Báb, *Selections from the Writings of the Báb*, no. 3:15.3, 115.

2   Abdu'l-Bahá, *'Abdu'l-Bahá in London*, 18.

3   From a letter of the Universal House of Justice dated August 9, 1984, to an individual believer, cited in *The Bible: Extracts on the Old and New Testaments*, compiled by the Research Department of the Universal House of Justice.

4   *'Abdu'l-Bahá in London*, 80.

5   'Abdu'l-Bahá, *The Promulgation of Universal Peace*, 155.

6   Victor H. Matthews and Don C. Benjamin, *Old Testament Parallels: Laws and Stories from the Ancient Near East*, 22. The Gilgamesh legends were first unearthed during an archeological excavation of the ancient site of Nineveh, 1848–49 CE. The stories of Gilgamesh are believed to have originated about 3300 BCE. They were written in Akkadian cuneiform on clay tablets, which are preserved today in the British Museum. Portions of the story in this book were taken from a Babylonian version written sometime between 2000 and 1550 BCE. Matthews is dean of the College of Humanities and Public Affairs and professor of religious studies at Missouri State University in Springfield, Missouri, where he has taught since 1988. Benjamin teaches biblical and Near Eastern Studies at Arizona State University.

7   *Selections from the Writings of the Báb*, no. 4:10.6, 162.

8   Bahá'u'lláh, *The Tabernacle of Unity*, no. 2.48, 47.

9   Bahá'u'lláh, *Gleanings from the Writings of Bahá'u'lláh*, no. 31.1, 74.

10 Bahá'í International Community, *A Statement on Bahá'u'lláh*, endnote no. 50.

11 Ginsburg, Rabbi, *The Legends of the Jews*, vol. 1, 11. There were wave offerings and heave offerings. The wave offering was a repeated horizontal motion, right to left. The heave offering consisted of an up-and-down motion. A wave offering was given to the Lord as

ruler of the earth; a heave offering was given to the Lord as ruler of heaven.

12 *The New England Primer*, the first reading primer designed for the American colonies. First published in 1690 for the American colonies, this primer combined the study of the alphabet with biblical verses. It became the foundation of most schooling and was used until the nineteenth century.

13 *Promulgation*, 219–20.

14 'Abdu'l-Bahá, *Some Answered Questions*, no. 30.2–13, 137–42.

15 Letter written on behalf of the Guardian to an individual believer, October 4, 1950, *Lights of Guidance*, no. 1696, 504.

16 *Selections from the Writings of the Báb*, no. 6:5, 200.

17 Bahá'u'lláh, "Tablet of Aḥmad," *Bahá'í Prayers: A Selections of Prayers Revealed by the Báb, Bahá'u'lláh, and 'Abdu'l-Bahá*, 210.

18 Elena Maria Marsella, *The Quest for Eden*, 66. Marsella was an American Bahá'í who pursued careers as a pianist, a member of the Foreign Service, and a teacher. She was a Knight of Baha'u'llah to the Gilbert and Ellis Islands (now Kiribati and Tuvalu) and a member of the first National Spiritual Assembly of the Bahá'ís of the Hawaiian Islands and the National Spiritual Assembly of Central America and the Antilles. She served on the Board of Counsellors for Northeastern Asia. Marsella was known for her encyclopedic knowledge of the Faith.

19 Ibid., 69.

20 Ibid., 72.

21 Ibid., 62.

22 William Barnes, "Mythoi: Stories of the Origin, Fall and Redemption of Humanity: A Study in the Topology of the Holy Books," *Scripture and Revelation*, 310–11.

23 Ibid., 316.

24 *Gleanings*, no. 93.1, 184.

25 "Mythoi: Stories of the Origin, Fall and Redemption of Humanity: A Study in the Topology of the Holy Books," *Scripture and Revelation*, 312.

26 *Some Answered Questions*, no. 64.3, 272.

27 John S. Hatcher and Amrollah Hemmat, *Adam's Wish: Unknown Poetry of Ṭáhirih*, 9.

28 Ibid., 163.

29 Ibid., 129.

30 Ibid., 125.

CHAPTER 5. NOAH AND HIS FLOOD

1 William P. Collins, "Sacred Mythology and the Bahá'í Faith," *Journal of Bahá'í Studies*, vol. 2:4, 1990, 1. Collins served on the Editorial Board of the *Bahá'í Studies Review*. He is the author of *Bibliography of English Language Works on the Bábí and Bahá'í Faiths, 1844-1985* (George Ronald Publisher, 1990) and many articles about Bahá'í history and beliefs.

2 "Ages of Adam, Seth, Methuselah and Noah," from a memorandum dated May 7, 2009, prepared by the Research Department at the Bahá'í World Centre at the request of the Universal House of Justice.

3 From a letter dated November 25, 1950, written on behalf of Shoghi Effendi to an individual believer, *Lights of Guidance*, no. 1659, 495.

4 R. H. Charles, *The Book of Enoch*, Chapter LXXXII, no. 1. The book of Enoch is included in the canons of the Ethiopian Orthodox Tewahedo Church and the Eritrean Orthodox Tewahedo Church but not by any other Christian groups. The Beta Israel Jews in northern and northwestern Ethiopia are the only Jews who include it in the Hebrew canon.

5 William B. F. Ryan and David C. Pitman, *Noah's Flood: The New Scientific Discoveries about the Event that Changed History*, 251–52. Ryan and Pitman are senior scientists at the Lamont-Doherty Earth Observatory of Columbia University (LDEO) and recipients of the Francis P. Shepard medal for marine geology from the Society for Sedimentary Geology. Ryan is a Doherty Senior Scholar in marine geology and geophysics and a special research scientist in biology paleoenvironment at LDEO and an adjunct professor at Columbia

University for earth and environmental sciences. Pitman is a senior scientist emeritus at LDEO and a fellow of both the Geological Society of America and the American Geophysical Union, which awarded him its Maurice Ewing Medal (1996). He also received the Alexander Agassiz Medal of the National Academy of Sciences (1998).

6   'Abdu'l-Bahá, *The Promulgation of Universal Peace*, 459–60.

7   *Bahá'í News*, No. 228, February 1950, 4.

8   Victor H. Matthews and Don C. Benjamin, *Old Testament Parallels: Laws and Stories from the Ancient Near East*, 21.

9   Bahá'u'lláh, *The Kitáb-i-Íqán*, no. 162, 142.

10 Ibid., no. 162, 142–43.

11 Ibid., no. 7, 7–8.

12 Bahá'u'lláh, "Tarazát" ("Ornaments"), *Tablets of Bahá'u'lláh revealed after the Kitáb-i-Aqdas*, 33.

13 *Glossary of Bahá'í Terms.* From the glossary in *Messages from the Universal House of Justice 1963–1986: Third Epoch of the Formative Age*, the Universal House of Justice.

14 The word Babylon is derived from Akkadian bab (gate) plus ilu (god). John L. MacKenzie, Dictionary of the Bible. (New York: Touchstone, 1965), s.v. "Tower of Babel."

15 The NAS Old Hebrew Lexicon, s.v. "Balal," https://www.biblestudytools.com/lexicons/hebrew/nas/balal.html

16 Wade Fransson, *The Rod of Iron*, 106–07.

17 Ibid., 34.

CHAPTER 6. ABRAHAM, INTO THE FUTURE

1   'Abdu'l-Bahá, *Selections from the Writings of 'Abdu'l-Bahá*, no. 25.3, 59.

2   From a letter written on behalf of Shoghi Effendi, dated November 25, 1950, to an individual. "Buddha, Krishna, Zoroaster, and Related Subjects," *Compilation of Compilations*, vol. 1, no. 23.

3   He was known as Abram until Genesis 17:5: *"No longer will you be called Abram; your name will be Abraham, for I have made you a father of many nations."* The footnotes to Abram and Abraham in the NIV version

THE COMING OF THE GLORY

of the Bible state that Abram means *exalted father* and Abraham means *father of many*.

4   The texts of Hinduism, Buddhism, and Zoroastrianism foretold the coming of Bahá'u'lláh. "To Him Zoroaster must have alluded when, according to tradition, He foretold that a period of three thousand years of conflict and contention must needs precede the advent of the World-Saviour Sháh-Bahrám, Who would triumph over Ahriman [evil, also non-reality] and usher in an era of blessedness and peace. He alone is meant by the prophecy attributed to Gautama Buddha Himself, that *'a Buddha named Maitreye, the Buddha of universal fellowship,'* should, in the fullness of time, arise and reveal *'His boundless glory.'* To Him the Bhagavad-Gita of the Hindus had referred as *'The Most Great Spirit,'* the *'Tenth Avatar,'* the *'Immaculate Manifestation of Krishna.'"* Shoghi Effendi, *God Passes By*, 95.

5   From a letter of the Universal House of Justice to an individual dated February 8, 1998. Posted on the website the Bahá'í Covenant | The Covenant of Bahá'u'lláh.

6   Bahá'u'lláh, *The Kitáb-i-Íqán: The Book of Certitude*, no. 11, 10.

7   Cahill, *The Gifts of the Jews*, 63.

8   Frances Worthington, *Abraham: One God, Three Wives, Five Religions*, 16–17.

9   Ibid., 17.

10   Bahá'u'lláh, *Gleanings from the Writings of Bahá'u'lláh*, no. 32.1, 75–76.

11   Ibid., no. 36, 85.

12   Bahá'u'lláh and his wife Asíyih Khanum had seven children, of whom only three survived to adulthood. They were sons 'Abdu'l-Bahá and Mírzá Mihdí and daughter Bahíyyih Khánum.

13   Shoghi Effendi, *God Passes By*, 188.

14   Ibid.

15   Ibid.

16   *Abraham: One God, Three Wives, and Five Religions*, 109. The wilderness of Paran, known today as the Hejaz, refers to the desert that runs down the western edge of the Arabian desert to the east of the

Red Sea. Paran was located in the northwest corner of this wilderness. Mecca is located two-thirds of the way from Jordan to Yemen, about 23 miles inland from the Red Sea.

17 'Abdu'l-Bahá, *The Promulgation of Universal Peace*, 362.

CHAPTER 7. JOSEPH, AN ALLEGORY
OF DIVINE BEAUTY

1 Bahá'u'lláh, *The Seven Valleys and the Four Valleys*, no. 17, 9. He is referring to the second valley, the Valley of Love.

2 The Pentateuch, also known as the Torah, is the first five books of the Bible—Genesis, Exodus, Leviticus, Numbers, and Deuteronomy.

3 Bahá'u'lláh, *Gleanings from the Writings of Bahá'u'lláh*, no. 14, 30.

4 Ibid., no. 53, 208. "Joseph is the subject around which revolves the Súrih of Joseph in the *Holy Qur'an*. In the Báb's weighty Commentary on that book He interprets it as foreshadowing the difficulties which Bahá'u'lláh would suffer at the hands of his half-brother, Mírzá Yahyá, who was the Arch-Breaker of the Covenant of the Báb." Anthony Joy, *Exploring Gleanings: Commentary on Gleanings from the Writings of Bahá'u'lláh*, 153.

5 Bahá'u'lláh, *Gems of Divine Mysteries*, no. 29, 23–24.

6 The following articles are written by two Bahá'í scholars, Todd Lawson and Jim Stokes. Lawson is Professor Emeritus of Islamic Thought at the University of Toronto. His articles pertinent to Joseph include "The Bible, The Qur'an and the Bahá'í Teachings all tell the story of Joseph,"
https://bahaiteachings.org/author/todd-lawson;
"Interpretation as Revelation: The Qur'an Commentary of the Báb," *Journal of Bahá'í Studies*, vol. 2:4, 1990,
https://bahai-studies.ca/wp-content/uploads/2014/05/2.4-Lawson.pdf;
"The Báb's 'Sura of the Bees': A Commentary on the Qur'an 12:93 from the Sura of Joseph," Occasional Papers in Shayki, Bábí and Bahá'í Studies No. 5, November 1997,
https://www.h-net.org/~bahai/bhpapers/vol1/nahl2.htm;

"The Bahá'í Tradition: The Return of Joseph and the Peaceable Imagination," Chapter 6 of *Fighting Words: Religion, Violence, and the Interpretation of Sacred Texts* by John Renard, https://bahai-library.com/lawson_Joseph_peaceable_imagination; and "Typological Configuration and the Meaning of 'Spiritual': The Qur'anic Story of Joseph," *Journal of the American Oriental Association*, 132.2, 221–244 (2012), DOI: 10.7817/jameroriesoci.132.2.0221, https://www.jstor.org/stable/10.7817/jameroriesoci.132.issue-2. Stokes was a Professor of English at the University of Wisconsin, Stevens Point, from 1981 to 2002. He wrote: "The Story of Joseph in the Bábí and Bahá'í Faiths," *World Order Magazine*, 1997–98, vol. 29:2, 25–42, https://bahai-library.com/stokes_joseph_babi_bahai and "The Story of Joseph in Five Religious Traditions," *World Order Magazine*, 1997, vol. 28:3, 35–46, https://bahai-library.com/stokes_joseph_five_ religions.

CHAPTER 8. A COLLAPSE AND A CALL

1 'Abdu'l-Bahá, *Bahá'í Prayers: A Selection of Prayers Revealed by Bahá'u'lláh, the Báb, and 'Abdu'l-Bahá*, 153.
2 The Levant refers to the eastern Mediterranean region that today consists of Cyprus, Israel, Jordan, Lebanon, the West Bank and Gaza, Syria, and part of southern Turkey.
3 Cemal M. Pulak and Mrs. Ray H. Siegfried II, "1994 Excavation at Uluburun: The Final Campaign," Institute of Nautical Archeology. *The INA Quarterly*, Winter 1994, vol. 24:1. Mark Cartwright, "Uluburun Shipwreck," *Ancient History Encyclopedia*, September 12, 2017.
4 Eric H. Cline, *1177: The Year Civilization Collapsed*, 143. Cline is a professor of classics and anthropology at George Washington University and is the director of the GWU Capitol Archaeological Institute. He has conducted fieldwork throughout the Middle East and has authored sixteen books as well as more than one hundred articles and book reviews.

5   Dafna Langgut, Israel Finkelstein, and Thomas Litt, "Climate and the Late Bronze Collapse: New Evidence from the Southern Levant," Abstract, *Journal of the Institute of Archaeology of Tel Aviv University*, vol. 40:2, Nov. 2013, 149–75. Isabel Kershner, "Pollen Study Points to Drought as Culprit on Bronze Age Mystery," *The New York Times*, October 22, 2013.

6   Noah Wiener, "Bronze Age Collapse: Pollen Study Highlights Late Bronze Age Drought," *Biblical Archeological Review*, April 3, 2018.

7   Bahá'u'lláh, *The Kitáb-i-Íqán*, no. 57, 50–51. *Salsabíl* is a heavenly spring, fountain, or river referred to in the Qur'an.

8   Glossary and Notes prepared by George Townsend and appended to *Gleanings from the Writings of Bahá'u'lláh*, first pocket-size edition 1983.

9   The Báb, *Selections from the Writings of the Báb*, no. 2:57, 95. The word fane is medieval English for temple or shrine.

10   Ibid., no. 2:53.1, 92.

11   Ibid, no 2:14.4, 64.

12   Nader Saiedi, *Gate of the Heart: Understanding the Writings of the Báb*, 76–77. The verse is from the Qayyúmu'l-Asmá' and is found in the Iranian National Bahá'í Archives (INBA), no. 3:76.g. The Arabian Youth is one of the designations of the Báb.

13   Ibid., 98.

14   Bahá'u'lláh, *The Kitáb-i-Aqdas*, no. 103, 57. Note no. 129 in *The Kitáb-i-Aqdas* states: "The term 'Mother Book' is generally used to designate the central Book of a religious Dispensation. In the Qur'an and Islamic Ḥadíth, the term is used to describe the Qur'an itself. In the Bábí Dispensation, the Bayán is the Mother Book, and the Kitáb-i-Aqdas is the Mother Book of the Dispensation of Bahá'u'lláh. Further, the Guardian, in a letter written on his behalf has stated that this concept can also be used as a 'collective term indicating the body of the Teachings revealed by Bahá'u'lláh.' This term is also used in a broader sense to signify the Divine Repository of Revelation."

15   Shoghi Effendi, *Unfolding Destiny*, letter dated 19 October 1947 to the Bahá'ís of the United Kingdom, 448.

16   'Abdu'l-Bahá, *Some Answered Questions*, no. 39.5, 177.

CHAPTER 9. A SPIRITUAL EXODUS

1 'Abdu'l-Bahá, *Paris Talks*, 119.

2 'Abdu'l-Bahá, cited in *Lights of Guidance*, no. 1678, 500. ('Abdu'l-Bahá: *Daily Lessons Received at 'Akká*, 1979 ed., 45)

3 Israel Finkelstein and Neil Asher Silberman, *The Bible Unearthed: Archaeology's New Vision of Ancient Israel and the Origin of Its Sacred Texts*, 62–63. Finkelstein is an Israeli archeologist and academic, the Jacob M. Alkow Professor of the Archeology of Israel in the Bronze and Iron Ages at Tel Aviv University. He is widely regarded as a leading scholar in the archeology of the Levant and a foremost applicant of archeological data in reconstructing biblical history. Silberman studied Near Eastern archeology at the Hebrew University of Jerusalem and pursued archeology of the Middle East from the perspective of history and politics. He spent 2000 to 2007 in Belgium working at the Ename Center for Public Archeology and Heritage Presentation on heritage projects in Europe, the Middle East, and Asia. He taught at the University of Massachusetts Amherst, where he helped establish its Center for Heritage and Society.

4 Carol A. Redmount, "Bitter Lives: Israel In and Out of Egypt," *The Oxford History of the Biblical World*, 87. Redmount is Chair of Near Eastern Studies and Associate Professor of Egyptian Archaeology at the University of California, Berkeley. She is also Director of Publications for the Harvard Semitic Museum.

5 Bahá'u'lláh, *The Kitáb-i-Íqán*, no. 12, 10–11. Moses said in His final speech to the people: *"The Lord came from Sinai and dawned over them from Seir; he shone forth from Mount Paran."* (Deut. 33:2)

6 'Abdu'l-Bahá, *Selections from the Writings of 'Abdu'l-Bahá*, no. 206.15, 271.

7 These ten plagues, in order of occurrence, were the turning of Egyptian waters into blood, frogs, swarms of gnats, swarms of flies, diseased livestock, boils, hail and extreme weather, swarms of locusts, darkness for three days, and the deaths of all firstborns.

8 'Abdu'l-Bahá, *Some Answered Questions*, no. 11.17, 58.

9   Jo Ann Borovicka, "The Ten Plagues of the Exodus in Light of the Bahá'í Writings," 21. *Lights of 'Irfán – Papers Presented at the 'Irfán Colloquia and Seminars, Book Sixteen.*

10 'Abdu'l-Bahá, *Tablets of 'Abdu'l-Bahá*, vol. 2, 350.

11 'Abdu'l-Bahá, cited in *Lights of Guidance*, no. 1678, 500. ('Abdu'l-Bahá: *Daily Lessons Received at 'Akká*, 45, 1979 ed.)

12 The number forty figures prominently in scriptures. A few examples related to trials and testing are the rain that fell for forty days and nights during Noah's flood, and the prophet Elijah walking forty days to reach Mount Horeb and fasting there for forty days before beginning his ministry. In the New Testament, Jesus withdrew to the wilderness for forty days of prayer before starting His ministry.

13 "The Code of Hammurabi," translated by L. W. King, the Avalon Project, Lillian Goldman Law Library, Yale University.

14 Ibid.

15 'Abdu'l-Bahá, *Promulgation of Universal Peace*, 106.

16 *"It is forbidden for you to trade in slaves, be they men or women. It is not for him who is himself a servant to buy another of God's servants, and this hath been prohibited in His Holy Tablet. Thus, by His mercy, hath the commandment been recorded by the Pen of justice."* The *Kitáb-i-Aqdas*, no. 72, 45.

17 Thomas Cahill, *The Gifts of the Jews*, 154–55.

18 Eric Toussaint, "Debt Cancellation in Mesopotamia and Egypt from 3000 to 1000 BC." Global Research, September 4, 2012. Toussaint is a senior lecturer at the University of Liege, President of the Committee for the Abolition of Third World Debt (CADTM, an international network based in Liege), a member of the International Council of the World Social Forum since it was founded in 2001, and a member of the Presidential Commission of Integral Audit of Public Credit (CAIC) in Ecuador.

19 Michael D. Coogan, "The Exodus," *The Oxford Companion to the Bible*, 667. Coogan is a lecturer on the Hebrew Bible at Harvard Divinity School, Director of Publications for the Harvard Semitic Museum, Editor-in-Chief of Oxford Biblical Studies Online, and Professor Emeritus of Religious Studies at Stonehill College, Easton, MA.

CHAPTER 10. JUDGES, PROPHETS, AND KINGS

1 William G. Dever, *Who Were the Early Israelites and Where Did They Come From?*, 71. Dever was a professor of Near Eastern Archaeology and Anthropology at the University of Arizona from 1975 to 2002. He held the title of Distinguished Professor of Near Eastern Archaeology at Lycoming College in Pennsylvania from 2002 until his retirement.

2 Israel Finkelstein and Neil Asher Silberman, *The Bible Unearthed*, 104.

3 *Who Were the Early Israelites and Where Did They Come From?*, 74.

4 *The Bible Unearthed*, 114–15.

CHAPTER 11. A KINGDOM UNITED AND DIVIDED

1 Israel Finkelstein and Neil Asher Silberman, *David and Solomon*, 32.

2 Hershel Shanks, "Ancient Jerusalem: The Village, the Town, the City," *Biblical Archaeology Review*, May/June 2016. Shanks draws on the work of Hillel Geva of Hebrew University of Jerusalem and the Israel Exploration Society, and states that Geva "bases his estimates on 'archeological findings,' rather than vague textual sources." Hillel Geva, "Jerusalem's Population in Antiquity: A Minimalist View," *Tel Aviv* 41 (2014), 131–160.

3 Bahá'u'lláh, *The Proclamation of Bahá'u'lláh*, 89–90.

4 Michael E. Dever, *The Lives of Ordinary People in Ancient Israel*, 80.

5 Ibid., 55.

6 'Abdu'l-Bahá, *Some Answered Questions*, no. 43.5, 188.

7 Ibid.

CHAPTER 12. LEND AN EAR
UNTO THE SONG OF DAVID

1 J. E. Esslemont, *Bahá'u'lláh and the New Era*, 211. Esslemont spoke these words regarding the prophet Daniel when he was told, *"But you, Daniel, roll up and seal the words of the scroll until the time of the end"* (Dan. 12:4). Some prophecies cannot be interpreted until the events occur. By the same token, Psalms 22, 24, 45, and 60 could not have been understood before their time of fulfillment.

2   Jeffrey Kranz, "The 10 most popular books of the Bible (and why)," blogsite Overview Bible Project, April 1, 2014. The other nine most read books of the Bible, in order, are Matthew, John, Romans, Proverbs, Genesis, Luke, 1 Corinthians, Isaiah, and Acts.

3   Jeffrey Krantz, "Which Old Testament book did Jesus quote most?" blogsite Biblia, April 30, 2014. Kranz states that Jesus quoted Psalms eleven times, Deuteronomy ten times, Isaiah eight times, and Exodus four times.

4   Emil G. Hirsch, "Psalms," blogsite Jewish Encyclopedia. The Latter Day Saints provide an excellent resource for finding attributions for the psalms.
     https://www.churchofjesuschrist.org/study/scriptures/ot/ps/32?lang=eng
     The Blue Letter Bible provides helpful information about the probable occasion on which each psalm was composed.
     https://www.blueletterbible.org/study/parallel/paral18.cfm

5   Bahá'u'lláh, "The Tablet of the Holy Mariner," verse 2, *Bahá'í Prayers: A Selection of Prayers Revealed by Bahá'u'lláh, the Báb, and 'Abdu'l-Bahá*, 221–29.

6   Shoghi Effendi, *God Passes By*, 184.

7   Ibid., 95.

8   Bahá'u'lláh, *The Summons of the Lord of Hosts*, no. 1.128, 66.

9   Ibid., no. 1.102, 54–55.

10   Bahá'u'lláh, *The Epistle to the Son of the Wolf*, 144.

11   'Abdu'l-Bahá, *Some Answered Questions*, no. 35.3–4, 156–57.

12   Bahá'u'lláh, *The Hidden Words of Bahá'u'lláh*, no. 2 from the Arabic.

13   Lady Blomfeld, *The Chosen Highway*, 39. Lady Sara Luisa Blomfeld (1859–1939) was an early Bahá'í. During her first trip to Haifa in 1922, she started writing notes from the verbal reminiscences of the female members of the family of 'Abdu'l-Bahá, including his sister, who gave Blomfield information about her parents' marriage and early years.

14   Ibid.

15   Ibid., 40.

16 Ibid.

17 Shoghi Effendi, *Messages to America*, letter dated December 21, 1939, 35.

CHAPTER 13. A STILL SMALL VOICE

1 'Abdu'l-Bahá, *The Secret of Divine Civilization*, 77–78.

2 William G. Dever, *The Lives of Ordinary People in Ancient Israel*, 292. Chapter 8, "Religion and Cult," 249–93, provides extensive archeological evidence for the prevalence of household shrines to the gods, fertility worship, and the veneration of Asherah throughout Israel and Judah. Dever reports that archeologists have found 3,000 Asherah artifacts in Judah alone.

3 'Abdu'l-Bahá, *Foundations of World Unity*, 95–96.

4 Edward F. Campbell, Jr., "A Land Divided: Judah and Israel from the Death of Solomon to the Fall of Samaria," *The Oxford History of the Biblical World*, 222.

5 'Abdu'l-Bahá, *Some Answered Questions*, no. 33.6, 150.

6 Shoghi Effendi, *God Passes By*, 276.

APPENDIX A: E. G. BROWNE

1 Edward G. Browne, Introduction to *A Traveller's Narrative Written to Illustrate the Episode of the Báb*, xxxix.

APPENDIX B: SHOGHI EFFENDI

1 Shoghi Effendi, *God Passes By*, 281–82.

Bibliography

WORKS OF THE BÁB

Selections from the Writings of the Báb. The Universal House of Justice. Compiled by the Research Department of the Universal House of Justice and translated by Habib Taherzadeh with the assistance of a Committee at the Bahá'í World Centre. Haifa, Israel: 1982; 1st pocket-size ed. Wilmette, IL: Bahá'í Publishing Trust, 2006.
https://www.bahai.org/library/authoritative-texts/the-bab/selections-writings-bab/

WORKS OF BAHÁ'U'LLÁH

Epistle to the Son of the Wolf. Trans. by Shoghi Effendi. 1st pocket-size ed. Wilmette, IL: Bahá'í Publishing Trust, 1988.
https://www.bahai.org/library/authoritative-texts/bahaullah/epistle-son-wolf/

Gems of Divine Mysteries. Haifa: Bahá'í World Centre, 2002.
https://www.bahai.org/library/authoritative-texts/bahaullah/gems-divine-mysteries/

Gleanings from the Writings of Bahá'u'lláh. Trans. by Shoghi Effendi. 1st pocket-size ed. Wilmette, IL: Bahá'í Publishing Trust, 1983.
https://www.bahai.org/library/authoritative-texts/bahaullah/gleanings-writings-bahaullah/

The Hidden Words. Trans. by Shoghi Effendi. Wilmette, IL: Bahá'í Publishing, 2002.

https://www.bahai.org/library/authoritative-texts/bahaullah/
hidden-words/

The Kitáb-i-Aqdas: The Most Holy Book. Haifa: Bahá'í World Centre,
1993.
https://www.bahai.org/library/authoritative-texts/bahaullah/
kitab-i-aqdas/

The Kitáb-i-Íqán: The Book of Certitude. Trans. by Shoghi Effendi. 1st
pocket-size ed. Wilmette, IL: Bahá'í Publishing Trust, 1983.
https://www.bahai.org/library/authoritative-texts/bahaullah/
kitab-i-iqan/

Prayers and Meditations of Bahá'u'lláh. Trans. by Shoghi Effendi. Wilmette:
Bahá'í Publishing Trust, 1987.
https://www.bahai.org/library/authoritative-texts/bahaullah/
prayers-meditations/

The Proclamation of Bahá'u'lláh. Wilmette, IL: Bahá'í Publishing Trust,
1978.

The Seven Valleys and the Four Valleys. Translated by Marziel Gail in consultation with Ali-Kuli Khan. 3rd ed. Wilmette, IL: Bahá'í Publishing
Trust, 1986.
https://www.bahai.org/library/authoritative-texts/bahaullah/
seven-valleys-four-valleys/

The Summons of the Lord of Hosts. Haifa: Bahá'í World Centre, 2002.
https://www.bahai.org/library/authoritative-texts/bahaullah/
summons-lord-hosts/

*The Tabernacle of Unity: Bahá'u'lláh's Responses to Mánikchí Ṣáḥib and Other
Writings.* Bahá'í World Centre, 2006.
https://www.bahai.org/library/authoritative-texts/bahaullah/
tabernacle-unity/

Tablets of Bahá'u'lláh Revealed after the Kitáb-i-Aqdas. Compiled by the
Research Department of the Universal House of Justice. Trans. by
Habib Taherzadeh et al. 1st pocket-size ed. Wilmette, IL: Bahá'í
Publishing Trust, 1988.
https://www.bahai.org/library/authoritative-texts/bahaullah/
tablets-bahaullah/

WORKS OF 'ABDU'L-BAHÁ

'Abdu'l-Bahá in London. London: Bahá'í Publishing Trust, 1982.
http://bahai-library.com/abdulbaha_abdulbaha_london

Foundations of World Unity. Wilmette, IL: Bahá'í Publishing Trust, 1979.
http://bahai-library.com/abdulbaha_foundations_world_unity

Paris Talks. 11th ed. London: Bahá'í Publishing Trust, 1972.
https://www.bahai.org/library/authoritative-texts/abdul-baha/paris-talks/

The Promulgation of Universal Peace: Talks Delivered by 'Abdu'l-Bahá during His Visit to the United States and Canada in 1912. Compiled by Harold McNutt. Wilmette, IL: Bahá'í Publishing Trust, 2007.
https://www.bahai.org/library/authoritative-texts/abdul-baha/promulgation-universal-peace/

The Secret of Divine Civilization. Translated from the Persian by Marzieh Gail in consultation with Ali-Kuli Khan. First pocket-size ed. Wilmette, IL: Bahá'í Publishing Trust, 1990.
https://www.bahai.org/library/authoritative-texts/abdul-baha/secret-divine-civilization/

Selections from the Writings of 'Abdu'l-Bahá. Compiled by the Research Department of the Universal House of Justice and translated by a committee at the Bahá'í World Centre and by Marzieh Gail, and originally published by the Universal House of Justice in Haifa, Israel, in 1978. 1st pocket-size edition. Wilmette: Bahá'í Publishing Trust, 1997.
https://www.bahai.org/library/authoritative-texts/abdul-baha/selections-writings-abdul-baha/

Some Answered Questions. Compiled and translated from the Persian by Laura Clifford Barney. Newly revised by a committee at the Bahá'í World Centre. Haifa, Israel: Bahá'í World Centre, 2014.
https://www.bahai.org/library/authoritative-texts/abdul-baha/some-answered-questions/

Tablets of 'Abdu'l-Bahá Abbas, 2nd ed., Chicago: Bahá'í Publishing Society, 1919.

BIBLIOGRAPHY

A Traveler's Narrative: Written to Illustrate the Episode of the Báb. Wilmette, IL: Bahá'í Publishing Trust, 1982. With E. G. Browne and translated by E. G. Browne.
https://www.bahai.org/library/authoritative-texts/abdul-baha/travelers-narrative/

WORKS OF SHOGHI EFFENDI

The Advent of Divine Justice. 1st pocket-size ed. Wilmette, IL: Bahá'í Publishing Trust, 1990.
https://www.bahai.org/library/authoritative-texts/shoghi-effendi/advent-divine-justice/

Citadel of Faith. Wilmette, IL: Bahá'í Publishing Trust, 1980.
https://www.bahai.org/library/authoritative-texts/shoghi-effendi/citadel-faith/

God Passes By. Rev. ed. 1974, second printing 1979. Wilmette, IL: Bahá'í Publishing Trust, 1979.
https://www.bahai.org/library/authoritative-texts/shoghi-effendi/god-passes-by/

Messages to America. Wilmette: Bahá'í Publishing Trust, 1947.
http://bahai-library.com/shoghieffendi_messages_america

The Promised Day Is Come. Wilmette, IL: Bahá'í Publishing Trust, 1980.
https://www.bahai.org/library/authoritative-texts/shoghi-effendi/promised-day-come/

The Unfolding Destiny of the British Bahá'í Community: The Messages of the Guardian of the Bahá'í Faith to the Bahá'ís of the British Isles. London: Bahá'í Publishing Trust, 1981.
http://bahai-library.com/shoghieffendi_unfolding_destiny

The World Order of Bahá'u'lláh: Selected Letters. 2nd rev. ed. Wilmette, IL: Bahá'í Publishing Trust, 1974.
https://www.bahai.org/library/authoritative-texts/shoghi-effendi/world-order-bahaullah/

THE UNIVERSAL HOUSE OF JUSTICE

Letter dated February 8, 1998, from the Universal House of Justice to an individual.

http://covenantstudy.org/issues-related-to-the-study-of-the-bahai-faith/8-february-1998/index.html

Messages of the Universal House of Justice 1963–1986. Compiled by Geoffry Marks. Wilmette, IL: Bahá'í Publishing Trust, 1996.

https://bahai-library.com/uhj_messages_1963_1986

BAHÁ'Í INTERNATIONAL COMMUNITY

A Statement on Bahá'u'lláh. New York: May 1992.

https://bahai-library.com/bic_statement_bahaullah

COMPILATIONS

'Abdu'l-Bahá on Divine Philosophy. Compiled by Elizabeth Fraser Chamberlain. Boston, MA: Tudor Press, 1918.

http://bahai-library.com/abdulbaha_divine_philosophy&chapter=all

Bahá'í Prayers: A Selection of Prayers Revealed by Bahá'u'lláh, the Báb, and 'Abdu'l-Bahá. Wilmette, IL: Bahá'í Publishing Trust, 1954/1970.

Bahá'í Prayers and Readings: Selected Writings of Bahá'u'lláh, the Báb and 'Abdu'l-Bahá. Australia: Bahá'í Publications, 2011.

https://www.bahaiprayers.org/mariner.htm

The Bible: Extracts on the Old and New Testaments by Bahá'u'lláh, 'Abdu'l-Bahá, Shoghi Effendi, and the Universal House of Justice. Research Department of the Universal House of Justice. (publication date not given) www.

http://bahai-library.com/uhj_old_new_testaments

Compilation of Compilations, vols. 1 and 2. Compiled by the Research Department of the Universal House of Justice. rev. ed. Mona Vale: Bahá'í Publications Australia, 1991. https://bahai-library.com/compilation_compilations_1 and

https://bahai-library.com/compilation_compilations_2

Lights of Guidance: A Bahá'í Reference File. Compiled by Helen Bassett Hornby. 3rd revised ed. New Delhi, India: Bahá'í Publishing Trust, 1994.

BIBLIOGRAPHY

HOLY SCRIPTURES

The Bible, King James Version

The Bible, New International Version

The Koran. Trans. by J. M. Rodwell. An unabridged republication of the work first published by J. M. Dent & Sons Ltd., London, 1909. Mineola, NY: Dover Publications, Inc., 2005.

OTHER SOURCES

"Ages of Adam, Seth, Methuselah and Noah," a memorandum dated May 7, 2009, prepared by the Research Department at the Bahá'í World Centre at the request of the Universal House of Justice. Sent to author by letter dated January 29, 2019.

Angel, J. Lawrence. "Health as a Crucial Factor in the Change from Hunting to Developed Farming in the Eastern Mediterranean." *Paleopathology at the Origins of Agriculture*, edited by Mark Nathan Cohen and George J. Armelagos. University of Florida Press. Gainesville, FL: 2013.

Bahá'í News. National Spiritual Assembly of the Bahá'ís of the United States, no. 228, 4, 1950.
https://bahai.works/Baha%27i_News/Issue_228

Balyuzi, H. M. *Bahá'u'lláh: The King of Glory*. Second Edition (revised). Oxford, UK: George Ronald Publisher, 1991.

Barnes, William. "Mythoi: Stories of the Origin, Fall and Redemption of Humanity: A Study in the Topology or the Holy Books." *Scripture and Revelation*. Bahá'í Studies Vol. III. Papers presented at the First Irfán Colloquium, Newcastle-upon-Tyne, England, December 1993, and the Second Irfán Colloquium, Wilmette, USA, March 1994. Ed. Moojan Momen. Oxford, UK: George Ronald Publisher, 1997.

Blomfeld, Lady (Sitárih Khánum). *The Chosen Highway*. London: Bahá'í Publishing Trust, 1940. Reprinted by George Ronald Publisher, 2007.

Borovicka, Jo Ann M. "The Ten Plagues of the Exodus in Light of the Bahá'í Writings." *Lights of 'Irfán – Papers Presented at the Irfán Colloquia and Seminars*, Book Sixteen. Ed. Iraj Ayman. Darmstadt, Germany: 'Asr-i-Jadíd Publisher, 2015.
http://bahai-library.com/borovicka_ten_plagues_exodus.pdf

Bottéro, Jean. *Religion in Ancient Mesopotamia*. Trans. by Teresa Lavender Fagan. Chicago and London: The University of Chicago Press, 2001.

Cahill, Thomas. *The Gifts of the Jews: How a Tribe of Desert Nomads Changed the Way Everyone Thinks and Feels*. New York: Talese / Anchor Books, Hinges of History series, 1999.
http://irfancolloquia.org/pdf/lights16_borovicka_plagues_exodus.pdf

Campbell, Edward F., Jr. "A Land Divided: Judah and Israel from the Death of Solomon to the Fall of Samaria." *The Oxford History of the Biblical World*. Oxford, UK: Oxford University Press, 2001.

Cartwright, Mark. "Uluburun Shipwreck." *Ancient History Encyclopedia*. September 12, 2017.
https://www.ancient.eu/Uluburun_Shipwreck/

Charles, R. H. *The Book of Enoch*. Postomorrow Books, 2013.
https://www.sacred-texts.com/bib/boe/boe085.htm

Cline, Eric H. "The Collapse of Civilizations: It's Complicated." *The Huffington Post*, May 19, 2014.
http://www.huffingtonpost.com/eric-h-cline/the-collapse-of-civilizations-its-complicated_b_4995479.html

———. *From Eden to Exile: Unraveling Mysteries of the Bible*. National Geographic, Washington, D.C., 2007.

———. *1177 B.C.: The Year Civilization Collapsed*. First volume in the series Turning Points in Ancient History. Princeton: Princeton University Press, 2014.

Club of Rome. *The Limits of Growth: A Report for the Club of Rome's Project on the Predicament of Mankind*. A Potomac Associates book. NY, NY: Universe Books, 1972.

Collins, William P. "Sacred Mythology and the Bahá'í Faith." *Journal of Bahá'í Studies*, vol. 2:4, 1990. https://bahai-studies.ca/wp-content/uploads/2014/05/2.4-Collins.pdf

"The Code of Hammurabi." Trans. by L. W. King. The Avalon Project, Lillian Goldman Law Library, Yale University, New Haven, CT, 2008.
http://avalon.law.yale.edu/ancient/hamframe.asp

Cohen, Mark Nathan and George J. Armelagos, eds. *Paleopathology at the Origins of Agriculture.* Gainesville, FL: University Press of Florida, 2013.

Coogan, Michael D. ed. *The Oxford History of the Biblical World.* Oxford, UK: Oxford University Press, 2001.

Coogan, Michael D. and Bruce M. Metzger, eds. *The Oxford Companion to the Bible.* Oxford Companions. Oxford, UK: Oxford University Press, 1993.

Curry, Andrew. "Göbekli Tepe: The World's First Temple?" *Smithsonian Magazine*, November 2008. https://www.smithsonianmag.com/history/Göbekli-tepe-the-worlds-first-temple-83613665/

Dever, William G. *The Lives of Ordinary People in Ancient Israel: Where Archeology and the Bible Intersect.* Grand Rapids, MI: Wm. B. Eerdsman Publishing Co., 2012.

———. *Who Were the Early Israelites and Where Did They Come From?* Grand Rapids, MI: Wm. B. Eerdsman Publishing Co., 2003.

Esslemont, J. E. *Bahá'u'lláh and the New Era.* Wilmette, IL: Bahá'í Publishing Trust, 1980.

Finkelstein, Israel and Neil Asher Silberman. *The Bible Unearthed: Archeology's New Vision of Ancient Israel and the Origin of Its Sacred Texts.* New York: Touchstone, 2002.

———. *David and Solomon: In Search of the Bible's Sacred Kings and the Roots of the Western Tradition.* Free Press, book imprint publisher of Simon & Schuster, 2007.

Fransson, Wade. *The Rod of Iron.* Madison, WI: Something Or Other Publishing, LLC, 2019.

Friedman, Richard Elliott. *Who Wrote the Bible?* New York, NY: Harper Collins, 1989.

Ginzburg, Rabbi Louis. *The Legends of the Jews: From the Creation to Jacob, vol. 1 of The Legends of the Jews.* Philadelphia, PA: Jewish Publication Society of America, 1909. http://www.sacred-texts.com/jud/loj/

Goodall, Helen A. and Alla Goodall Cooper. *Daily Lessons Received at Akka: January 1908.* Wilmette, IL: Bahá'í Publishing Trust, 1979.

Harlan, Jack R. "From Foraging to Farming: Explaining the Neolithic Revolution." Institute of Economics, University of Copenhagen. http://citeseerx.ist.psu.edu/viewdoc/download?doi= 10.1.1.454.5998&rep=rep1&type=pdf

Harris, Benjamin. *The New England Primer.* Boston, MA, 1690. https://www3.nd.edu/~rbarger/www7/neprimer.html

Hatcher, John S. and Amrollah Hemmat. *Adam's Wish: Unknown Poetry of Ṭáhirih.* Wilmette, IL: Bahá'í Publishing, 2008.

Heun, Manfred et al. "Site of Einkorn Wheat Domestication Identified by DNA Fingerprinting." *Science Magazine*, Vol. 278, November 14, 1997. http://www.sciencemag.org/content/278/5341.ful

Hirsch, Emil G. "Psalms." Jewish Encyclopedia. http://www.jewishen-cyclopedia.com/articles/12409-psalms

Hodder, Ian. *The Leopard's Tale: Revealing the Mysteries of Çatalhöyük.* London: Thames and Hudson, 2006.

———. *Religion in the Emergence of Civilization: Çatalhöyük as a Case Study.* Cambridge University Press, Cambridge, UK, 2010.

———. *Religion at Work in a Neolithic Society: Vital Matters.* Ed. Ian Hodder. Cambridge University Press, NY, 2014.

Hurriyet Daily News, The. "New temples, stones found in Turkey's Göbekli Tepe site." July 15, 2018. http://www.hurriyetdailynews.com/new-temples-stones-found-in-turkeys-Göbeklitepe-site-134583

Joy, Anthony. *Exploring Gleanings: Commentary on Gleanings from the Writings of Bahá'u'lláh.* New Delhi, India: Bahá'í Publishing Trust, 2013.

Kershner, Isabel. "Pollen Study Points to Drought as Culprit in Bronze Age Mystery." *The New York Times*, October 23, 2013. http://www.nytimes.com/2013/10/23/world/middleeast/-pollen-study-points-to-culprit-in-bronze-era-mystery.html

Kranz, Jeffrey. "The 10 most popular books of the Bible (and why)," blogsite Overview Bible Project. April 1, 2014. http://overviewbible.com/popular-books-bible-infographic/

———. "Which Old Testament book did Jesus quote most?" blogsite Biblia. April 30, 2014.
http://blog.biblia.com/2014/04/which-old-testament-book-did-jesus-quote-most/

Kershner, Isabel. "Pollen Study Points to Drought as Culprit on Bronze Age Mystery." *The New York Times*, October 22, 2013.
http://www.nytimes.com/2013/10/23/world/middleeast/pollen-study-points-to-culprit-in-bronze-era-mystery.html

Lambden, Stephen. "The Word Bahá: The Quintessence of the Greatest Name." *Bahá'í Studies Review*, 3:1, Bahá'í Studies for English-Speaking Europe, 1993.
https://bahai-library.com/lambden_quintessence_greatest_name

Langgut, Dafna, Israel Finkelstein, and Thomas Litt. "Climate and the Late Bronze Collapse: New Evidence from the Southern Levant." *Journal of the Institute of Archaeology of Tel Aviv University*, vol. 40, issue 2 (November 2013), 149–75,
http://archaeology.tau.ac.il/wp-content/uploads/2014/01/Langgut_et_al_LB_Collapse_2013.pdf

Leick, Carolyn. *Mesopotamia: The Invention of the City.* New York: Penguin Books, 2003.

Lewis-Williams, David and David Pearce. *Inside the Neolithic Mind: Consciousness, Cosmos and the Realm of the Gods.* New York: Thames & Hudson, 2005.

Luckert, Karl W. *Stone Age Religion at Göbekli Tepe: From Hunting to Domestication, Warfare and Civilization.* Karl W. Luckert, 2013.

Marsella, Elena Maria. *The Quest for Eden.* New York: Philosophical Library, 1966.

Matthews, Victor H. and Don C. Benjamin. *Old Testament Parallels: Laws and Stories from the Ancient Near East*, 3rd ed. Mahwah, NJ: Paulist Press, 2006.

Mírzá Abu'l-Faḍl Gulpáypání. *Miracles and Metaphors.* Trans. from the Arabic and annotated by Juan Ricardo Cole. Originally published in Cairo, Egypt, in 1900. Los Angeles, CA: Kalamát Press, 1991.

Mithen, Steven. *After the Ice: A Global Human History 20,000–5,000 BC.* Cambridge, MA: Harvard University Press, 2006.

Nabíl-i-A'ẓam [Muḥammad-i-Zarandí]. *The Dawn-breakers: Nabíl's Narrative of the Early Days of the Bahá'í Revelation.* Translated and edited by Shoghi Effendi. Wilmette, IL: Bahá'í Publishing Trust, 1932.

http://bahai-library.com/nabil_dawnbreakers

Nesbitt, Mark. "Where Was Einkorn Wheat Domesticated?" *Trends in Plant Science*, March 1998, Vol. 3, no. 3.

http://www.ancientgrains.org/nesbitt1998einorn.pdg

Pulak, Cemal M., and Mrs. Ray H. Siegfried II. "1994 Excavation at Uluburun: The Final Campaign." Institute of Nautical Archeology. *The INA Quarterly*, vol. 24:1 (Winter 1994).

https://nauticalarch.org/projects/uluburun-late-bronze-age-shipwreck-excavation/

Pulak, Cemal M. "The Uluburun Shipwreck and Late Bronze Age Trade." *Beyond Babylon: Art, Trade, and Diplomacy in the Second Millennium B.C.* by J. Aruz, K. Benzel, and J. M. Evans, eds. New Haven and London: Yale University Press, and New York: Metropolitan Museum of Art, 2008.

http://berlinarchaeology.files.wordpress.com/2013/01/-pulak-2008289-310-uluburun.pdf

Redmount, Carol A. "Bitter Lives: Israel In and Out of Egypt." *The Oxford History of the Biblical World.* Oxford, UK: Oxford University Press, 2001.

Ryan, William and Walter Pitman. *Noah's Flood: The New Scientific Discoveries about the Event that Changed History.* New York, NY: Simon & Schuster, 1998.

Saiedi, Nader. *Gate of the Heart: Understanding the Writings of the Báb.* Waterloo, ON, CA: Wilfred Laurier University Press, 2010. Co-published with the Association for Bahá'í Studies.

Sahlins, Marshall. "The Original Affluent Society." *Stone Age Economics.* Chicago: Aldine, 1974.

http://www.eco-action.org/dt/affluent.html

BIBLIOGRAPHY

Scham, Sandra. "The World's Oldest Temple." *Archeology*, vol. 61, no. 6, November/December 2008.
https://archive.archaeology.org/0811/abstracts/turkey.html

Shanks, Hershel. "Ancient Jerusalem: The Village, the Town, the City." *Biblical Archaeology Review*, May/June 2016.
https://www.biblicalarchaeology.org/daily/biblical-sites-places/jerusalem/ancient-jerusalem/#note01

Sherratt, Andrew. "Plough and Pastoralism: Aspects of the Secondary Products Revolution," *Pattern of the Past: Studies in Honour of David Clarke*, eds. Ian Hodder, Glynn Isaac, and Norman Hammond. Cambridge: Cambridge University Press, 1981. Also, *Journal of World Archeology*, Vol. 22, 2010, Issue 1.
https://www.tandfonline.com/doi/abs/10.1080/00438240903429722

Simmons, Alan H. *The Neolithic Revolution in the Near East: Transforming the Human Landscape*. Tucson. AR: University of Arizona Press, 2010.

Standage, Tom. *An Edible History of Humanity*. New York, NY: Walker Publishing Company, Inc., 2009.

Symmes, Patrick. "Turkey: Archeological Dig Reshaping Human History." *Newsweek*, world edition: 18 February 2010.
http://www.newsweek.com/turkey-archeological-dig-reshaping-human-history-75101

Taherzadeh, Adib. *The Revelation of Bahá'u'lláh, Volume 1: Baghdad: 1853–63*. Rev. ed. Oxford, UK: George Ronald Publisher, 1976.

———. *The Revelation of Bahá'u'lláh, Volume 3: 'Akká, The Early Years 1868–77*. Oxford, UK: George Ronald Publisher, 1983.

"Texts, Sacred, Numbers, and Classifications by/on Behalf of the Universal House of Justice," *Lights of 'Irfán*, vol. 10, 350. http://bahai-library.com/uhj_numbers_sacred_writings

Toussaint, Eric. "Debt Cancellation in Mesopotamia and Egypt from 3000 to 1000 BC."
http://www.globalresearch.ca/debt-cancellation-in-mesopotamia-and-egypt-from-3000-to-1000-bc/5303136

Wells, Spencer. *Pandora's Seed: The Unforeseen Cost of Civilization.* New York: Random House, 2010.

Westenholtz, Joan Goodwin. *Legends of the Kings of Akkade: The Texts (Mesopotamian Civilizations.* University Park, PA: Penn State University Press, 1997.

Weisdorf, Jacob L. *Crops and Man.* Madison, WI: American Society of Agronomy, 1992.

Wiener, Noah. "Bronze Age Collapse: Pollen Study Highlights Late Bronze Age Drought." *Biblical Archeological Review*, April 3, 2018. http://www.biblicalarchaeology.org/daily/-ancient-cultures/ancient-near-eastern-world/bronze-age-collapse-pollen-study-high-lights-late-bronze-age-drought/

Worthington, Frances. *Abraham: One God, Three Wives, Five Religions.* Wilmette, IL: Bahá'í Publishing Trust, 2011.

CPSIA information can be obtained
at www.ICGtesting.com
Printed in the USA
BVHW092034090223
658214BV00004B/370

9 781732 451186